The Guide to Successful Short-Term Programs Abroad

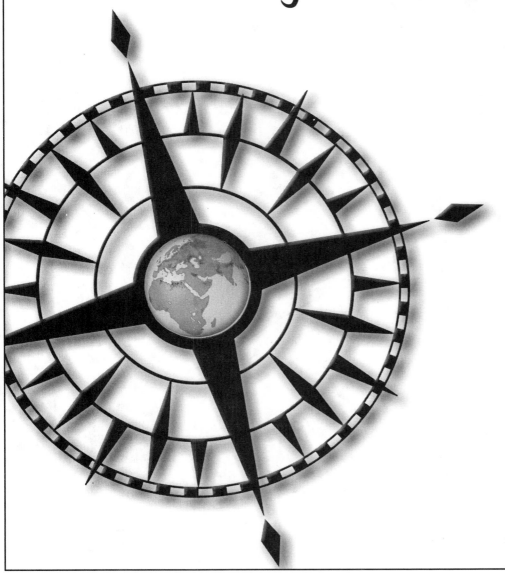

The Guide to
Successful Short-Term
Programs Abroad

edited by Sarah E. Spencer
and Kathy Tuma

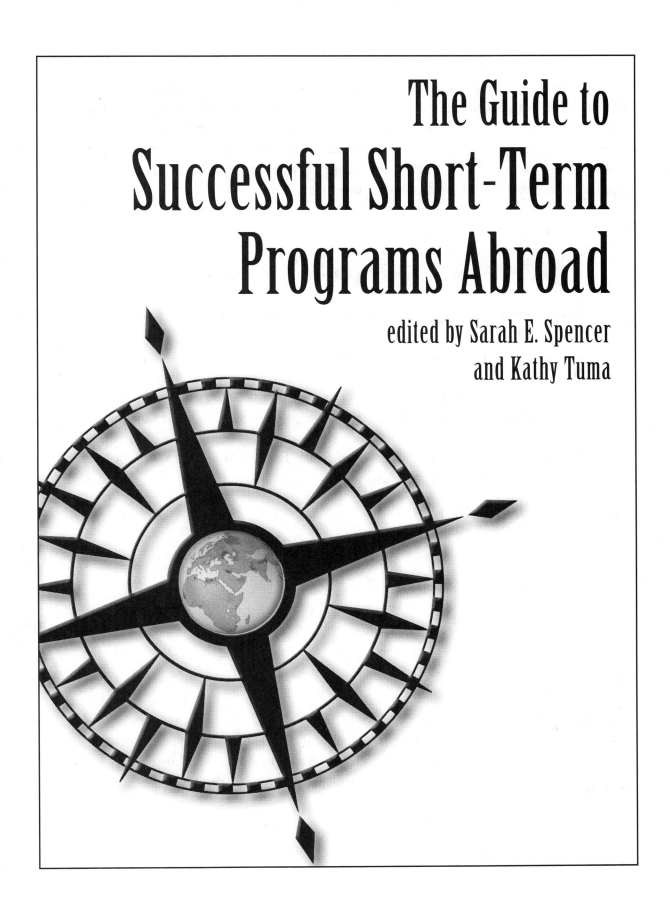

NAFSA: Association of International Educators promotes the exchange of students and scholars to and from the United States. The Association sets and upholds standards of good practice and provides professional education and training that strengthen institutional programs and services related to international educational exchange. NAFSA provides a forum for discussion and awareness of and support for international education in higher education, in government, and in the community.

International Standard Book Number: 0-912207-86-8

Library of Congress Cataloging-in-Publication Data

The guide to successful short-term programs abroad/edited by Sarah E. Spencer and Kathy Tuma.
     p. cm.
   Includes bibliographical references and index.
   ISBN 0-912207-86-8
   1. Foreign study—Administration—Handbooks, manuals, etc. 2. American students—Travel—Handbooks, manuals, etc. 3. College students—Travel—Handbooks, manuals, etc. 4. Faculty advisors—Handbooks, manuals, etc. 5. College administrators—Handbooks, manuals, etc. I. Spencer, Sarah E. II. Tuma, Kathy. III. NAFSA: Association of International Educators (Washington, D.C.)

LB2376 .g75 2002
370.116—dc21
                                                 2002070126

NAFSA

Association of International Educators

Table of Contents

Introduction

Sarah E. Spencer and Kathy Tuma

For students who are older, of minority background, employed (46 percent of full-time students under age 25 are employed at least part-time), disabled, or have limited funds, study abroad is not perceived to be an option. The more typical study abroad models and structures mostly ignore the needs of such students.
1990 National Task Force on Undergraduate Education Abroad[1]

Amazingly, a mere 12 years ago many students, especially those who could not take advantage of a semester or academic year overseas, did not study abroad. Today is a very different story. Short-term off-campus programs—credit-granting, volunteer, internship, international, domestic, summer, embedded in a semester—create opportunities for a far greater range of students to leave their homes to access another culture and educational opportunity.

Our goal in producing this volume is to enable anyone—education abroad professionals, teachers in secondary or higher education, volunteer or church group leaders—to learn how to develop and safely administer short-term off-campus programs. Whereas readers from international organizations can gain knowledge and use this book for their own programs, it has been written from the perspective of U.S. higher education.

Because short-term programs differ from one another in location, length, topic and goals, time of year, and audience, we hope you will use this book as a guide. We provide the tools to build successful short-term programs, but it is up to you to decide what is the best structure and fit for your participants and your organization.

Within higher education, the definition of short-term programs abroad has changed significantly over the last 50 years. First considered as year-long, and then as a semester, they are now considered one- to eight-week programs (less than a term), usually faculty-directed and sponsored by a home institution or a consortium. Short-term program models are in abundance, taking place during the January or May term, in the form of a 2-week study tour embedded in a regular term or semester-length class, or as a 6-week summer program. The programs can be based in one city, one country, or travel to multiple sites or countries. And, though they are not taught abroad, many short-term domestic programs face the same issues and challenges.

Although we assume the readers of this book will be primarily those working in higher education, the tools found in specific sections can be used by a variety of groups. All of the audiences noted below have two things in common beyond creating short-term programs: they need logistical and group support and they need to function in the cross-cultural context. This guide provides the information needed to succeed in both areas.

---

1 *A National Mandate for Education Abroad: Getting on With the Task.* Report of the National Task Force on Undergraduate Education Abroad (ERIC Document Reproduction Service No. ED 331 340)[t], May 1990.

Service Learning/Volunteer: These programs may be academic or purely experiential. Focus on Parts III and IV, but do not miss Mike Klein's advice on service learning programs in Part II, Chapter 6.

High School: These groups may also be credit-granting or experiential. Parts III and IV provide resources for program development and orientation, but also consider using Tips on Guiding Students to Cultural and Intellectual Mileposts found in Part II, Chapter 6.

College Alumni: Short-term programs catering to alumni groups are increasingly popular. Most are experiential, but may use a seasoned faculty director who has taught academic courses overseas. See Parts II, III, and IV and also Working with Graduate Students in Chapter 8, Logistics. There are similar issues for both groups.

Nonacademic Groups (e.g., musical organizations, sports groups, and religious groups): Depending on the program objectives, focus on Parts III and IV, because logistics, financial matters, and orientation are important for all group travel.

Higher Education (e.g., faculty, education abroad or international programs offices, senior administrators): Because this volume was inspired, developed, and authored by higher education professionals, each chapter addresses a need, issue, or solution in designing and administering short-term programs. We hope that faculty who do not have the support of an international office find this volume useful as well.

Positioning Short-Term Programs Abroad

Most of us would agree that the longer the encounter a student has with another country and culture, the better. But the reality is that fewer and fewer students are willing or able to spend a term, semester, or full year abroad. For these students, it is important to provide quality academic experiences of shorter duration. The reasons students seek short-term opportunities are numerous, and as participation and programs grow, so do the motivations. Examples of students seeking short-term programs abroad include the following:

- Nontraditional undergraduate students with home, job, and family responsibilities.
- Undergraduate students who are double or triple majors with very structured and tightly scheduled degree plans.
- Students who cannot afford the loss of income from an on- or off-campus job for a semester, but who can take 3 to 4 weeks off to participate in a short-term program.
- Working graduate students seeking study and professional opportunities who cannot be released from job and family responsibilities.
- Students who are simply not willing to take the leap to study abroad for a longer period of time without first having some exposure of a shorter duration.
- Semester or academic year returnees who convince themselves (and sometimes their parents) that they can go abroad (again) during their senior year.
- Students with increased curricular restrictions in their major/minor field and core areas.

Whatever the reason, it is clear that the market for short-term programs has dramatically increased in the last decade, and there are no indications that it is or will be decreasing. Recent data from *Open Doors: Statistics on International Student Mobility* show that nearly 50 percent of all students studying abroad participated in short-term programs (http://www.opendoorsweb.org, March 2002).

Why a Book on Short-Term Programs?

A quick literature review will show comprehensive information on traditional study abroad issues, such as that found in *NAFSA's Guide to Education Abroad for Advisers and Administrators, Second Edition*, but little has been published on short-term programs abroad. As you will discover in the opening chapters of this book, short-term programs differ from other traditional models.

For readers who work with college students, Part I: Working Within Higher Education will be an invaluable resource for identifying your allies, creating efficient administrative processes, and recruiting a community of colleagues.

Part II: Principles of Academic Course Design focuses on available models as well as design issues for academic courses, particularly for teaching on the road.

Logistics and financial management, the backbone of a short-term program, are explained in Part III: Program Development and Evaluation. Without experience or sufficient staff, how do you plan programs such as these? Whereas the final three chapters are again focused on higher education, marketing ideas, participant selection, and assessment are valuable for any program administrator.

We consider Part IV: Preparing to Travel to be a very useful guide in making a short-term program abroad successful. Intercultural and logistical preparation of the leadership team and the participants can make the difference between a been there, seen that attitude, and a truly cross-cultural experience.

The volume concludes with Part V: Reflections from the Field, written by a retired long-term faculty director.

We are pleased to have the opportunity to share the knowledge we have gained in our many years of administering short-term programs. We sincerely hope this guide proves useful to the many people directing and administering such programs.

Good luck and good planning!

Acknowledgments

For initial inspiration: Mickey Slind, Scott Lomas, Janis Perkins

For additional review and contribution: Nik Wilson, Adrienne Kaufmann, Anne King, Sommer Leonard, Ruth Mason, Sue Moro, Pam Nice, Ana Scofield, Catherine Spaeth, Susan Verdi Webster, Dawn White

For listening and ideas: Maynard Tuma, Nik Wilson, Martha Johnson, Mary McGuinness, George Dordoni

Our current workshop team: Peter Hovde, Allison Keith, Susan MacNally, Anders Uhrskov

Our past presenter colleagues, the countless participants at NAFSA national and regional conferences, and the faculty directors we have worked with.

For the support of our offices: International and Off-Campus Studies, St. Olaf College, Northfield, MN (Pat Quade, Helen Stellmaker, Barbara Walters, Jane Weis, Synneva Zempel), and International Education, University of St. Thomas, St. Paul, MN (Colleen Carey, Ann Gemmell, Eleni Hoffhines, Ann Hubbard, Sommer Leonard, Ruth Mason, Ana Scofield, Catherine Spaeth, Sarah Stevenson)

SECUSSA National Team, especially Susan Thompson, University of Nevada-Las Vegas

NAFSA's Education and Training Department, especially Wes Maekawa

NAFSA's Publication Department, especially Steve Pelletier and Jan Steiner

Chapter 1

Opening Doors: Alternative Pedagogies for Short-Term Programs Abroad

Peter Hovde

Goethe once said: "The only way to see Rome is through the keyhole of the Aventino." Thousands of travelers heed his advice each year, lining up at the large, heavily painted green door blocking entrance to the former palace of the Knights Templar. Standing on their tiptoes, squinting through the keyhole of the ancient lockset, each traveler can see a walkway braced by a precisely trimmed hedge on either side. As the hedges converge at the end of the walkway, they form an arch, an arch that perfectly frames the dome of St. Peter's basilica standing across the Tiber. So many travelers, in fact, that the heavy green paint around the keyhole is worn away, its brass brushed bright by the eyelashes of all those tourists following Goethe's advice.

The travelers squint through the keyhole, turn, and walk away. After our students have had their looks through the keyhole, the bolt of the lockset is heard to move aside, and the great green door swings open…

What Is to Be Gained?

If the goal of study abroad is restricted to student gains in factual and conceptual content assessed by measurements tapping the extent of cognitive learning alone, then study abroad might come up short in a cost/benefit analysis. Indeed, cognitive content gains in the near term may be better accomplished in the campus classroom. This is not to say that cognitive learning does not occur during study abroad experiences. It clearly does, and if decades of impressions are any evidence, that learning "sticks" better in students. More important, however, is that if more permanent gains in "higher-end" goals are considered important—the kinds of attributes our college catalogs claim are nurtured by the four years of matriculation—study abroad can be far more effective than the campus classroom in producing such outcomes. If critical thinking skills and value-reflective thinking are enhanced as the result of study abroad, not to mention increased interest in intellectual pursuits and enhanced motivation to learn, along with a decreased need for certitude and a greater tolerance of ambiguity, then sending students abroad is a very good idea. Or if increased world-mindedness, cosmopolitanism, and international-mindedness are worthy goals, as well as increased interest in world affairs, awareness of interdependence of nations, increased cross-cultural interest and decreased ethnocentrism, and greater empathy and concern for others, then study abroad is clearly worth doing. If students' self-confidence (and possibly self-esteem) and their sense of well being is improved, if they sharpen their sense of interdependence and autonomy, if their flexibility and adaptability to changing circumstances are enhanced, and if their vocational goals are clarified as they become aware of the far greater occupational opportunities the world has to offer, then students need study abroad experiences.[1]

---

1 For these research citations, see Chapter 2: Building Institutional Support, footnote 4.

But how long do students have to study abroad to make these gains? It was not all that long ago that the "junior year abroad" with the student immersed in the study of (or immersed in a course of study in) a second language was held to be the only legitimate study abroad experience. Indeed, there are those in the international language community today who still hold that position. However, for most of us, the spectrum of legitimate study abroad experiences is far broader, admitting of a far greater variety of approaches to study abroad.

A Departure from the Ideal?

The international education community has moved toward short-term programs abroad in a big way. As a community, international educators recognized that if the goal of giving vastly more students an overseas experience was to be realized, then short-term programs were the only vehicles that could accomplish that goal. The vast majority of U.S. students are simply not willing to spend a year (or even a semester) studying overseas. (Nor, for that matter, are most colleges and universities willing to send vast numbers of their students overseas in the face of the realities of tight budgets, empty dorm rooms, and lowering student/faculty ratios.) It began to dawn on the community as evidence—both anecdotal and quantitative—began pouring in, that short-term study abroad could be done in academically legitimate ways. The conclusion was that if done right, short-term study abroad can have an extraordinary impact on students, an impact beyond what they can derive from the campus classroom.

How Long Need the Program Be? How Short Can It Be?

The most common short-term programs are scheduled in January, May, or the summer months, and are usually 3 to 6 weeks in length. Increasingly, however, schools are experimenting with "embedded" or "nested" seminars abroad, experiences usually scheduled for mid-semester breaks, usually about a week in length.

The learning abroad is enhanced in these short-term programs if the experience is preceded by preparatory study. The preparatory study needs to include the logistics of travel, but far more importantly, it must include the academic content that gives focus to the course. Such study allows the students to "hit the ground running," to have an intellectual context into which to fit what they learn abroad.

Some short-term programs abroad require prerequisite learning. This requisite learning can be gained by a set of on-campus courses (such courses as art appreciation and comparative religion to prepare for the study of religious artistic expression of the Mediterranean, for example) or a single campus course dedicated directly to that focus of learning abroad. Some weeklong programs are simply scheduled during mid-semester break, but many are embedded into a normal on-campus semester-length course. With the longer short-term programs, the preparatory courses enhance the subsequent learning abroad. With the shorter nested seminars, learning in the first half of the semester prepares the students for the experience abroad, whereas the experience abroad enhances the subsequent classroom learning. In both types of programs, the prior study enhances the legitimacy of the short time abroad. How many of those higher-end developmental goals can be served by the nested seminar remains to be seen (by future impact research), although its furtherance of classroom goals seems assured.

What Can We Study Abroad?

Three types of study abroad courses can be defined by their academic focuses.

Topical

One focus is topical. The possibilities are nearly as numerous as a department's course offerings. Here, the content of disciplinary courses is enhanced by either adding material from other contexts or by comparing our practices and experiences with those of other cultures. For example, museum or site visits could add understanding of the Battle of the Somme to a course on international conflict. On the other hand, comparison of the social impacts of the Somme to those of the Vietnam War can enhance understanding of each nation's social experience, as well as the human impact of war.

Language Training and Cultural Learning

Another set of course focuses is language training and cultural learning. Although honing one's skills in a second language is justification enough for study abroad, such study should be designed to lead to intercultural understanding as well. Here the hoary but enduring framework of Robert Hanvey's "attainable global perspective" gives both vision and goals.[2] Students should minimally become aware of the "diversity of the ideas and practices found in societies around the world, of how these cultures compare, and of how our practices and behaviors might be viewed from the perspective of other cultures." The third of these three goals especially is a very tall order, for it requires empathy. As Hanvey notes, empathetic understanding is difficult enough to achieve within one's own culture, but it is a much tougher task when the target of one's understanding is the people of another culture. So much more difficult a task than empathy, in fact, that Hanvey gives it another name: "transpection," the capacity to imagine oneself in a role within another culture.

Immersion in another culture is the usual pedagogical vehicle for improving language skills and cultural understanding. Immersion requires time, as language learning takes time, though intensive language instruction has long ago proven its worth. Immersion in another culture (e.g., home stays) can and should be a very intense experience. Done right and with preparation, significant gains can be made in both language and cultural learning abroad in 3 to 4 weeks. Embedding a week abroad into on-campus language or cultural instruction at minimum should motivate students to further instruction and to longer-term study abroad by giving them a taste of the world's diversity.

Interdisciplinary Understanding

A third focus of study abroad is interdisciplinary understanding. Many such courses would deal with issues deemed global, issues such as ethnicity and global diversity, economic development, human ecological sustainability, and war and peace.[3] Hanvey is again helpful here. Study of the "state of the planet" begins with the "analysis of global issues, awareness of those prevailing world conditions, and emergent trends." Step two is to gain awareness of "how the world works," with an "emphasis on theories that explain global change." Step three is awareness of the impact of human choice in creating and resolving these problems, and of the range of options available.

---

[2] Hanvey, Robert G. (1979). *An Attainable Global Perspective*. New York: Center for Global Perspectives. The essay is found in summary form in *Theory into Practice* 21 (1982), 162-167, and his (1979b). "Cross-Cultural Awareness" in *Toward Internationalism: Readings in Cross-Cultural Communication,* edited by Elise C. Smith and L. F. Luce. Rowley, MA: Newbury House.

[3] The typology is from Ann Kelleher and Laura Klein (1999) *Global Perspectives: A Handbook for Understanding Global Issues.* Upper Saddle River, NJ: Prentice Hall.

Study abroad of any length can immerse students in global problems. It is one thing to study global issues such as pollution in the classroom. It is quite another to see, feel, hear, and smell those pollutants in the real world. Further, the abstract nature of theories explaining the links of both cause and consequence can be made more real to students when heard from practitioners working in the field to determine the impacts of human interventions such as industrial pollution. Finally, experiencing the surreal reality of a wind farm can give students both awareness of alternative choices and a measure of hope that at least partial solutions can be found to these pressing problems.

Each of these points of academic focus—topical, language-culture, and interdisciplinary—provides subjects that can legitimately be studied abroad on a short-term basis. Indeed, study abroad can vastly enhance student learning about such themes.

However, one of these foci, cross-cultural understanding, deserves special emphasis. Knowledge of the world's diversity and the capacity for empathetic understanding should pervade all study abroad, be it disciplinary or interdisciplinary. This priority is based not on an ideological foundation, but on simple pedagogical pragmatism. Without cross-cultural understanding, the fruits of comparison of cultures or experiences will never ripen. The different ways of doing things abroad can look silly and inefficient to the uninformed Westerner. Without the ability to see problems from the perspective of another, attempts to resolve problems on a global scale will inevitably founder. Proposals by First World people to enhance the environment are seen by those in the Third World as attempts to limit economic development in their part of the world, for example.

Sadly, the instructional reality in topical and interdisciplinary courses often finds these cross-cultural imperatives ignored as more "important," "pressing," or "rigorous" contents elbow out intercultural issues. Intercultural understanding should pervade all courses abroad, and the only way ensure that is to make such learning a more explicit part of the course.

That said, the "be all and end all" of international education is not cross-cultural or intercultural education. (I'm sure a more heretical statement could not be penned, but I wrote it because it needs to be stated.) The primacy of cultural understanding is that it must be part of all learning abroad, but not that it is posited as the ultimate goal of international education.

What is the ultimate goal of international education? Going back to the ancient Greeks, the ultimate goal is gaining an understanding of ourselves and of our self. We see that happening to our returning students, the irony that they go abroad to study others and come back learning more about their own country and themselves. No ideological or pedagogical commitments of teachers and study abroad administrators can change that outcome. Study abroad is perhaps the best way to attain the injunction of the oracle to "know thyself." For Hanvey, what is critical to know about ourselves is awareness that we have a perspective (or, more accurately, perspectives). This "perspective consciousness" is not so much a dimension of a global perspective as were the other four, but its foundational prerequisite. Without an awareness that we have a "view of the world that is not universally shared, and that others have views of the world that are profoundly different from our own," attempts at gaining understandings of other cultures, of the state of the planet, of how the world works, and of the impact of human choice on the globe are doomed to be incomplete and superficial.

Alternative Pedagogical Approaches: Or, What's Behind the Green Door?

A wide variety of pedagogical approaches have been developed to assist student learning overseas. One basic consideration concerns the site of the program.

Consideration 1: Residential or Travel Experience?

Should a short-term study abroad experience be located at one site (the residential model) or involve extensive relocation (the travel model)? Single-site short-term study abroad is held by some as an inherently superior model.[4] Clearly, if immersion in a culture is the primary goal of the experience, a single-site residential program may be the better way. On the other hand, a single-culture travel seminar (in which the travel itinerary is confined to a single country or cultural area) could be enriched by the many exposures to important sites (cultural breadth) at a modest cost to immersion (cultural depth).

As we have noted, however, exposure to other cultures is not the only legitimate reason to study abroad. Disciplinary or interdisciplinary foci can more than justify the traveling study abroad model. For example, a seminar abroad in theater or opera needs to go to where the action is, be it London, Paris, Vienna, or Prague. A course in environmental problems needs to visit both sites of environmental degradation and to organizations producing solutions to the problems. A seminar on conflict needs to hit the road, visiting historical sites (battlegrounds or museums) as well as organizations involved in conflict resolution (be they military organizations or peace nongovernmental organizations [NGOs]). Quite literally, Muhammad must go to the mountain.

What is the best design for short-term study abroad—residential or travel? It depends, and the answer clearly depends on the topic of the course, as well as its learning goals. In some instances, the residential and travel models may be productively combined. For example, learning about a former colony in depth clearly calls for a residential experience. However, passing up a comparatively brief visit to the former mother country in the name of pedagogical purity would seem a wasted opportunity for fuller understanding.

Consideration 2: Who Teaches—Us or Them?

In its purest form, the "transplanted" or "offshore" classroom finds the U.S. faculty director responsible for all instruction. The topic of instruction often is intimately related to the surrounding culture or historical place, but it need not be. Those of us more enamored of experiential education need not sneer at the offshore model in pure form. For example, understanding of the novels of Kazansakis is enhanced when the reading and discussion is done in Crete, especially if local site visits complement the classroom learning.

Academic rigor and control of classroom content is clearly enhanced in the transplanted approach. The potential risk this model runs is its social isolation and the resulting insulation of students from the local culture.

There is one outcome that the transplanted model in its pure form will inevitably gain. Its exclusively U.S. instruction will be greeted with skepticism at best by local people, be they academics or ordinary citizens. For that reason alone, local instructional resources should be employed at least to some extent.

---

[4] Such criticism of travel seminars derives from those who hold the junior year abroad experience as ideal, and that shorter-term study abroad models ought to imitate the junior year abroad experience as best they can.

There are a variety of means to offset the enclave proclivities of the offshore classroom, including living arrangements (locally managed flats or home stays), which can produce a measure of cultural immersion and conversation. Hiring local academics to give some of the lectures can introduce an alternative cultural view, a view the faculty director can exploit by comparison to produce cross-cultural understanding in students. Or, overseas universities or providers can supply the entire academic enterprise.

The Site As a Stage

"All the world's a stage," said the Bard. Countless faculty directors have followed his advice, using important cultural or historical sites as backdrops for lectures. The seats of the Roman Coloseum or the walls of St. Paul's Cathedral fairly ring with the echoes of lectures ranging from architecture to religion.

Faculty directors often farm out such responsibilities to their charges, assigning a student or team of students to research each site and proffer the fruits of their research to their colleagues on site. As with the offshore classroom, cross-cultural perspective can be gained by hiring local academics or local guides. Increasingly, such local assistance is required at sites (to protect the jobs of local guides in Greece or Italy, for example), and faculty or students providing their own lectures do so at some legal risk. Faculty directors can also expect the need for some postpresentation elaboration or corrective to the site reports of either their students or local guides.

Using the site as a stage is not without its inefficiencies, and these magnify as the group size gets larger. It is difficult for all students to catch the entire lecture, as the group gets strung out as some artifact diverts individuals' attention or students become exhausted by the hot sun. Despite all the problems, however, the site as stage can produce an emotional moment that can "fix" the learning in students.

Being There

Something similar can happen when the stage alone is the instructor. Simply being at an historical site can have profound effects on students and faculty alike. The process of "historical immersion" is a bit of a mystery (at least to this writer), but something meaningful occurs in each of us when we stand in the exact spot where the Prince of Darkness stood across the Seine from the Eiffel Tower on his only visit to the City of Light. Or when we are moved as we gaze on the exact scene that moved Van Gogh to apply his tortured brush strokes to canvas. Or when we trod the exact cobblestones in an ancient Roman city that St. Augustine frolicked over as a youth. Or how the coals of our motivation to learn are fanned to flame when we visit the sites of the intellectual foundation of our civilization in Greece.

I do not know if we will ever fully understand how the mixture of cognition and emotion produce both the subjective understanding and the motive for further learning these memorable moments provide. I do know that they happen, both predictably and unexpectedly, in such frequency as to warrant visits to such sites just to be there. For the experience to be recognized for what it is, much less for it to be meaningful, some form of intellectual preparation is required. That preparation can occur any time prior to the experience, or even during the experience itself.

So, What Was Going on Behind That Green Door in Rome?

The Aventino these days is occupied by the Sovereign Military Order of Malta, home of the fabled Knights of St. John Hospitallers (the "Knights of Malta" in common parlance). Tracing their organization's roots all the way back to the crusades, these present-day aristocrats sally forth, delivering health care to those in need around the world. Our students spent a golden Roman afternoon learning not only of the order's history and functions, but pondering the noblesse oblige that drives these privileged few to take at times extreme risks to serve the needs of the less fortunate of the world.

The Sovereign Military Order of Malta is but one example of what resources the world has to offer short-term study abroad. The Knights of Malta represent all the variety and diversity of educational opportunities that await the request of leaders and administrators of such programs. Yet what role awaits faculty directors as teachers, if they mobilize the full spectrum of overseas educational resources for their students?

If All the World's a Stage, What's the Teacher Doing in the Pit?

How international education ought to be done depends absolutely on its goals and what the situation has to offer. Any particular pedagogy—be it classroom lecture or service learning—ought be selected not because of some instructional or ideological commitment, but only because of its effectiveness in serving the goals of international education. Simply put, what is good is what works best in attaining the range of goals of study abroad. Usually that means a mix of pedagogies. Oftentimes that mix means that the teacher is not the star of the show, but rather its director. A director is seldom on stage. Rather, a director is gathering the needed resources for the performance, assembling the cast, interpreting the script, and coordinating the efforts of all toward a common end.

We academics are often loath to give up the limelight. In my formative years of teaching, a very wise man suggested that I spend my efforts thinking up ways to teach my students "more than I know." More often than not, that meant stepping out of the instructional spotlight to bring reality into my campus classroom, or to bring my students into a reality overseas. Directing short-term programs abroad and later administering a program has given me a career's worth of opportunities to think up a variety of ways to teach more than I know. These experiences have opened up many doors for me—to learn about other people and global problems, and about the processes of teaching and learning—than I would ever have otherwise.

PART I
Working Within
Higher Education

Chapter 2

Building Institutional Support

Peter Hovde

One of the first things I did following my appointment as director of our study abroad programs was to read all the published advice I could find in books like this one about how to do the director's job. One common piece of advice was this: that a director will (sadly, but necessarily) devote more time and attention to building institutional support for the program than to creating and managing programs abroad.

I just did not believe that advice. Far more daunting was the thought of negotiating agreements overseas and managing programs from a distance; comforting was the certainty that all elements of the campus community would pull together in common effort to make our college a national leader in study abroad. My naiveté sprang eternal.

It did not take many years' experience as director to demonstrate the veracity of all that published advice. Luckily, my naiveté was offset by a professional career in political science. Though not a practiced politician, my discipline had at least given me an eye for politics, and having a political perspective proved very useful. In my experience, directing study abroad programs is a very political process, and being director a very political position.

Neither this chapter, nor any other chapter in this book, is a simple checklist for success for someone creating or managing short-term programs abroad. This chapter does contain perspectives and principles—filched from my discipline and derived from my experience, gained from both successes and failures—that should, or at least could, apply to your situation as well. I have tried to write what I wish I could have read when I took on the task of director over a decade ago.

Your situation is probably unlike mine. Your institution may be public, whereas mine is private. Your university may be vastly larger than my college, or your college smaller.[1] Your institutional culture may be more attuned to globalization than mine, or less so. And the director's position at your school may be less politicized (though it's hard to imagine it being more so).

I do not think those differences in institutional context matter very much. Each of us has the same task: make it possible for as many students as possible to have the best overseas learning experience possible. To attain that end, we each have to get a large number of people with their diverse institutional interests to

---

[1] The terms "college" and "university" are used interchangeably in this essay.

do what they otherwise would not do. That process—of getting others to do what they should have the good sense to do anyway, as Harry Truman would say—is politics. To accomplish that end by remaking your institution in important ways, as James McGregor Burns would say, is leadership.[2]

Two things to remember before we set off. First, as a political scientist, I see the world through a set of political lenses, which give me insights others do not see. Remember that your training and your experience—be it as economist or educator, partner or parent—have given you lenses and insights that you can bring to this task. Your unique combination of lenses and insights will serve you well if you hark back to them. Second, remember that those who stand in your way on the road to success—indecisive dean, irascible faculty, inflexible bureaucrat—are (probably) not the malicious louts they may appear to be. They are nearly always well-intentioned, committed people possessed of the responsibilities and agendas of the offices they occupy. To build institutional support for your program, it is your task to expand those sets of responsibilities and to place study abroad high on their agendas. Or, put more simply, to change their institutional outlook, and to modify their motivations. That's all....

The Goal Is to Build a Winning Coalition

In politics, the side with the most votes wins. The trick in politics is to get more people, and more committed people, on your side than any other side. Bringing diverse people with different perspectives, motives, and incentives into a coalition under one banner or behind a candidate is a real trick. In short, coalition building is the essence of politics. And so it is with building institutional support for a study abroad program.

Colleges and universities are composed of diverse people with different perspectives, motives, and incentives, all messily contending for recognition and resources. Trying to go it alone in this sea of hard-fought politics relying only on the "obvious" merit of your study abroad cause is a recipe for failure. A study abroad director needs many people, committed people, and important people on his or her side, and needs budgetary input. The trick is finding allies to build a winning coalition out of all that diversity and difference, a coalition whose members—your allies—will help you get what you need to run a successful study abroad program. In this section, we will look first at the foundation of any study abroad program, the office staff, and conclude with the most crucial of your allies, the faculty.

Your Allies: the Director's Coalition Partners

Staff

Hire the best staff you can find. For a number of reasons, there has been an oversupply of people in our society with travel agency experience. Former travel agents bring the skills and perspectives that are a natural fit for an international office. On the other hand, study abroad is not rocket science, so hiring someone with a willingness to learn and a commitment to the mission is of greater importance than extant skills. However they arrive or develop, committed and skilled staff are the bedrock of success for any study abroad program.

All study abroad staffs are vastly overworked, due the nature of the enterprise. Most staff members are underpaid as well. Getting better pay and promotion for the staff helps to maintain that necessary

---

[2] Burns, J. McGregor (1978) *Leadership*. New York: Harper & Row.

commitment to job performance and skill enhancement, but that is difficult to accomplish in the tight-fisted modern university. You may need to seek other incentives. One is to make sure that each staff member has a challenging and satisfying set of tasks. Another is to insure that each staff member finds out what it is like to study abroad. If a staff member can handle an overseas assignment, it is better that he or she goes than the director. Staff who make travel arrangements will do a better job if they know what the situations they are sending students into are like "on the ground." There is no reward of greater importance to staff development and morale than the chance to find out what it is like "over there."

Program Providers and Vendors

Services needed from program providers and vendors can range from the purchase of group airline tickets to contracting all logistics. Most published advice and some university regulations would keep the relationships with these support organizations distant and competitive, always looking for the lowest bid.

A minority of directors take a different approach, looking for agencies and agents who are consistently cost effective and reliable, and bringing them into the fold as coalition partners. When things go wrong at the worst possible time—which they do with stimulating regularity in this business—the cost of a service does not seem like such an important criterion after all. Far better to have an agent whom one can contact day or night, and on whose ability and judgment one can rely.

Things can get a bit too cozy with service providers, of course. If prices begin to creep up a bit more than they should, a little competition needs to be injected back into the mix. Just raising the specter of another competitor usually is enough to bring prices back into line.

Administrative Offices

Sending students abroad requires the active participation of many of the college's administrative offices, the business office, the financial aid office, and the registrar's office chief among them. Unfortunately, short-term programs abroad place new sets of demands on these offices that do not fit well in either time frame or task with their standard operating procedures. In short, the international office represents more work for these offices, work that is seen as an overload (more students to deal with) and is more labor intensive (often requiring individual attention to a student or problem). In short, other administrative offices see the study abroad office as a big pain. That is, unless these offices (their directors and staffs) are brought into your coalition.

Bringing these offices on board requires a three-pronged strategy. First, assign a liaison to these offices. The Machiavellian director must not perform this task. Rather, appoint the nicest and most naturally friendly person on your staff as liaison. He or she will unavoidably get to know, on a personal basis, the staff who work in the trenches of those other offices that are key to your program success. Your liaison will get to know the needs of both the people and the processes of those offices, which is key to the second step in bringing these partners into the coalition. The second prong of the strategy is to "ease their pain." That is, design your office procedures to conform to theirs, and do your work in such a way that it does a lot of the work for them. For example, simply designing and modifying a financial worksheet for international office use that exactly meets the informational needs of the financial aid office can warm and strengthen the bond between the two offices. Third, these people who labor in the administrative trenches of universities are its unsung heroes. In my view, our colleges would fall apart without them. Singing their praises at every opportunity—both to their faces and to those higher up (and to the faculty)—is not only the effective thing to do, it is the right thing to do.

The Image Makers

It is crucial to make your program as visible as possible. It is difficult to be visible, because so much of the action in study abroad occurs out of sight, overseas. It is imperative to use every medium possible (from brochures to the Web), in as compelling a way as possible, to parade your program in front of all customers (i.e., students and parents) and all constituencies (e.g., top administrators, faculty). It pays to have these messages look as professional as possible, and it helps if you can get professionals to help you create the messages.

Professional communications people are creative people looking for outlets for their creativity. Study abroad is an attractive topic to these people, because the case is so compelling, and the topic so photogenic. In short, your needs match their interests, and great things can happen with that synergistic alliance. The only problem is that production and the publication can cost a lot of money, and your budget may not have a publications line item. At a minimum, you can at least get advice and assistance from the communications professionals on campus, and you can produce the advertisements on your office computers.

How much promotion is enough? In campaign politics, you know that half of your promotional effort is wasted. The problem is, you do not know which half has been a waste, so you must try every promotional activity that you can afford.

Students (and Parents)

The direct targets of your promotional activities are the students themselves, and for undergraduates, their parents. Convincing students to go abroad is the obvious task, but convincing parents that their child going abroad is a good idea may be even more important. And it is easy to overlook the parents in the flurry of your recruiting efforts. Talking to groups of parents during summer advisement about the importance of study abroad in a global age is very well received. Sending mass mailings to parents either promoting programs or reassuring them in troubled times is both the effective and the right thing to do. Calling each parent to inform them that their child's group has arrived safely at its destination, and that everything is fine, will pay big dividends. That a few parents will contact the university's president to express their appreciation for the thoughtfulness of your office for that phone call will not hurt your institutional support one bit.

The strategy to build institutional support among students is pretty simple. It is a principle contained in the motto of our program: "Your experience of a lifetime." Do whatever you can to insure that outcome for each and every student, and then ask them to help you convince the next generation of students to follow in their footsteps.

Prospective Students and Parents

Whether they intend to participate during their matriculation or not, many students use the existence of a study abroad program as a marker of the quality of the institution. This is even more true of parents, who are quite receptive to the idea that students need to be prepared to succeed in the global culture, and who are quite willing to believe that study abroad is the best way for their children to prepare for the future. The same is true for most college and university ranking systems, even those ranking systems that use a rather short list of evaluative criteria.

It does not seem to matter much to students whether the college operates its own programs or farms them out to providers, nor does the extent of study abroad offerings seem to matter all that much. That students have easy access to study abroad options is what matters most. However, colleges and universities without a study abroad program place themselves at a competitive disadvantage, content to be considered second rate by many prospective students and parents.

On the other hand, requiring one's students to study abroad—except for some schools with exceptional constituencies—can dampen the enthusiasm of prospective students and parents for the college. U.S. students often bridle at "having" to do something, even something they otherwise might like to do, and requiring students to go abroad will give more cautious parents pause. For some students and their parents, just going off to college is a step big enough. Simultaneously signing up for both higher education and education overseas is a step too far.

Some middle ground would offer the best approach—a program of either encouraging or inducing students to study abroad, rather than requiring it. That way, more hesitant students and students for whom study abroad is a low priority when they enter the university will get a chance to discover why study abroad is so important and beneficial as they rub shoulders with older students who have already studied overseas. A college that either encourages or induces study abroad is likely to have better success in retaining its students as well, for the prospect of overseas experience can tie students to the institution, overcoming other factors that might push them toward another university.

It does not necessarily follow that one's admissions office will hold the same level of enthusiasm about study abroad, however. Admissions officers are often loath to fiddle with a formula that has brought success to this point, and study abroad often does not show up as a high priority in prospective-student surveys. Data and anecdotes confirming the pull of study abroad for prospective students, and the retaining force of overseas study for matriculated students may help convince them. Reminding admissions officers of the integral part that study abroad plays in a modern higher education and the duty we have as educators to prepare our students for the global world can help as well. However, it may take the intervention of a higher university authority to get admissions officers to see this clearly.

Alumni and Friends

Alumni can lend powerful support to your study abroad recruiting efforts. Those graduates who were program participants are not hesitant about singing the praises of study abroad to important constituencies, both on campus and beyond its confines. Alumni can sell your program to prospective participants and their parents, either face-to-face (during a family weekend, for example) or in your promotions and advertisements (either printed or electronic). More persuasively than anyone, alumni can explain how the study abroad experience affected the trajectory of their lives—how it made them much more confident in such a very short time, how it altered their perspective on the world, and how it changed their career path. And nothing sells better to students and parents these days than careers—that a student is more likely to find the right one, or a better one, because of study abroad. Even those alumni who did not go abroad and regret missing out on the experience do not mind telling others that they made a mistake.

It is never too late to create alumni. Short-term programs abroad for "alumni" and "friends" can be especially popular with graduates of your college, as well as its friends (even if that friendship just got started with the deposit for a program abroad). Such programs can stand on their own, or they might tag along with a university musical ensemble on its overseas tour. Such experiences can build close relationships among alumni, friends, and faculty members, and current students on the performance tours.

It might be too much to expect older alumni and friends to have the kinds of transforming experiences that younger students often take away from study abroad. However, if alumni tours are made sufficiently and engagingly academic, the experience can open the minds, the hearts, and even the wallets of those old dogs who have learned new tricks. Development directors will sometimes send along an officer, ever ready to help those opening processes along, although this tactic might seem a bit transparent.

Especially powerful alumni can be especially powerful allies of study abroad when they are asked to participate in curricular reform or strategic planning for your university. These alumni did not attain their success by being hesitant or timid, so they are likely to have either studied or traveled abroad and are convinced of the merits of such experience for all students. It is difficult to overestimate the value of the support of powerful alumni, both for your programs and for your college.

Senior Administrators

The important directions of any college or university are generally set by a rather small group of people, the senior administrators (presidents and provosts, deans and directors), or more colloquially, the "big boys" (be they male or female). Their support is essential for the maintenance and defense of your programs. Their support is absolutely crucial for the expansion of your programs.

The numbers game. "How many students do you send abroad?" Reporting a large number in response to that question is the measure of success these days. That question is asked in either absolute terms or percentage terms, and answered in the way that makes the school look best.

Large universities can support a wide array of programs of their own, and send large numbers of students overseas. Smaller colleges have the advantage of being able to send larger percentages of their students overseas on fewer programs. Success in either numbers or percentages can go nearly as far as the photographs, the prose, and the poetry of students' experiences abroad in building solid support for your program.

A director at a small college would have the advantage of having greater access to top-level decisionmakers. That kind of personal relationship with the top administrators is an advantage that builds institutional support all on its own. The darker side of that advantage, however, is that the director will be directly involved and responsible when something goes wrong.

Crisis management. An old U.S. State Department hand once said that crisis comes at you "like a tiger out of the night." In more technical terms, a crisis is generally a surprise, is a direct threat to major institutional values, and normally demands quick decisions made in the absence of complete information. Crises seem most often to start with a phone call in the middle of the night. They threaten our highest values—the safety of our students and staff, and secondarily our college's legal liability and reputation—and force us to try to predict the future with precise clarity while groping around in a fog of inadequate information.

Experienced study abroad directors do not really need such a definition of crisis, having experienced those "tigers out of the night" with a depressing and increasing regularity in recent years. Study abroad crises can range in focus from an individual physical or emotional problem on a single program all across the spectrum to the worldwide impacts of the Gulf War and September 11 on the entirety of our programs. Crisis management also means anticipating crises, planning for contingencies, and building safety into one's programs.

Crisis management for study abroad could fill its own volume. Our topic here is building institutional support. Crises do contain great danger, but they also contain great opportunities to build institutional support, if you are a good crisis manager. And if you are lucky.

The least bad kind of crisis to have is the anticipatory crisis. In such a case, something has happened overseas in a place where you are planning to send students, but the students are not there yet. This gives you a chance to get a briefing on the desks of the president and other top-level crisis decisionmakers first thing in the morning. Examples would be a terrorist group announcing they would begin including tourists on their list of terrorist targets just as you are about to send your students to Turkey, or the Luxor massacre occurring just as your students are about to depart for Egypt. The briefing would include the nature of the situation, alternative courses of action, your recommended course of action, and a few supporting documents from the media or the Web with important information highlighted.

In the examples just described, your office and your crisis team[3] had an opportunity to show how professionally it handled a major problem. This kind of organizational performance is highly valued by the top administrators, and will build organizational support for your programs and office like few other accomplishments. With each successive crisis, your reputation will build and your institutional support will increase. The dark side, however, is that you will be expected to perform just as effectively in any future crisis and a failure will not be quickly forgiven. Welcome to the world of 24-hour on-call.

Like so many other things on the director's plate, building institutional commitment through the numbers game and crisis management diverts one from the tasks of creating and maintaining programs.

Faculty

In their attitudes toward the study abroad enterprise, faculty come in four stripes: hostile, indifferent, supporting, and active. Think of faculty as forming four concentric rings around the international office, with hostile faculty on the periphery, and active faculty forming the protective inner ring.

Faculty who are *hostile* to international education and question its legitimacy and its drain on university resources usually prefer subversion to public expression of their antagonism toward study abroad. Hostile faculty seem to have a way of worming their way onto curriculum committees where they can use their votes to obstruct study abroad initiatives. Efforts to persuade hostile faculty of the folly of their ways pretty much fall on deaf ears, and are usually a waste of time. Isolating and marginalizing hostile faculty by the statements of your important allies showing how out of step they are with trends in higher education is the most effective strategy.

Indifferent faculty members are not a major problem, unless they compose the vast majority of the faculty. There is potential in this ring, however. Indifferent faculty can be roused from their lethargy by the realization that their discipline has gone global, or that their focus of professional passion is threatened by some international issue or has some important contribution to make to the global human condition. Such realizations can be engendered by, for example, dangling grant money in front of this faculty to explore the international implications and contributions of what they do, or more effectively (but more haphazardly) by some serendipitous self-realization.

---

[3] If you do not have a crisis team, form one comprising people with cool heads and clear-eyed judgment who are willing to drop everything, including their personal lives if need be, until some resolution of a crisis has been attained.

Supporting faculty are those who recognize the importance of study abroad, yet are not actively involved in taking students overseas. Supporting faculty are crucial to any initiative in study abroad, from helping to get the program passed by the faculty senate to assisting in recruiting students whom others will take overseas. All that is required to arouse their support is information about programs and initiatives, and simply being asked to help.

Active faculty are those who direct programs abroad. They are the backbone of the international office. Their efforts determine not only the existence of a short-term program, but its quality as well. Spare no effort in support of your active faculty.

So, the strategic approach to faculty is really quite simple: narrow the widths of the outer rings and broaden the widths of the inner rings. A simple strategy, but not so easy to accomplish. Tactically, that means isolating and marginalizing the hostile faculty, ignoring or arousing the indifferent, engaging the supporting faculty, and doing everything you can for the active faculty. That last task—doing everything you can for the active faculty—is of such importance that its discussion takes up most of the rest of this chapter.

There are two key principles that will bring about the faculty support and participation a successful program requires.

1. Make your study abroad program unassailably academic. In contrast to the numbers game needed for outside recognition, the road to success with faculty is paved with academic quality. Faculty bred to respect the classroom as the only place where true learning can occur are initially suspicious that real learning can occur residentially immersed in a culture or on the road. They must be shown otherwise.

At the beginning, it takes masses of documentary evidence to convince skeptics. Learning assessment surveys and reentry interviews, logs of contact hours, examples of papers and exams, syllabi, texts, and so on, all will be examined with the skeptics looking for chinks in the case for short-term study abroad. But when the best of the faculty come on board your program as directors, as they inevitably seem to, their leadership insures the academic quality of the program offerings. With their arrival, the evaluation game changes. Acceptable evidence of learning moves from the quantitative to the qualitative, even to the anecdotal. In our own case, logs of contact hours faded before the realization that something memorable happened to almost every student almost every day of the program, whether it was planned in the itinerary or not. With institutional experience, the realization dawns that study abroad is the most effective means of engendering the higher-end outcomes—the "education of the whole person" kinds of goals—many of our colleges claim to produce.[4] These shifts occur because of the reputations of the finest faculty, and because of the creative ways

---

[4] Koester, J. (1985). *A Profile of the U.S. Student Abroad.* New York: Council on International Education Exchange. Nicely summarized research concerning the effects of study abroad.
Other examples are as follows:
Carlson, J. S. and Widaman, K. F. (1988). The effects of study abroad during college on attitudes toward other cultures. *International Journal of Intercultural Relations, 12,* 1-17.
Carsello, C. and Greiser, J. (1975). How college students change during study abroad. *College Student Journal, 10,* 276-278.
Hansel, B., and Grove, N. (1986). International student exchange programs: Are the educational benefits real? *NASP Bulletin, 70,* 84-90.
Juhasz, A. M., and Walker, A. M. (1988). The impact of study abroad on university student's self-esteem and self-efficacy. *College Student Journal, 22(4),* 329-341.
Kauffman, N. L. (1983). The impact of study abroad on personal development of college students. (Doctoral dissertation, Indiana University, 1983). *Dissertation Abstracts International, 44,* 1350A.
Nash, D. (1976). The personal consequences of a year of study abroad. *Journal of Higher Education, 47,* 191-203.
Sell, D.K. (1983). Attitude change in foreign study participants. *International Journal of Intercultural Relations, 7,* 131-147.
Stitsworth, M. H. (1988). Personality changes associated with sojourn in Japan. *The Journal of Social Psychology, 129,* 213-224.

they design learning experiences abroad for your students, and simply because of the way learning outside the comfort of our own culture affects us all. But skeptics will continue to be hired as faculty, so we all must continue to collect evidence of the obvious.

2. Focus on faculty first (last, and always). That principle simply means to get faculty what they need to do the job of giving students an experience of a lifetime. You cannot have a good program without good faculty. No matter what directors and other administrators do, your study abroad program is only as good as the faculty who direct it. The best way to improve a program is to make good faculty even better and more numerous. Faculty development is the best investment a college or program can make in its future.

Faculty need to become more skilled and better at directing students abroad. Faculty also need to be able to overcome their understandable fear of taking students abroad.

Summer workshops, monthly briefing sessions on various leadership topics during the academic year, and one-on-one meetings with staff can all assist faculty in gaining the skills and the confidence required to take students overseas. Veteran faculty directors are your key resource here. They are the human capital of your program, the repository of the wealth of experience and insight about delivering the benefits of short-term study abroad to students.

However, on-campus learning can only go so far. As with students and staff, the best international education for faculty can only occur overseas, for the gains in learning skills and gaining confidence are far greater abroad than at home. This approach to faculty development costs money, however. There are two potential sources for this faculty development money—external and internal.[5] There are few external funding agencies that will fund faculty leadership training overseas. It just looks too much like a boondoggle. Internal funding is more flexible, but far more limited in supply. Beyond that, there is the issue of what skill or quality the faculty need to develop. Is it familiarity with the site to be visited, or is it learning how to direct short-term programs in a succession of sites? Our faculty prefer the latter. The most efficient method we have found to develop future faculty directors is to bring them on existing seminars abroad as assistant directors so they can learn the ropes on site. There is no mechanism that produces greater support for the program among faculty than a "free" trip abroad.[6]

Second, make faculty full partners in all stages of the study abroad process, from planning and costing through assessment and evaluation. Such partnership will shrink the faculty/administrative divide, and reduce the conflict between the international office and the faculty, who always want all the extras on their seminar at less than actual cost.

Finally, provide the most incentive possible for faculty to participate in short-term study abroad. Gaining these incentives for faculty is not easily done, however. Our summer program directors get a greater salary than faculty who teach summer school on campus, reflecting the greater contact time and added responsibilities of directors abroad. However, the college did not always find that case compelling, and it took more than 20 years for that policy change to be made. Nonfinancial incentives to faculty—such as specific credit toward promotion and tenure for study abroad leadership—seem even more difficult to obtain.

---

[5] For a comparative discussion of the impact of three models of international faculty development, see Hovde P., Ellig N., Krejci M., Rice M., and Sandgren D. (1997). An evaluation of faculty study abroad: a response to Lambert's strategic questions. *International Education Forum* 17, 23-31.

[6] "Free" in a very qualified sense. Our faculty go abroad with a clear expectation that they will be directing their own seminar in the near future.

In summary, development of both the faculty and curriculum are the most important accomplishments to building institutional support for short-term programs abroad. How one does those jobs is far less important than that the jobs themselves get done. Make sure that all your efforts to develop faculty and curriculum are visible to faculty and administration alike.

Eroding Institutional Support

There are many ways and means to dissipate the institutional support for international education that has accumulated. Circumstances can do it, your adversaries can do it, and you can do it.

Circumstances

Global events such as the Gulf War and September 11 have and will temporarily decrease enrollments and erode psychological support for study abroad. None of the many types of allies noted above is immune. Trends, both global (e.g., inflation abroad) and national (e.g., consumer confidence), can diminish support as prices of programs and costs to the college increase. Conflicts among senior administrators can put you between a rock and a hard place. Most of these circumstances are outside your control, but their impact can be lessened. Imposing cost-containment measures on program budgets can help, as will building safety measures into your programs, but only if you are *seen* to be doing these things. Notice has to be given via various media to the college at large (ranging from mass mailings to parents to memos to the top administrators) describing what you are doing and why your actions are going to solve the problem.

Adversaries

Harry Truman said that a leader without enemies is not much of a leader. Burns says that leaders "Must be willing to make enemies—to deny themselves the affection of their adversaries. They must accept conflict. They must be willing and able to be unloved."[7] But a long list of enemies does not a leader make, and I would advise making as few enemies as possible.

Resistance to your study abroad administration often comes from within the campus international education community itself. Foremost is the faculty member who wants to run his or her program free of any interference from your office, and above and apart from the university rules that govern all study abroad programs. A secondary source of resistance can be the directors and coaches of musical organizations and sports teams, who often do not want their concertizing or game schedule cluttered by cross-cultural experience and learning. All such resistance is difficult to fight directly, because it seldom is done in the open. A better approach is to get the top administrators to do the job for you by policy edict. The issue of centralization is discussed in Chapter 3, Administrative Processes.

Self-Destruction

The actions and inactions of the director can do a lot of damage to the institutional support of his or her programs. Damage can come from either the substance of the director's policies or the symbolism of his or her actions. For example, flying business class while faculty directors are back in coach is a surefire way to reduce your institutional support. Inattention to the ideas or needs of each and every faculty or staff member—stated or not—will erode support. This problem haunts almost every overworked and overstressed office of international education, and at best it can only be ameliorated, not resolved. Inattention

---

[7] Burns, J. McGregor (1978) *Leadership*. New York: Harper & Row, 34.

to budgetary detail can kill you, and submitting financial audits with red numbers on the bottom line will find senior administrators questioning the need for the entire study abroad program.

The Director

Finally, we directors ourselves are major players in our own coalitions. The position and status of the director within the university, the experience he or she brings to the task, and his or her leadership style, are all important factors in the success of the study abroad programs, and the institutional support that coalesces behind the international education office.

Position and Status

Most program directors have little authority inherent in their organizational position. Responsibility for any problem with the name "international" associated with it, yes. Possession of the authority to do anything about the problem, no. A word of caution: if you are one of the few anointed with the real authority that the term "director" implies, be very careful. Exercise this authority very sparingly, and only as a last resort. Rely instead on the use of persistent and elaborate persuasion that all of the rest of us must use to get the job done. In the long run, that more complex approach works better at building institutional support anyway.

To be frank, it helps if the director has faculty status, the more senior the better. Faculty have a strong tendency to view "mere" administrators as unsophisticated meddlers in academic affairs about which such interlopers know only superficially at best. If you do not have faculty rank, there is a better strategy than running out and getting a quick Ph.D. from some virtual university. The better way is to form a small group of highly respected supportive or active faculty who are willing to be your "kitchen cabinet." Listen to the advice they have to give you, and do what they recommend. Let them front for you in any academic setting, explaining to the rest of the faculty why some new initiative, policy, or pedagogy is good for the program and the institution. In my own experience, even as a senior faculty member, my kitchen cabinet has given me invaluable advice, and has prevented me from doing some really dumb things.

Formative Experience

Few study abroad administrators have been educated specifically for the task. Most of us were diverted from some other career path to take on this job. Having some other previous experience is really a reservoir of learned talents that you can employ in this job. In my own case, I draw daily on what I learned from being an auditor, a naval flight officer, taking students overseas as a faculty director, and raising two wonderful children as a single parent. So, if you are new to this game, take heart. Your previous experience has taught you far more than you realize about how to run a program and build institutional support for that enterprise.

Leadership Style

For Harry Truman, a leader was "someone who gets others to something they should have had the good sense to do in the first place." By necessity, a director of international programs has a lot of leadership on her or his to-do list.

James McGregor Burns[2] would tell us there are three approaches to leadership in any institution. The first is power wielding, the kind of heavy-handed authoritarian approach designed primarily for the benefit of the one exercising the authority. We have all seen administrators with that style come (and thankfully mostly go) at our colleges. It is an approach to leadership that is inherently corrupting and ineffective, and just will not work in a modern "multiversity" of any size or complexity.[8]

The next type of leadership Burns identifies is "transactional" leadership. Transactional leadership is exchange theory in action, for each side gets what it wants in an exchange of nonequivalent resources. For example, when you ask your communications office for help in designing a program brochure, you get your brochure and they get their creative outlet. Both parties got what they wanted, and both are happier than they otherwise would have been.

If you should keep coming back asking for more brochure design, your requests may start to wear a little thin, and the communications office may begin asking you for your college budget number. Or you might wrangle some funding to send the graphic designer overseas to see how your programs operate from the inside, and to bring back text and pictures for brochures for some time to come. That experience will be appreciated, but even appreciation will soon fade and the expectation for future funded trips raises the value bar of exchanged goods.

Transactional leadership is leadership's most prevalent form. It is extremely useful in forming coalitions by building a series of mutual assistance pacts with the players. But as transactional leadership really rests on a "What have you done for me lately?" foundation, the networks of appreciation that are built on that style of leadership are rather tenuous, and require continuous nurturing to maintain them.

Much more enduring, and much more difficult to achieve, is the "transforming" leadership style. Here it is not the exchange of resources but a mutual raising of motivation. The motives of both the leader and the led are raised to qualitatively new heights.

> ...Transforming leadership is dynamic leadership in the sense that the leaders throw themselves into a relationship with followers who will feel "elevated" by it and often become more active themselves, thereby creating new cadres of leadership.[9]

Alliances based on transforming leadership may have had a transactional beginning, likely based on the "webs of appreciation" you created among your allies. But somewhere along the line, motivations changed, and networks of appreciation became "networks of affection." Somehow colleagues are transformed into friends, friends who would do anything for you, as you have done and would do for them. This is leadership at its most satisfying. This leadership produces the kind of institutional support that endures the long haul, and is there when you need it most. And, if you are foolish enough to still want to become director of a short-term study abroad program after reading this chapter, this is the kind of support you are eventually going to need.

How will you know when your leadership has had some effect? For Burns, leadership is measured by "the production of intended effects," the degree of actual accomplishment of promised change.[10] So feel justifiably proud of your accomplishments as new programs accumulate, as more faculty are "internationally

---

[8] Indeed, Burns does not call power wielding a type of leadership at all. He references the term leadership, reserving it for the two higher-level and productive types of behavior.

[9] Burns, J. McGregor (1978) *Leadership*. New York: Harper & Row, 20.

[10] Burns, J. McGregor (1978) *Leadership*. New York: Harper & Row, 22.

developed" or "globalized," and as increasing numbers of students enjoy an "experience of a lifetime" under your tutelage. All of these accomplishments will build and bank institutional support for you and your program. But do not rest too easy on your laurels, for the job of study abroad director has real transactional leadership or "What have you done for me lately?" quality about it. Institutional support can evaporate far more quickly than all your hard work took to build it up.

Becoming a transforming leader is a pretty tall order. Burns uses Gandhi as his best example. Transforming leadership is at least a goal to which we lesser lights can aspire. But know that a director cannot do all this alone. For Burns, leadership occurs in a relationship among leader and followers. Transforming leadership occurs only when followers and the leader are transformed, when "leaders help make their followers into leaders. Only by standing on their shoulders can true greatness be achieved."[11]

That is the kind of leadership that builds "webs of affection" among allies, allies who have become the kind of friend you are to them. The kind of friend who anticipates your needs and acts without having to be asked. These are friendly followers who have become the kind of leaders you need, those who will build the kind of institutional support that will get you through the tough times that will surely come along.

Conclusion

As a brief summary, the basic principles that have structured this essay are printed below. They are guidelines that I have found valuable in building institutional support for study abroad programs.

- Build and nurture webs of affection among your allies.
- Make your programs and activities visible.
- Make your programs unassailably academic.
- Focus on faculty first (last, and always).
- Give students an experience of a lifetime.

I would very much appreciate hearing about principles you have derived, so I may learn from your experience. Please e-mail me at hovde@cord.edu.

---

[11] Burns, J. McGregor (1978) *Leadership*. New York: Harper & Row, 443.

Chapter 3

Administrative Processes

Julie Taylor

Once you have determined that a need for short-term study abroad programs exists on your campus, where do you begin planning a program? What critical questions should you be asking and of whom? The purpose of this chapter is to examine the administrative processes necessary to plan, implement, and sustain a short-term program abroad and to highlight policy issues that should be considered when starting up such a program.

Developing and administering quality short-term programs abroad requires at least as many resources and as much attention to the myriad of details as demanded in study abroad programs or exchanges of a longer duration. In order to create a sustainable short-term program, careful consideration must be given to administrative and academic processes, policies, and resources. Here is a sample of responsibilities that a program administrator may undertake:

- Build support on campus for short-term programs abroad.
- Determine program model and design; establish criteria for successful programs.
- Determine timing for proposal review and development.
- Recruit faculty.
- Create committee to review proposals.
- Market the program: design flyers, brochures, electronic media; conduct promotional activities, including fairs and classroom presentations.
- Make logistical arrangements, including arranging for transportation, lodging, activities, classroom, research, computer facilities.
- Assess risk factors of location and program activities; inform students and faculty on health, safety, responsibility, and insurance issues.
- If working with consortia: recruit for, accept, and process applications from outside institutions.
- Review applications; notify students of acceptance decisions.
- Maintain student records.
- Arrange payment to program providers, including travel agents, tour guides, program providers, or organizations contracted for lodging, classroom space, and so on.
- Register students.
- Collect program fees, including deposits; issue refunds.
- Prepare program, faculty, and student budgets.

- Provide training for faculty directors and other leaders, such as staff or teaching assistants.
- Provide predeparture orientation for students and faculty.
- Prepare program handbooks for students and faculty.
- Respond to emergencies or problems during program.
- Conduct program evaluations.
- Respond to the questions and concerns of faculty, students, parents, administrators, and other staff.
- Close budget at end of program; manage excess program funds or budget deficits, reimburse faculty expenses.
- Provide reentry support to students and faculty.
- Maintain contact with service providers in anticipation of future programs.

The administration of short-term programs abroad may flow easily into the current structure and calendar of administration for longer-term academic study abroad and exchange programs. It may, however, require that you create new or different administrative structures such as separate application deadlines, an additional application review process, and different timelines for students to pay deposits or withdraw from the program.

You may also receive applications from students outside of your institution or from noncredit participants. These applications may necessitate a different approach to fee collection, the participants may have different financial aid and credit processing needs, and even group travel may be affected.

Keeping the many responsibilities outlined above in mind as you create an administrative structure will help you determine which tasks the international office or faculty director can manage, which are best handled by another office on campus, and which tasks will require an outside service provider.

Laying the Groundwork for Administrative Structure

Building Support on Campus for Short-Term Programs Abroad

The previous chapter examined different constituencies on campus that may assist you in endorsing short-term programs abroad as another avenue of meeting the institution's international mission; this section briefly considers which offices on campus should be consulted when establishing administrative procedures. Most international educators realize that it does indeed take a campus to run a study abroad program. Chapter 4 thoroughly examines how many departments—from the registrar's office to campus publications—can support these programs.

It is crucial that you know your campus before you establish an administrative structure for short-term programs abroad. Who are the key decisionmakers within each academic or administrative department? Who will have a say or has a vested interest in how these programs are set up and managed? Taking the time to identify and meet with these individuals and working to establish supportive relationships will make for a successful program.

Key Offices	Important Questions
Academic deans	Is there support at the highest levels for short-term programs abroad? Can the dean secure funding for faculty salaries?
Department chair/ school directors	Are there faculty with study abroad leadership experience or others with similar experience who can be recommended? Are there suggested majors to target for faculty recruiting? How will short-term programs abroad affect faculty load, salaries, and full-time enrollments for the department? Is there an ideal time for short-term programs?
Registrar	Will the short-term course require a special registration code? How will students register for the course? Will the transcript reflect study abroad? If off-campus students are participating, which office will prepare and distribute a transcript?
Business office	Which office will manage the budget for the short-term program abroad? Who will negotiate contracts for goods and services? Who will conduct financial wire transfers? Which office will issue deposits to service providers, provide faculty with meal allowances and discretionary funds? What is the refund policy for study abroad program fees? For tuition? Which office will issue refunds of program deposits for students who withdraw? Who will reconcile accounts at the end of the program? Where will excess program funds be placed or deficits managed?
Financial aid	Can participants in short-term programs abroad apply for financial aid? Is there a separate application, a different process, or time frame? If eligible, will students receive financial aid monies prior to the start of the program?
Risk management	Is emergency medical and/or health insurance required of all participants? Does a contract with an insurance provider need to be negotiated? Will the risk management office need to assess the health and safety conditions of a program location?
Legal counsel	Do program-specific releases and/or an acknowledgment of risks need to be drafted? Do contracts with service providers need to be reviewed and approved by legal counsel? Can legal counsel clarify the responsibilities of the faculty director and the relationship of the program to the service providers and guest lecturers?
Continuing education; existing departmental programs	Are there short-term programs abroad in existence at your institutions? How are they administered? Can you work in collaboration? How do you avoid duplicating effort? Are there turf issues of which you should be aware?

Working Within Existing Administrative Structures

It is essential to determine if short-term study abroad academic and administrative models are already in place elsewhere on campus. You will save time and resources by not duplicating efforts already at work within your institution. You also need to be sensitive to turf issues and to departments and faculty that are already involved with existing programs.

The continuing education or summer session office may be involved in administering short-term programs for academic credit and may have experience in working with off-campus participants. These offices could be a source of collaboration and may be able to absorb some of the administrative and fiscal responsibilities that the international office cannot manage.

Models of Administration

Until the last quarter of the 20th century, individual faculty and departments facilitated most study abroad activity. With the large increases in student participation and the number of programs available, many institutions have created and staffed international or study abroad offices. Since most administrative processes focus on the role of the study abroad office, the institution must determine the services and level of administration that can be provided by this office. This is often a balancing act between what the resources will allow and the expectations of faculty directors and their academic units. This section will present and discuss three models of program administration: decentralized, centralized, and hybrid.

Institutional Setting

The location of the international office within the organizational structure of the institution will largely determine the administrative model used in creating and managing short-term programs abroad. An office under the umbrella of academic affairs may have greater credibility and visibility than an office under student affairs. This is significant when reaching out to academic units or departments for assistance in program development. An office within academic affairs is usually under the leadership of a dean, or under a director who reports to the senior academic leadership. Some international offices report directly to a dean or vice president of international programs, who report directly to the provost.

If the international office is within a college (typically, the college of liberal arts) or within a department (e.g., foreign languages, area studies center), the administration of short-term programs abroad may be restricted to the departments or schools within that college. For small colleges, a staffed office may not exist, and faculty in each department must manage programs without support. An office that is located within student affairs may have a broader reach throughout the institution, but may not have a credible voice in program development, as such offices are often limited to general study abroad and travel advising.

Decentralized Model

In a decentralized model of administration, an individual faculty member, department, or college will manage its own short-term programs abroad, with little or no input or assistance from the international office. An example is a program run out of the foreign language department. These may be longstanding summer programs with solid relationships at language institutes abroad and that regularly rotate faculty directors. An attempt by the international office to draw such programs into a centralized process may be seen as interference and unwanted treading on academic and political turf.

On the other hand, established programs can serve as resources when you are seeking to develop a program model and administrative processes. The department may have established procedures for working with program providers, designing predeparture orientation for students and faculty, and managing program budgets, and there may be precedents for using financial aid and grantings of credit. Preexisting short-term programs may also have useful contacts, such as host institutions, service providers, and travel agencies, which can be valuable to the international office for future program development.

There may be situations when a faculty member or academic unit moves ahead with program development without requesting or after rejecting the assistance and input of the international office. Once again, knowing your office's role and its standing within your institution is crucial. Some institutions require, via the mandate of senior administration, that all off-campus academic programs be monitored to some extent by the international office. The relationships you have built with key academic decisionmakers may allow you to assert influence over the assessment of risk factors at the program location and other areas where the institution may be liable.

An additional decentralized model is that in which another administrative unit on campus provides services and support to the academic department. An office of continuing education or summer sessions may be responsible for the management of student records, including course registration, marketing, and making logistical arrangements for the group. In this case, the international office is still an important voice in assessing health and safety factors and in providing predeparture preparation, reentry support, and program promotion.

If your office is small, resources are limited, or the primary function of the office is general study abroad advising, a decentralized approach to short-term programs may be the most feasible.

Centralized Model

In a centralized model, the international office plays the primary role in developing and administering short-term programs abroad. These responsibilities may include:

- program design and development;
- requesting that a faculty committee is established;
- recruiting faculty directors;
- reviewing proposals;
- making all logistical arrangements and arranging payments to service providers;
- promoting the program;
- reviewing applications;
- managing student records;
- advising students;
- providing training to faculty and staff directors and predeparture orientation to students;
- conducting a program evaluation; and
- providing reentry support to students and faculty.

If several short-term programs are proposed and approved for the same term, a centralized office will need substantial resources of time and personnel.

The faculty director of the short-term program abroad should assist in the development of the program by contributing his or her knowledge of the region and any academic and logistical contacts at the program site; determining the program's academic content, itinerary and activities; creating or contributing to a program handbook; and participating in predeparture orientation.

In this model, most institutions require that programs be proposed, reviewed, and approved by a standing committee of the faculty, which may or may not have administrative staff or student representation. This specific process is outlined later in this chapter.

Advantages of a centralized model. The distinct advantage of a centralized model is the standardization of policies and procedures across programs, no matter which academic unit or department is granting credit for a program. A centralized model ensures that:

- faculty are aware of and operate under policies established by the administration and the international office;
- participants have been appropriately screened;
- procedures for the application and use of student financial aid have been clearly communicated and adhered to;
- pricing of short-term programs abroad follows a standard formula;
- billing and collection of fees are standardized;
- predeparture orientation for both students and faculty is conducted; and
- issues of liability, responsibility, risk management, insurance, and crisis management are addressed.

A centralized model means that the international office is aware of all program development and management issues as they occur.

Managing growth in a centralized model. The international office may find itself a victim of its own successes as short-term programs grow, with greater numbers of students participating and more faculty expressing interest in directing programs. It is imperative to have a plan for how to manage the growth of these programs. A division of responsibilities should be clearly spelled out from the beginning of the program development process. There must be support to either control growth or add additional resources. You may consider researching student-to-staff ratios—for example, 100 students abroad for every one full-time staff person—and asking schools with similar programs for their student/staff ratios.

Hybrid Model

Short-term program abroad administration at your institution may fall into the hybrid model category. The international office may be too small to handle the responsibilities of a centralized model, or there may be longstanding programs in academic units that resist being brought under the direction of the international office or that are well managed under the current system. Some units may be eager to have the international office manage all of the administrative details, whereas others may need assistance in certain areas but are able and willing to develop and administer their own programs.

Another administrative office, such as continuing education, may already be administering summer programs but will turn to the international office for assistance in predeparture orientation, preparing faculty, assessing health and safety risk factors, and finding contacts at potential program sites. You may find yourself juggling several or all of these scenarios if several short-term programs are in the works.

A hybrid model may allow you to work successfully with several different academic units, each of which may have a different history, program model, and administrative needs.

Moving Toward a Centralized Model

A degree of centralization and standardization is recommended, and in fact, is *essential* if short-term study abroad is to develop and become a sustainable international option at your institution. If your efforts to centralize are met with resistance by those already administering short-term programs abroad, you will need to call upon the support structure you have created among key decisionmakers.

First, you will need to create a credible argument for the standardization of policies and procedures for short-term program management, such as the one found at the end of this chapter. Areas of concern that will likely get the attention of the key decisionmakers are institutional liability, academic integrity, selection of participants, and collection of program fees.

Institutional liability. Faculty directors who have not had training or experience in supervising groups of students overseas, and who are not aware of health and safety issues or of procedures for responding to emergencies, put the institution at greater risk of liability. Students who have not received a predeparture orientation at which issues of health, safety, responsibility, insurance, cultural adaptation, and academic expectations are addressed are also a potential liability for the institution. Your goal should be to present areas of concern and to offer ways to prepare both faculty and students for the overseas experience, rather than to suggest that the international office make the decision about who is qualified to direct a short-term program abroad.

Academic integrity. Courses that are held overseas for institutional credit cannot simply replicate the on-campus experience in an off-campus setting. Without a standard approach to approving and evaluating short-term programs abroad, there is no guarantee that a course makes use of its locale or enhances the academic unit's existing curriculum. A faculty committee reviewing all proposals for short-term programs abroad, or a committee within each college organized by or with the participation of the international office, will ensure that these courses fulfill the academic mission of the institution. Similarly, a standardized evaluation form for the short-term program will demonstrate through reliable measures that the course met defined criteria for academic and intercultural effectiveness. See Chapter 12, "It Changed My Life": Strategies for Assessing Student Learning, for examples.

Selection of participants. Policies for participation in study abroad may already exist at your institution. Such policies usually prohibit participation in an off-campus program by students who are on academic or disciplinary probation. A faculty member or academic unit independently organizing a short-term program may not review student records to verify that the student is in good academic and conduct standing. Disregard for or ignorance of admissions policies puts the institution at risk by encouraging unqualified students to participate, and will ultimately cast a spotlight on disparate standards of acceptance. See Chapter 11, Student Selection and Enrollment.

Collection of program fees. A faculty member or academic unit independently administering a short-term program abroad may collect program fees in a way that does not comply with university policy. Students may be submitting payment directly to a faculty director or program provider not properly sought out and bid for by the institution.

If credit is granted for the course, the faculty director is essentially acting on behalf of the institution, and indirect payment for services makes the institution liable for any negligent behavior or policies of the third-party provider. Any direct collection of program fees by the faculty director or academic unit also means it is unlikely that the student will have access to financial aid monies to offset the cost of the program and may not receive an official transcript reflecting the course or study abroad experience. By not participating in a standardized billing system, the academic unit will have difficulty collecting delinquent fees or processing refunds.

The "Proposal for Standardizing Policies and Procedures for Short-Term Study Abroad Programs" at the end of this chapter can be partially or wholly adapted to suit your institution; simply insert your institutional data under "list student participation numbers" and "list courses offered."

Once you have established credible arguments for the standardization and/or centralization of policies and procedures, you must determine which services your office will provide to academic units developing programs. The document, "Program Development and Administration Responsibilities for Short-Term Study Abroad Programs," shows different models of the division of responsibilities among faculty directors, the administrator for study abroad programs, and program providers.

Course Approval Process

Once you have determined an administrative structure (assuming that it is a centralized or hybrid model), and clarified the responsibilities of the international office and faculty directors vis-à-vis the management of the short-term programs, it is time to consider the course approval process.

Depending upon the administrative structure of short-term programs at your institution, you may solicit course proposals campus-wide or from certain academic units (e.g., the college of liberal arts, area studies centers). If the structure is more decentralized, the academic units may take the full responsibility of selecting courses; the international office may be asked to consult on the administrative feasibility of a program, but not its academic content. See the flowchart, "Review of International Education Programs," at the end of this chapter for an example of a centralized review process for a private university.

Why a Course Proposal Process Is Needed

As discussed above, the course proposal process is an area to focus on when making an argument for a centralized approach to the development and management of short-term programs. A standard method of reviewing and evaluating program proposals ensures the following:

♦ The integrity of the academic work across units. It also asserts the value of international education to the institution as a whole, rather than belonging to one college, school, or department.

- The ability to review and the authority to reject courses based on factors such as assessment of risk in area or region, sound academic objectives, and the maintenance or insurance of academic quality.
- A process to manage the number of courses in one discipline or country.
- A method to manage growth. There may be more proposals than resources can support.

The course proposal process will require forming a review committee, developing criteria for selection, determining a timeline for submission and review, creating standardized proposal forms, and disseminating information about short-term programs to the faculty.

Proposal Review Committees

A committee that reviews study abroad proposals can serve many different functions, including the following:
- Review and approve academic content.
- Set unit or campus-wide policy for study abroad and exchange programs.
- Establish guidelines for program development.
- Create standards for admissions and for program budgets.
- Approve affiliation and exchange agreements.
- Review student program and scholarship applications.
- Evaluate existing programs.

The committee's charge may be identified as academic review, setting administrative policy, or both. Also confirm that the committee has sufficient time to carry out its responsibilities. Most members discover that this kind of committee work has a very high learning curve and unpredictable complexities. Members should have international experience, especially as faculty directors, and the committee must have strong leadership. See the "International and Domestic Off-Campus Studies Committee" outline at the end of this chapter.

Working with existing committees. If a study abroad committee already exists, you may decide to include the review of short-term program proposals in its set of responsibilities. If the short-term programs are developed through one academic unit, the committee may consist only of faculty and senior administrators from that unit, as well as a representative from the international office. The proposal process could be a two-step process, whereby the academic unit has the responsibility of determining the academic appropriateness of the course and the study abroad review committee has the task of examining the cultural integrity and administrative feasibility of the program. In the latter model, the program proposal would come to the study abroad committee after receiving approval from the department chair or school director and the academic or college dean.

The course being proposed for a short-term program may be an existing course or it may be a first-time offering from the academic unit. If it is a new course, faculty should complete the departmental process for proposing a new course well in advance of submitting the course for inclusion in a study abroad program. There may be a way to have the course approved on a trial basis for one program cycle, before going through a formal review to be added to the department's roster of courses. As short-term programs abroad grow, an academic unit may form a subcommittee from an existing curriculum committee to review the courses to be offered abroad.

Standing committee of the faculty. Regardless of the size of your institution, most international programs discover that a standing committee of the faculty or university is required to reinforce the *authority* to approve or reject proposals, and to make policy for these programs.

A standing committee focusing on off-campus programs can be a strong ally in advocating for a standardized, centralized approach to short-term program development. In addition, presenting key decisionmakers with sample criteria, proposal and budget forms with suggested guidelines, and a timeline will demonstrate that input from the study abroad office is necessary.

Course Proposals for Short-Term Programs

Again, depending on administrative structure, short-term program proposals may be an appendix to the standard on-campus proposal for new courses, or a separate, detailed document.

These proposals do three things: gather information, force the writer to articulate the academic or learning objectives of the program, and show how the site and learning objectives are integrated. Because these courses are in a nontraditional environment, as much focus is placed on what students will see or do as what the students will learn and how they will learn it.

Proposals offer an opportunity for faculty not only to think through the academic components, but also to focus on the logistics (e.g., how to get from site to site) and the general flow of the program. Is there too much free time, too much travel or programming, too little time for reading?

See the course proposal samples at the end of Chapter 6, Designing the Academic Course: Principles and Practicalities.

Timeline for Submission and Review

The deadline for review of course proposals must take into consideration the amount of time needed to develop and recruit for the course. Generally, *at least* 12 months is required for short-term courses to be developed. A detailed timeline for developing a short-term course can be found in Chapter 7, Feasibility Studies.

Criteria for Reviewing Proposals

The review committee will be charged with either approving or rejecting short-term program proposals, or making recommendations to a senior academic official who will make the final decision. A negative decision should be related directly to the program criteria established, with suggestions to improve the program for future consideration.

The academic, intercultural, and logistical standards for short-term programs abroad should be no less exacting than those for programs of greater duration. In fact, the program's objectives and the stated pedagogical methods of reaching the objectives must be even more specific, clearly articulated, and demonstrable, given the brevity and intensity of these programs.

General Criteria for Short-Term Programs[1]

Academic

- Is the academic rigor comparable to courses offered on campus? Are the prerequisites clearly stated and appropriate? Does the course enhance or supplement, rather than duplicate, on-campus curriculum? If this is a new course, has it been approved by the academic unit's curriculum committee?
- What are the intended academic goals of the program? Are these feasible goals given the program duration and the resources and facilities available to students?
- Who is the intended audience for the course? Does the course have a broad enough appeal (i.e., is it a general education course or a required course for majors or minors) to attract a sufficient number of applicants?
- What are the academic advantages to conducting this course abroad? What are the advantages to the specific location proposed?
- What are the qualifications of the faculty? Does the faculty director have prior experience in this country or region? Does the faculty director have prior experience in directing a group of students abroad? How were the host country faculty selected? What are their qualifications? Will a graduate teaching assistant be necessary? If so, how will that/those graduate assistant(s) be selected?
- What are the admissions requirements for the program? At a minimum, do they match admissions requirements for other institutional study abroad programs?
- Is the projected program size conducive to an effective learning environment, given the location, facilities, and proposed activities?

Cultural/Logistical

- How will this program integrate students into the local academic and community lives?
- What is the nature and degree of exposure to the host culture and language?
- How do the predeparture materials and session(s) prepare students for the academic and intercultural experience?
- Will international air travel be done as a group, or will students be expected to make their own arrangements?
- What is the nature of support services available to students? Have health clinics, a hospital, the nearest consulate or embassy been identified in case there is an emergency?
- What library, computer, and research facilities are available at the program site? Are these sufficient for students to complete assigned work?
- How will students be counseled to spend their free time? Will the faculty director be available after hours and on weekends?

General

- What evidence is there of student interest for this program (including its location and content)?
- How will this program be marketed? What student populations will be targeted for promotional activities?

---

[1] Based in part on criteria suggested in Hoffa, W. and Pearson, J., editors, (1997) *NAFSA's Guide to Education Abroad for Advisers and Administrators, Second Edition*, NAFSA: Association of International Educators, Washington, DC.

◆ Is this program sustainable (i.e., are faculty members interested in directing it in future years, are there other faculty who can take leadership on a rotating basis, are the facilities abroad able to host future groups)?

◆ How does the projected cost of this program compare with other study abroad programs of similar duration and in the same location offered by peer institutions? How does it compare with the cost of other study abroad programs at your institution?

◆ By what method will the participants evaluate the course and the program, and when?

◆ How does this program fit into the range of programs already offered by your institution? Are there other programs in this geographic area or with this academic content? Does this program compete with or complement those existing programs?

Proposals will often fall into a gray category, and with some tinkering—revising expectations, perhaps adding an on-site program provider—would be approved to run. The committee must determine if there is enough time for the faculty member to resubmit the proposal to be considered for the term currently under consideration. It may also happen that a well-composed, feasible proposal is submitted, but the evidence of student interest is not apparent or is in doubt. The committee can approve the program, with the caveat that if a certain quota is not met by the application deadline, the program will be canceled and applicants will receive a refund of any deposit monies.

Policy Issues

When developing policy for off-campus programs, always start with an existing *on-campus* policy (if available), and modify as necessary.

Credit

If the course falls within a regular academic term (e.g., summer session, January term, intersession), standards for the number of academic credits offered are probably already in place, with the credit hours determined by the academic unit offering the course. The course should be granted the same amount of credit as a comparable on-campus course. If graduate credit is available for an undergraduate short-term course, the graduate program will need to determine if and how much extra work is required.

Evaluation methods will need to be adjusted to fit the nature of a course conducted off-campus. If students are to produce research papers, will they have access to libraries or other research facilities, or computer labs? Will handwritten papers be acceptable? If the participants are to submit artwork, do they have adequate and appropriate studio space? Will final papers or projects be due before the end of the program, or will students have an opportunity to submit a final draft upon return to the United States? The chapter on academic course design (Chapter 6) will examine in detail various approaches to teaching tactics, guided free time, and evaluation methods for short-term programs abroad.

Faculty Load and Salary

The effect of a short-term program on a faculty member's teaching load is of critical importance to the academic unit sponsoring the course. At issue is the possibility that the faculty member will request or be entitled to a decrease in the teaching load during the regular academic year in order to direct a short-term course off-campus. This may decrease the department's on-campus course offerings during a given semester.

The issue of faculty salary is also examined in the section on financial matters (Chapter 9), but compensation must be determined before the budget is finalized. Possible salary models may include one of the following: the short-term course is counted into a regular teaching load and the faculty member receives his or her normal salary; the short-term course constitutes a teaching overload, so the faculty director receives a supplement; the short-term course is part of a summer or intersession term, with the department maintaining a separate budget for those terms; the faculty director's salary is covered on a per student basis by program fees; or the salary is covered by separate funding from within the department of record or study abroad office.

Program Size

Careful consideration must be given to the number of participants admitted to the short-term program abroad. The student/faculty ratio should be smaller than that of an on-campus course, as the role of the faculty director extends far beyond the classroom. His or her time on-site will be spent not only on instruction and evaluation, but on arranging logistics, dispensing travel advice, counseling students struggling with the demands of cultural adaptation, resolving housing and budget issues, and responding to problems.

First, confirm the on-campus minimum class size. Try to keep to that policy, unless there are field or research reasons to take fewer students. Another determining factor of the program size is the program budget. A minimum number of students may be required for the program to be fiscally feasible. An additional factor may be an agreed upon minimum set by the academic unit and the international office. The maximum number of students may be determined by the facilities available at the program site (e.g., housing, transportation, access to cultural sites, excursion arrangements). The faculty director may also have a preferred maximum number that he or she is willing to take, based on activities planned, coursework required, and evaluation methods. Typically, a course with one faculty director will have between 8 and 20 participants, but faculty have reported that two directors should not take more than 25 students. Ultimately, the specific discipline and course requirements will determine the program size. A geology field course may have a lower student/faculty ratio, based on intense supervision needs. Make sure that a consistent policy is established, and that if deviations occur, they are well documented and understood by all.

Nondegree Students

A policy should be set regarding if nondegree students may participate in off-campus programs. Most institutions will allow nondegree students to participate, based on the permission of the faculty director and on a space-available basis. If these students are allowed to participate, define the expectations for their inclusion and the payment process. The range of grading (letter grade, pass/fail, audit) and their different student status may affect the group dynamics.

Staffing

The participation of a second faculty member, staff member or graduate-level teaching assistant can be of tremendous help to the faculty director – most importantly in providing a second set of eyes and ears, and additional leadership support. This additional staff can be available to make logistical arrangements, lead excursions, conduct lectures, or provide backup in the event the faculty director is called away to respond to a problem.

Defining Roles of Additional Staff

The faculty director will need to clearly define the role of additional staff. It is best to have a job description or set of responsibilities and expectations available to possible candidates and the department, and to interview potential assistants. The leadership team should also spend time before departure discussing their interaction with students—the level of formality, use of titles or first names, and if staff will drink alcohol with students. Because these programs have such academic, intercultural, and social intensity, it is imperative that the leadership team understand each other's expectations.

The expenses for additional staff, including salary, travel costs, and meal allowances, may fall upon the academic unit of record or be factored into the program budget to be charged to the participants on a per student basis.

Participation of Family Members/Friends

The faculty director may desire to bring along family members, a partner, or a friend for part or all of the program. A policy regarding travel companions must be clearly stated in the program proposal guidelines. Some institutions may prohibit any participation of family members or any party not directly contributing to the academic or administrative content of the program; other institutions may have a more generous policy that allows nonfaculty and family members to accompany and even participate, as long as doing so does not interfere with the teaching of the course or the availability of the director to the students.

Similar to additional staff, the role of a travel companion must be carefully defined. They may have specific skills to contribute to the program such as proficiency in the language or knowledge of the host country. In these situations, there may be a role for them in the program, with some of their expenses supported by the program budget.

Status and Risk Management

If family or nonfaculty members are allowed to participate in the program, consideration must be given to their academic and financial status in the course: will they be required to register for the course and pay the tuition? If it is a family member, will he or she be required to pay the program fee, including a portion of the accommodation and board? It is necessary to consult with institutional counsel and/or the office of risk management to determine if any policies exist regarding the participation of family members and if there is any risk to the institution by allowing them to accompany the group.

Children

Policies and practice differ from institution to institution with regard to faculty bringing children on short-term programs abroad. Some colleges allow and encourage family participation, whereas others prohibit children under age 16 from accompanying the group. Not allowing children may limit the number of faculty who can direct programs, and many times children can bring an added benefit to the group, not to mention the growth experience for the children.

If faculty are allowed to bring their children, consider that short-term programs based in one site work better than programs that include more travel, and that children should be accompanied by another adult who is responsible for the child's supervision.

Planning for Round Two!

It is not likely that *all* of the policies and procedures for short-term programs abroad can be determined and an administrative structure established before the first program proposal is ready to be reviewed by the committee, or even before the first group of students is about to board the plane. You will encounter many unforeseen challenges and you will need to constantly and consistently revise your expectations, the administrative model, and the policies and procedures as the programs develop and grow.

By maintaining a working document of how well procedures are working, and by meeting regularly with key decisionmakers, you will ensure that all voices are heard in the planning process and that problems can be resolved as they occur. Even before the first program successfully concludes, you should be thinking about how to spread the word of its success, how to recruit faculty for the following program cycle, and to what other academic units you can reach out with the short-term program abroad model. Try to include "entrepreneurial" faculty, schools, and departments in the standardized policies and procedures you are creating.

Proposal for Standardizing Policies and Procedures for Short-Term Study Abroad Programs

The goal of international education is to provide all qualified students, graduate and undergraduate, with the opportunity to participate and succeed in a study abroad experience. One method to meet the needs of a diverse group of students is through short-term study abroad, which is defined as a 2- to 6-week, faculty-led program. Our short-term programs abroad have experienced tremendous growth over the past 4 years, including an increase in participation from 144 to 345 students and an expansion of programs from 20 to 28, with 35 programs in place for the 1997–98 academic year. This growth also translates into a sharp increase in administrative responsibilities for the international education staff. To meet our stated goals, we need consistent policies and procedures for all short-term programs abroad. Standardization means that we can better represent and protect the university, improve each student's experience, and facilitate the process for faculty. We propose the following policies and procedures:

1. Course Proposals
✓ All faculty will submit a *Course Proposal for a Short-Term Study Abroad Program*, outlining the course description, syllabus integrating how site visits enhance learning objectives, previous site experience, role in the teaching load, and approval by the department chair or program director.
✓ Guidelines for developing such proposals will be provided to faculty and chairs or directors by the international education office. These guidelines are not meant to be either prescriptive or binding. However, considering them will assist in the development of solid programs that are academically strong and feasible abroad.
✓ Department chairs or program directors will verify the academic rigor of the proposal and its place within department plans and staffing needs.
✓ Proposals must be accompanied by a tentative budget.
✓ The January term proposal deadline is December 1.
✓ The summer program deadline is May 1.

2. Review of Proposals
✓ The Academic Review Committee for International Education (ARCIE)—a standing committee of the faculty—will review and approve proposals as well as assessment programs. The committee's purpose in reviewing proposals is to examine logistics, preparation of the faculty, the viability of geographic areas, how site visits enhance the learning objectives of the course, and to approve courses.
✓ Budgets will be reviewed and approved to ensure that salary, stipends, and benefits are included, as well as emergency funds and other expenses.
✓ Curricular and academic issues, such as credit substitutions, prerequisites, and general education requirements must be resolved in the department *before* the proposal is submitted.
✓ A maximum of 35 (including all consortium) courses will be offered each year. If course proposals exceed this maximum, ARCIE will select courses or recommend additional resources.

3. Administration of Courses
✓ Courses will be administered by the staff of the international education office.

✓ Administrative responsibilities will include: coordinating program development, establishment and adherence to timelines, final budget approval, coordinating with faculty on marketing and promotion, facilitating the application and approval process, financial billing and disbursement of all funds, registration of students, organizing a general orientation session and providing orientation materials, preparation and facilitation of application, and evaluation and final report forms. As well, the international education office will provide mandatory faculty training.

✓ Faculty not working with a program provider will be responsible for presenting students with a full syllabus and detailed itinerary before departure.

4. Student Orientation

All short-term programs abroad will have a mandatory student orientation, with a general session coordinated by the international education office.

5. Evaluations

✓ Faculty will ask students to evaluate the academic component of the course by using the appropriate institutional or department forms. Students will also complete a questionnaire about the organizational and logistical aspects of the course.

✓ In addition, the international education office will ask faculty to convene a meeting upon their return, to document travel, accommodations, and unforeseen problems, and to provide a detailed financial accounting.

6. Policies for Short-Term Programs

Policies and procedures will be the responsibility of the international education office. Revisions and additions to the policy will be reviewed by the Study Abroad Advisory Committee or ARCIE, which will make appropriate recommendations to the appropriate committee.

Background for Proposal

Development

Short-term study abroad has been offered since the early 1970s and most student participation has occurred through consortia relationships. Our relationship with the consortium has been very satisfactory to date, as it has allowed faculty to teach courses abroad with substantial support regarding travel details.

On an annual or biannual basis, faculty have offered their own programs outside the consortium, which we refer to as "institutional courses," including courses sponsored by the Spanish, French, and Biology departments.

Enrollment

The last 3 years have seen an "explosion" in student participation.
List student participation numbers.
The increase continues for the following term. *List statistics.*

Proposal for Standardizing Policies and Procedures for Short-Term Study Abroad Programs (contd.)

Course Offerings

There has also been a notable increase in the number of courses offered in the last 3 years. *List courses offered.*

Problem Areas

The following areas have proven to be areas of concern for the international education office's staff:

Course Selection/Approval: Currently, there is no policy for the proposal, review, and administration of short-term programs abroad. This situation allows any faculty member to propose a course at any time and take a group of students abroad independent of any involvement from the international education office. Faculty has been operating under the general policies for the January term or summer courses, which require approval by the department chair. The international education office has offered administrative services and guidance on a resource basis, when it was requested, or we offer and encourage faculty to use our services. As a result, many faculty choose to work with our office, and when numbers were modest, we were able to respond on an ad hoc basis. However, as numbers have grown, so have the expectations for services. Given the current and increasing demand for international education office services, if we are to be efficient and effective we need to establish standard operating procedures.

Standard Rules of Participation: Study abroad policy states that students are not allowed to study abroad if they are on academic or disciplinary probation. Faculty who take students abroad do not necessarily request or verify academic and/or disciplinary records, and on most application forms, do not seek the authorization necessary from each student to verify their status.

Standard Approach to Pricing: At present, pricing is the decision of the faculty director. All short-term study abroad courses should have a stated program cost, which includes academic fees, travel expenses, and the university off-campus study fee. The registrar's office and the office of business affairs seek the international education office's direction in defining proper course and fee coding.

Facilitation of Financial Aid: If students wish to apply for or use current financial aid, they must work with student financial services. The international education office has developed a system to provide the registrar's office and student financial services staff with specific budget figures, official documentation from each student going abroad, and confirmation that student accounts have been cleared for additional billing. If faculty work independently, students will not benefit from the clear, seamless procedures that are in place for other study abroad programs, and this places undue, last-minute burden on staff from many different departments.

Standardized Billing: A system has been created to allow participants to be billed through their student accounts for programs. The many advantages to this system include the following: no individual or office functions as a bank or a collection agency; the designated individual (parent or student) receives the bill; financial aid matters can be considered by trained personnel, and students receive institutional credit for the course, paying the institution that transcripts the credit rather than an external vendor.

Collection of Fees by Proper Sources: Some faculty who work independently have collected monies directly from students and thus do not comply with the university policy that all funds collected on behalf of the university be administered by a department of the institution, not by individual faculty members.

Liability for the University: Because there are no standardized procedures, there is no guarantee that faculty who take students abroad independently but on the behalf of the university, are aware of risk management and insurance issues. Faculty must also take the proper steps to advise and educate students about their responsibilities as study abroad participants. Further, faculty need to be well informed so that they do not make decisions that could increase the risk of liability for the institution.

Coordinated Orientation Programs: Currently, there is no coordinated orientation program for students or faculty. As an institution, we want to ensure that students receive a *thorough* predeparture orientation and information on academic expectations, cultural issues, health and safety, travel and logistics, and behavioral expectations. In addition, there is no policy ensuring that faculty should be informed about issues of institutional liability.

[Source: Adapted from the University of St. Thomas.]

Program Development and Administration Responsibilities for Short-Term Study Abroad Programs

FACULTY	INTERNATIONAL EDUCATION	PROGRAM PROVIDER
GENERAL		
▪ Finalize itinerary. Notify International Education Center (IEC). ▪ Provide IEC with: Program dates, final course title, no. of credits, if non-UST students are welcome to apply, if family or guests will accompany program. ▪ Identify program provider. If program provider is not selected, faculty take responsibility for all logistical and academic arrangements, except IEC will coordinate airfare. ▪ Obtain written contract from program provider. ▪ Identify special health considerations. ▪ Notify IEC of any links to your own Web site, department, etc.	▪ Advise on selection of program provider. ▪ Assist with request for proposal, if required. ▪ Review and sign all contracts. ▪ Advise on special health considerations. ▪ Schedule travel clinic with health services department. ▪ Manage all Web site content.	▪ Provide contract. ▪ Identify special health considerations.
BUDGET/TRAVEL/LOGISTICS		
Budget		
▪ Submit budget figures to IEC (see example). ▪ Provide payment information (e.g., invoices). Provide receipts and the UST Employee Travel and Reimbursement form.	▪ IEC manages all financial issues. ▪ Review and create final budget. ▪ Approve program cost. ▪ Provide budget information to student financial services. ▪ Create student billing sheets for student financial services and business office.	▪ Provide budget numbers to faculty or IEC. ▪ Provide payment information and timeline to IEC (wire, draft, credit card). ▪ Submit final payment invoice to IEC.
Airfare		
▪ Identify airline departure and arrival dates and flight requests. Notify IEC.	▪ Notify airfare provider of required airline tickets.	▪ Process flight deviations.

- Pay all deposits on travel.
- Submit full names to airline or program providers.
- Obtain visa information and request visa forms.
- Coordinate all visas.
- Obtain or renew personal passport, if required. Submit copy to IEC.

Meals

- How many group meals? What meals will be provided?
- Complete student financial services database with expenses and number of meals provided.

MARKETING/RECRUITMENT

- Advise students.
- Recruit students for program.
- General recruitment of students through Web site, Bulletin Today, and a printed list of all short-term programs available.
- Create brief course description for Web.
- Create full course description.
- Edit course description.
- Post course description on Web site.

ENROLLMENT

- Decide on enrollment criteria.
- Establish all enrollment materials, including forms required by faculty and/or program provider as well as the number of photos required from students.
- Place enrollment procedures and materials on study abroad Web site.
- Notify IEC if additional forms are necessary (including liability waivers, etc.).
- Review application dossiers.
- Set up and conduct interviews (per procedures established by IEC).
- Make final selection of students. Notify IEC of those students selected or denied.
- Create and mail Notification of Status letters to students (accept, deny).
- Refund deposits.
- Manage student data for reporting.
- Communicate with faculty regarding all enrollment changes, issues, etc.
- Provide enrollment updates, etc., to program providers.
- Request enrollment updates as required.

ACADEMIC/REGISTRATION

- Advise on course content.
- Provide syllabus.
- Organize on-site classrooms, class schedule, and "processing" sessions.
- Order books.
- On-site classrooms and class schedule, if required.

Program Development and Administration Responsibilities for Short-Term Study Abroad Programs (contd.)

FACULTY	INTERNATIONAL EDUCATION	PROGRAM PROVIDER
▪ If part of course is taught on campus, request classrooms. Notify students and IEC. ▪ Submit course for major/minor and/or general requirement approval. Notify IEC of status. **Registration** ▪ Identify course number/section number. ▪ Notify IEC of course number.	▪ IEC notified of on-campus classroom, if used. ▪ IEC notified of major/minor and/or general requirement proposals and status. Assist faculty if necessary. ▪ Provide course number/section number to registrar. ▪ Provide student information for registration. ▪ Provider transcript "footer" information to registrar.	
ORIENTATION		
▪ Notify IEC of audiovisual needs for orientation (e.g., slide projector, VCR). ▪ Schedule course orientation if not held after general orientation session. Notify IEC and students. ▪ Hold additional individual group meetings. ▪ Provide course-specific information. ▪ Provide airline and itinerary information and enough copies for students and their emergency contacts. ▪ Attend faculty director's dinner. ▪ Attend other faculty director training events.	▪ Schedule general orientation session and breakout sessions. ▪ Create and distribute student handbook. ▪ Provide Culturegrams for all available locations. ▪ Provide passport information to students (via policies and procedures and Web site). ▪ Organize faculty director's dinner.	
PREDEPARTURE		
▪ Correspond with students. ▪ Provide IEC with photo and birth date for International Teacher ID card (form enclosed). ▪ Provide IEC with final syllabus and travel itinerary. ▪ If receiving a faculty stipend (not part of course load), consult with payroll on tax deduction issues. ▪ Distribute airline tickets to students at airport.	▪ Create and distribute International Student ID cards. ▪ Create student evaluations and give to faculty for distribution at end of course. ▪ Order credit card (if required). ▪ Prepare travel advance (if required). ▪ Request faculty stipends (if required). ▪ For summer courses, request salaries. ▪ Make advance payments. ▪ Disburse budgeted funds to faculty director.	▪ Continue to communicate details and planning with faculty and IEC.

- Convert funds advanced to foreign currency.

ON-SITE

- Conduct on-site orientation.
- Inform public safety:
  - o List of home phone numbers of IEC staff
  - o List of faculty/course/location
  - o Departure and arrival dates
- Prepare final faculty packets, including evaluations and student emergency contact info.
- Conduct on-site orientation with faculty (if on-site).
- Make on-site payments.
- Account for all expenditures of funds advanced and submit accounting and/or receipts.
- Distribute student evaluations. Identify student to bring to IEC upon return.

POST-RETURN

- Submit grades.
- Attend faculty debriefing session.
- Debrief with IEC regarding course details.
- Reconcile all budgets.
- Collect student evaluations. Share with department chair (per on-campus process), dean, and use in program assessment.
- Submit final bills to IEC.

[Source: Adapted from the University of St. Thomas]

International and Domestic Off-Campus Studies (IDOCS) Committee

A. The general purpose of the IDOCS committee is to consider, review, and promote courses, plans, and policies relating to international and domestic off-campus academic programs.

B. Responsibilities include

1. Granting probationary approval for first-time offerings, off-campus courses, and programs (both domestic and international). Approval of these courses will signify approval of all relevant additional requirements prior to the committee's approval:

    a) Department or program major credit

    b) General education credit

    c) Cross-cultural credit

    d) Area studies credit

2. Reviewing, evaluating, and recommending off-campus, noninterim courses and programs (both domestic and international) to the faculty for final approval during the second year of operation.

3. Reviewing, evaluating, and recommending off-campus field supervisor courses to the faculty for approval.

4. Acting on behalf of the faculty in approving as ongoing interim courses (both domestic and international) those courses offered for the second time (within 3 years of the first offering).

5. Advising on administrative policies and procedures for courses and programs administered by the international and off-campus studies office.

6. Promoting a global perspective through:

    a) encouraging scholarship and expertise supporting international and off-campus study;

    b) nurturing effective relationships between on-campus and off-campus study;

    c) fostering ties with other academic institutions that support international and off-campus study;

    d) advising on continuing education and alumni programs that further the aims of international and off-campus study;

    e) aiding the promotion of international career opportunities; and

    f) supporting recruitment, admissions, and integration of international students and scholars on campus.

C. Personnel

1. One elected faculty member from each of the five faculties of the college, two students elected by the student body, and the director of international and off-campus studies.

2. Term of office:

    The term of office for the elected faculty members is 3 years. One of the elected students will be a junior and one a senior. Both students should have had an off-campus experience.

[Source: Adapted from St. Olaf College]

Review of International Education Programs

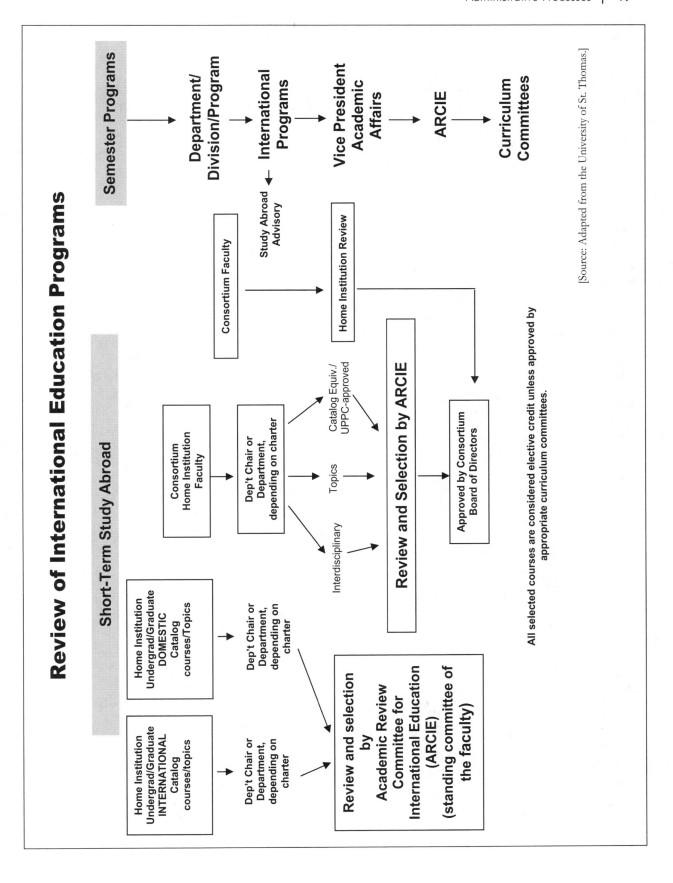

Semester Programs

Department/Division/Program → International Programs → Vice President Academic Affairs → ARCIE → Curriculum Committees

Study Abroad Advisory

Consortium Faculty → Home Institution Review

Short-Term Study Abroad

Home Institution Undergrad/Graduate INTERNATIONAL Catalog courses/topics → Dep't Chair or Department, depending on charter

Home Institution Undergrad/Graduate DOMESTIC Catalog courses/Topics → Dep't Chair or Department, depending on charter

Review and selection by Academic Review Committee for International Education (ARCIE) (standing committee of the faculty)

Consortium Home Institution Faculty → Dep't Chair or Department, depending on charter → Catalog Equiv./ UPPC-approved / Topics / Interdisciplinary

Review and Selection by ARCIE

Approved by Consortium Board of Directors

All selected courses are considered elective credit unless approved by appropriate curriculum committees.

[Source: Adapted from the University of St. Thomas.]

Chapter 4

Internal Support Systems: It Takes a Campus to Run a Study Abroad Program

Dawn White

By their very nature, short-term programs abroad intensify the relationship between the international office and administrative and academic units on campus. In most cases, these programs require modifications to policies and procedures already in place for longer-term study abroad programs as well as on-campus courses. Two elements that have a great impact on the extent to which policies and procedures need to be modified on your campus are (1) the degree to which study abroad is accepted by your institution as an integral part of a student's university experience, and (2) the amount of administrative flexibility inherent in or built into your institution's internal systems.

This chapter examines the relationship between the international office and the other departments on campus that are essential to the successful administration of short-term programs abroad.

Academic Affairs

As the office ultimately responsible for all academic programs on your campus, academic affairs is likely to take more than a passing interest in the shape and content of short-term programs abroad. Indeed, most international offices are regularly tapped for information on their programs as part of the institution's annual update to its regional accrediting body.

Information routinely requested includes the following:

- Where in the world programs are offered.
- Whether the programs carry graduate or undergraduate credit.
- The number of students enrolled.
- Whether there is an on-site administrator.
- Whether there is a cosponsoring organization.

Accrediting agencies are also interested in the existence of contractual relationships with nonaccredited organizations, which include most institutions and program providers abroad, and whether or not any substantive changes were implemented in existing programs or are planned for the coming year.

If your office is asked to provide this information, consider it an opportunity to promote awareness of your programs instead of a reporting burden. Use the information request as an opportunity to highlight the innovative opportunities your office is creating for students and faculty to gain international experience and expertise. If the university's mission is already geared toward a greater international profile, you have the perfect opportunity to promote short-term programs abroad as a way of enhancing that mission and positioning the international office as central to that effort. If the university does not focus on its international profile, you have yet another opportunity to make a case in favor of including study abroad in the university's mission.

Institutional Priorities

Keeping institutional priorities in mind as you work with faculty to develop short-term programs abroad or identify program providers will further enhance your relationship with the academic leaders on your campus. If service learning is a priority, seek to incorporate a service-learning element in some of your short-term programs. If student retention is a priority, assess how many of your short-term program participants have come back to graduate from your institution. If the percentage is high, which is likely, make sure your president and provost know that study abroad is a powerful retention tool. If diversity is a priority, show how international opportunities can be attractive to participants from underrepresented groups. Make it a point to link short-term study abroad with other campus initiatives, and keep campus leaders informed of those links.

Academic Deans

You will be recruiting faculty from individual colleges and may be asking the departments to fund faculty salaries for the programs. A dean is one of the most important sources of support, as he or she has the ear of the president or provost and the faculty as well as overseeing the budget, and he or she sets the mission for and tone of the college. The dean can assist in recruiting faculty and in helping you navigate the sometimes murky waters of college politics, turf, and faculty relations.

Academic Departments

Once you have sold the idea of short-term study abroad to an academic dean, the chair of a department or the director of a school can help determine which faculty will be enthusiastic and capable program directors and administrators; who has prior experience directing or teaching in a program abroad; what areas of the department curriculum could be enhanced by a short-term program; what potential for participation exists within the majors offered at the school; the appropriate timing such a program; and how a short-term program could fit into a faculty teaching load and existing salary.

Working with faculty in the creation and administration of short-term programs abroad can be one of the most enjoyable parts of your job. Faculty in academic departments support international offices in a number of ways: they review course proposals, they advise students about programs abroad, they publicize program opportunities in their classrooms, and they often evaluate coursework students bring back from abroad. If they also happen to be developing and directing programs abroad, their contributions are even greater.

Study abroad professionals tend to focus so much on the student experience of education abroad that it is easy to overlook the personal and professional gains that departments and faculty members can realize. A faculty member's experience directing a short-term program can:

♦ Culminate in the design of new courses, adding currency to a department's roster of course offerings and enriching its curriculum.

- Lead to the development of research interests or enhance existing ones. Although the work involved in directing most short-term programs usually precludes faculty from engaging in independent research opportunities while the program is underway, some faculty can extend their stays abroad to make the very best professional use of their time.
- Result in scholarly publications, an outcome highly valued in the promotion and tenure process.
- Contribute to an increase in student credit hours for the department. A charismatic teacher with a loyal following will attract program participants. In the same vein, students who have a truly positive experience abroad under the guidance of an excellent faculty member may take more courses from that professor once they are back on campus. Either way, the increase in student credit hours is a boon to the department.
- Spark innovative approaches in methods of teaching and evaluation that are suitable for transfer to the home campus setting. The experiential nature of short-term programs abroad—a feature that sets them apart from programs of longer duration—often serves as the driving force behind the development of new approaches to student learning and assessment.

All of these outcomes have the potential to enhance a faculty member's portfolio. This is especially true on campuses that have gone through the process of internationalization: teaching abroad is more likely to be valued, incorporated as one criterion of faculty scholarship, and reflected in the institution's promotion and tenure guidelines.

There is potential for a mutually beneficial relationship between academic departments and international offices. Faculty members appreciate the expertise of study abroad professionals in preparing budgets, orienting students, and providing logistical support. Study abroad professionals appreciate the fact that the academic content of a faculty-directed program is the province of the department. Because each unit understands what it can offer the other, a complementary relationship is established that feeds the development of short-term opportunities abroad for students and faculty.

Yet the relationship between international offices and academic departments is not without its challenges. One challenge surfaces, for example, in the form of the faculty member who for years has run a proprietary program abroad without the involvement of any campus office and who wants the situation to stay that way, even if policies and procedures established on campus in the interim warrant a change. Campus politics will usually determine how such a situation is addressed.

Relations with academic departments can also be tested when a short-term program takes place during a term or semester, requiring students to miss regularly scheduled courses. This puts a burden on faculty members to make special arrangements for the students missing class, but the argument can reasonably be put forth that this is the same kind of accommodation that is made for athletes and band members who are out of the classroom for brief periods of time. Faculty members who know of these situations well in advance are more likely to be accommodating.

An additional challenge comes from faculty members who think that the only place students can learn is in their own classrooms. Such faculty are not likely to be supportive of any type of study abroad program, even short-term, if it takes students off campus. Fortunately, such faculty are exceptions to the rule. Most people engaged in the business of educating students understand and appreciate that study abroad professionals are dedicated to creating opportunities for students *and* faculty to gain overseas experience.

Academic Advising

Academic advisers often form long-lasting relationships with students, guiding them through the entire course of their academic program on your campus. These advisers are likely to know a great deal about the personal lives of their advisees. If they are made aware of the reasons students have for not participating in traditional study abroad programs (e.g., financial obligations or family commitments) the advisers are in a powerful position to recommend a short-term program abroad as a feasible and attractive alternative.

A strong selling point for students participating in short-term programs abroad is that their progress toward graduation is unlikely to be interrupted by a brief sojourn abroad. Indeed, this is one of the reasons short-term study is so attractive to today's university students. A pressing issue for students is how the credit earned abroad will apply toward graduation requirements. Will it fulfill a general education requirement, a distribution requirement, a major or minor requirement? Will it qualify for internship or service-learning credit? Or will it fall into that general category of "elective credit?"

A student's academic adviser, who might be a faculty member in the student's major department or an administrator assigned to a larger unit, can be instrumental in influencing or even determining how credit will be applied.

Because one of the goals of academic advisers is to guide students toward timely completion of their degree programs, it is in their best interests to facilitate the process of program participants getting useful academic credit applied toward their graduation requirements. Inviting suggestions from academic advisers about the possibilities for credit earned on short-term programs during the program development stage may even yield more student participants: the advisers are more likely to be invested in the success of the program if they helped shape it.

The Registrar's Office

The sheer number of administrative tasks that directly affect students on programs abroad, ranging from the way courses are coded internally to the way grades earned abroad are recorded on student transcripts, makes the registrar's office a key player.

Building Courses into the System

A given course is "built" by the registrar's office when certain elements—including but not limited to the title, level, beginning and ending dates, instructor of record, and grading options—are entered into a computer program using information supplied by the appropriate academic unit. Departures from the norm usually require special handling, and short-term courses abroad often fit this category.

Timelines

As the short-term courses abroad are built, information is added that distinguishes them from on-campus courses. For example, a special mechanism may be developed to override regular tuition and fee charges if tuition for a program abroad is included in the program fee. And because the timeline for developing and administering short-term programs abroad is often completely independent of regular university processes, the timeline for building them in the registrar's office may be different as well, creating an additional reason for special handling. Also, the timeline for registering students, processing grade reports, and generating transcripts varies greatly according to the actual dates of the short-term program.

Blocked Registration

The registration process must be controlled so that only program participants are able to register. There are probably as many ways to do this as there are institutions. If the course is listed in the school's schedule of classes or available online, certain information such as the course registration number can be withheld, or the consent of the instructor can be required to complete the registration process. On many campuses, registration is completed not by the student but by the program administrator, because students must be approved to participate in the course. This is especially effective if registration is tied to payment of program fees or other administrative processes, such as allocation of financial aid. On the other hand, registration is a good double check for the international office—if a student fails to register, it may mean that his or her plans have changed but he or she neglected to notify your office.

Temporary or "Dummy" Courses

Several course registration issues need to be considered. Temporary or "dummy" courses—to be replaced later by courses reflecting the student's actual enrollment—are often used in situations where course registrations are not finalized until students are well into the program or where the registration triggers a program charge on the student's university account. Due to their limited duration and the fact that fewer courses may be involved, short-term programs abroad are more likely to have discrete course names and numbers assigned, but there may be valid reasons to use temporary registrations, such as when a course's credit comes from another institution. If this is the case, the registrar's office then relies on the international office to submit paperwork to replace the temporary registration with a student's "real" courses and credits. Often this happens at the time grades are ready to be recorded on the student's permanent academic record, which may be sometime after the program has ended.

Business Office (Including Bursar, Accounts Payable, Grants, and Contracts)

Especially for institutions that administer their own short-term programs, creating and maintaining a partnership with the business office is key. Why? The management of budgets for short-term programs is often very complicated.

As discussed in Chapter 8, Logistics, it is likely that your office will need to place deposits for accommodations, group flights, arranged activities, or conduct site visits long before any program revenue is generated to allay these costs. Where will these monies come from?

If wire transfers need to be made to overseas accounts, which office will conduct the transactions? There may be rules about signing contracts and negotiating fees and payments, particularly if the service provider is overseas. You may be able to make arrangements up to a certain dollar limit (e.g., arranging group travel with your preferred travel agent); above that amount, services must be sent out for bid and your office may not be able to use its preferred provider. What about "corporate" credit cards? Can your faculty director get one in the institution's name?

If there is more than one program, will the fees be placed into separate program accounts or one general fund? Who will process refunds for students? Which office will provide the faculty director with a per diem advance and monies needed during the program? Which office will reconcile the accounts upon completion of the program?

Be sure to check out Chapter 9, Financial Matters: Collecting and Disbursing Monies, for a discussion on easy, clear reporting systems for faculty directors.

Whenever possible, use the existing account system to bill students for their short-term programs abroad. In the past, short-term programs were billed separately from the standard on-campus billing system, with an invoice sent directly to the student studying abroad, and the student making payment to the international office or the faculty director's personal checking account to cover travel logistics.

It is obvious that this independent system does not work for many reasons, including the increased liability of handling students' money outside of the normal institutional channels.

Student Accounts

If students are not billed through their student accounts at your institution, consider advocating to the business office for the following reasons:

- The international office does not function as a bank or collection agency.
- There is increased time to collect final payments.
- The designate person(s) receives the bill, including parents.
- Financial aid matters can be considered by trained personnel, by working directly with the financial aid office.
- Students are receiving institutional credit for the course and therefore should be paying the institution that grants the credit.
- By billing students through their on-campus accounts, the process parallels the usual billing procedures for longer-term study abroad.

The Financial Aid Office

When it comes to financial aid, many students do not leave home without it. Increasingly, students rely on federal, state, and institutional grants and loans to help finance their study abroad programs. The compressed nature of short-term programs abroad and their unique organizational characteristics create a need for the financial aid office and the office or individual responsible for the short-term program to work closely together to make sure the financial aid process encourages rather than hinders study abroad. This is especially important if an off-campus course is offered through a program provider, which mixes a third party into the equation.

Program Budgets for Financial Aid Counselors

The financial aid office determines the amount of financial aid a student is eligible to receive based on the cost of tuition and estimated living expenses in the local community. A short-term program abroad necessitates the creation of a separate budget, not only because living expenses abroad can vary dramatically from those on the home campus but also because instructional costs are not the same. These budgets, typically prepared in the international office or by the faculty director and sent to financial aid, break down the program fee into student, instructional, and administrative expenses. Students often have the opportunity to apply for additional aid, usually in the form of loans.

Maintaining Student Eligibility

Since the financial aid office must also receive documentation that students passed a requisite number of credits before their aid for the next term is released, the administrator needs to develop procedures that allow students to maintain their eligibility for aid. For example, one of your students is on a short-term program involving intense field work on site but also requiring a written report to be submitted when the student is back on campus for the next term. Failing to receive a grade for the study abroad course may prevent that student from getting aid for the following term, since the student will technically be seen as not having completed a full academic load.

One creative way to address such an issue is to assign the student an "in progress" or temporary passing grade, based on successful work on site and the presumption of a final project to be turned in. This kind of creative solution requires trust and a partnership between the financial aid office, the registrar's office, and the international office, and depends on careful record keeping and appropriate follow-up in all three offices.

How to Modify On-Campus Procedures

What is clear from the descriptions above is that someone is going to extra effort on behalf of the study abroad participant—and it is usually more than one person in more than one office at various times in the short life cycle of a program abroad. If you find that policies and procedures on your campus impede short-term study abroad, it may be time to overhaul them. These may be the legacy of a previous generation of administrators who were resistant to change, or they may simply be outdated. If the answer to every question regarding a given procedure is "because it's always been done that way," it is clearly time to reevaluate the procedure. Advances in technology can serve as a springboard to innovation. Advances in mindsets can do the same.

To start building these important relationships, propose a meeting with the registrar, the business office, and the financial aid officer. After first expressing gratitude for the assistance and cooperation these key people provide in making study abroad possible for so many deserving students, you can suggest a review of procedures with the goal of streamlining the process. Busy administrators embrace timesaving measures. Encouraging innovations leads to outcomes that everyone can support. It is important for you to remain flexible throughout this process and to be willing to listen. Your ideas for streamlining the system may need to be adjusted.

Do not overlook the power of anecdotal evidence to assist your cause. Point out other campuses whose offices have endorsed streamlining measures. Suggest that the administrators talk to their colleagues on other campuses who can provide reassurance that they are not going out on a limb while at the same time providing models worthy of emulation. The bottom line: if your campus administrative officers equate streamlining a process with reducing the effort they have to expend—without relinquishing control—you may find them extremely receptive allies.

Dean of Students/Division of Student Affairs

The dean of students and your student affairs colleagues can provide invaluable support to off-campus programs.

Because of the group structure and the larger pool of students going abroad, conduct or behavioral issues may become a problem while overseas. A process to send students home is described in Chapter 16, Safeguards: Crisis Management, but you must first work with your dean of students office to write student conduct procedures, such as those also found in the Sample Disciplinary Rights and Procedures for

Study Abroad Programs, Academic and Nonacademic, at the end of Chapter 16. Behavioral expectations should be an integral part of any general student policy handbook.

Most institutions do not allow students to apply for or participate in study abroad programs if they are on conduct probation. You may have a student who is put on probation after being accepted and approved to study abroad. Work with the dean of students office to negotiate the case. Sometimes students are placed in the conduct system at the end of the term, right before departure. Depending on the situation, a student may be allowed to depart for the off-campus program after signing a behavior contract and discussing the case with the faculty director and the dean of students.

As discussed in Chapter 11, Student Selection and Enrollment, the dean of students office may provide student disciplinary records (with permission from the student) for past infractions, or provide an endorsement to study off campus. See sample Consent to Release at the end of this chapter.

New Student Orientation/Residence Halls

Recruit your student affairs professionals to help promote study abroad opportunities at new student orientations, especially short-term programs abroad aimed at first or second year students. Also make sure that resident hall personnel, such as resident assistants, know what opportunities are available, and ask them to promote study abroad.

Health and Wellness

Fortunately, many services offered to students on campus can be extended to participants of short-term programs abroad. Professionals in the health center and the counseling center possess knowledge that is valuable in preparing students for aspects of their brief sojourns abroad that they had not considered. They may welcome opportunities to share their expertise and to develop country-specific or program-specific plans for students to stay healthy while abroad. These colleagues can also be useful in faculty director orientations and training, so faculty can ask questions and work through situations before going abroad with students.

Health Services

Health service professionals (i.e., nurses and doctors) can play a key role in preparing students to study abroad. Work with the health services department to identify required immunizations for region-specific areas (see the Costa Rica example in Chapter 16, Safeguards: Health Issues), and propose that they offer these prescriptions or inoculations at the health center. Also ask them to participate in predeparture orientations and review written materials such as handbooks and Web sites.

Your health services colleagues may also work with students after they return, when symptoms may appear and need to be diagnosed.

Counseling Center

Counseling professionals also play a role in preparing both faculty and students to go abroad, as well as assisting with situations while the group is overseas.

Be sure a representative from the counseling center is available to talk to faculty directors and other staff responsible for short-term programs abroad. The counselor can discuss how to deal with certain situations, such as a student going off prescription medication or refusing to eat. If circumstances that warrant counseling develop abroad, make sure a counselor and the program's on-site personnel talk to each other. Confirm that some members of the counseling staff have current passports, in case one of them needs to bring a student home.

Human Resources

Your human resources department can provide information on the benefits available to faculty directors and other leaders such as staff or teaching assistants while they are out of the country. Remember to discuss appropriate levels of medical evacuation for all international sites. Like students, faculty and staff should understand their health insurance and how it travels abroad.

General Counsel/Risk Management

Great strides have been made in the last decade in establishing guidelines and best practices with health, safety, and risk management. With short-term programs abroad, where so many aspects of these issues are condensed, there is less time to deal with emergencies of any kind.

As documented in Chapter 16, Safeguards: Crisis Management, your institution's legal counsel and risk management personnel can help you prepare contingency plans to deal with the unexpected: medically evacuating a student or faculty director, notifying a student of a family emergency at home, dealing with a natural disaster in the field, or coping with a political crisis at home or abroad.

Legal Services

The legal affairs or services office should be made aware of the short-term programs abroad and their locations. Program-specific waivers of responsibility and acknowledgment of risks forms may need to be drafted; any new waiver should be reviewed and approved by the general counsel of your institution. In addition, any contracts for goods and services provided by third party agencies or organizations (e.g., travel agency, host institution, local transportation company) may need to be reviewed and approved by institutional counsel.

Risk Management

The risk management office can play an important role in supporting a decision to reject a program proposal that presents too great a health or safety risk, based on its location or proposed activities. This office can also negotiate emergency medical and/or health insurance coverage for students and faculty. It can also assist in creating a budget line for emergency contingency funds for a single or a set of short-term programs abroad.

Publications/Communications

International offices are well versed in publicity strategies for their programs, but often they do not think about publicity beyond the immediate need of using it to recruit students. Tapping into the vast network of communication lines across campus is an extremely effective way not only to promote a particular short-term program abroad but also to advocate for study abroad in general. Ask your publications department to create materials and brochures that will carry the institution's "image" and highlight your programs.

Contributing to Internationalization

The success of a program is determined not just by what happens to the students on site but also by the educational value placed by the institution on the students' experiences. Campus leaders and colleagues need to know about these students' experiences in order to *value them*. The more the institution and its members value these experiences, the more they will promote them, especially if short-term study abroad is viewed as a significant contributing factor in the process of internationalization. Keeping the campus informed also draws attention to international offices as leading agents in facilitating opportunities for students to have meaningful intercultural experiences.

When the latest statistics on short-term study abroad are published in the annual Institute of International Education's *Open Doors* report, send notes to your campus media office and your government relations officer, indicating your institution's role in participating in significant study abroad trends.

Staff/faculty newsletters and daily bulletins are obvious places to advertise opportunities for faculty to direct programs abroad as well as to call for proposals. They are also excellent venues to carry follow-up stories on program participants and faculty directors.

Student newspapers can serve the same function for students and faculty. Invite the campus editor to visit your office at least once a year. Ask the editor to assign a reporter to check in on a regular basis. Invite a campus reporter to predeparture orientations and reentry sessions. (Be prepared to get a phone call if a student is sent home from the program, a political situation arises, or complaints about your enrollment process surface.)

If your students were in programs that included a service-learning component, facilitate opportunities for students to share their experiences with the campus community on return. Ask your campus media office for assistance in developing public service announcements to publicize student presentations of their experiences abroad.

If your campus has its own radio station, suggest that the station interview students and faculty before they go and after they come back.

Alumni Magazine

Editors of alumni magazines are always on the lookout for story ideas that reflect well on the university, even if they do not specifically feature alumni, so suggestions are likely to be well received. The unique features of short-term programs abroad make good copy.

On-Campus News Services

Occasionally, media sources will contact your institution wanting an interview either of general interest or pertaining to some global crisis. Have a plan for dealing with these requests. Especially if the interview is dealing with a particular crisis issue, it may be better for the communications director to deal with the media since your office will be busy dealing with the crisis.

Admissions

Admissions counselors routinely visit local high schools and community colleges. Ask your admissions staff to highlight short-term study abroad as an exciting option for new and transfer students.

Career Center

Ask the career center advisers on your campus to talk to students about how study abroad can enhance employment prospects and how short-term study, with its frequent emphasis on field work and experiential learning, can help them develop skills beyond the academic framework. Invite alumni who participated in short-term programs abroad to talk about how their experiences abroad shaped their career paths.

Instructional Technology

Computers are so much a part of campus life now that students are forced to make major adjustments when they go abroad on programs where computer access is limited. Unless students have the comparative luxury of ready access to laptops, the opportunity to use computers is even more limited on short-term programs abroad.

Laptops Abroad

You might consider making it an institutional policy that the faculty director be equipped with a laptop to take along lecture notes, to keep a running report throughout the program, or to facilitate e-mail access for emergency communication. A faculty director's department might be a resource for portable computer equipment. Program providers are often one step ahead of universities in offering this level of support. Check with your university's instructional technology office to assess institutional policies regarding borrowing computer equipment to take abroad.

Program Web Site

Often a Web-savvy student member of the study abroad group will be willing to build a program Web site. The site can contain both academic and logistical information. Access to a laptop (and digital camera) allows the site to be updated regularly for the home campus, family, and friends.

Digital Cameras

Many faculty directors find it useful to take a digital camera along to visually document students on site. These photos can assist in the recruitment process for the next program and be used for publicity materials and creative academic journals. Check with your university's instructional technology or communication department to see if a digital camera is available to take abroad, or advocate to have one purchased specifically for the program abroad by the academic department, the international office, or the institution.

The welfare of students and faculty abroad, couched in phrases about liability concerns, can bolster arguments for institutional investment in instructional technology equipment for short-term programs.

Conclusion

This chapter has looked primarily at the offices on campus that can and do provide essential support for short-term programs abroad. Your institution's internal organization, including whether it is largely centralized or decentralized, will also have an impact on how your programs are run. Nothing will influence the success of your programs and the level of collaboration you can expect as much as campus attitudes about the intrinsic value of short-term study abroad programs and their place in a student's academic experience.

A short-term program is characterized by the brevity of the actual time spent abroad, but an enormous amount of time still goes into its planning, and the academic and cultural impact it has on students is long term and far reaching. Keeping offices across campus in the communication loop and actively pursuing every avenue of publicity that draws positive attention to the uniqueness of short-term programs will reap rewards for the international office and reflect favorably on the university. That is why it is important to think "long range" and "big picture" when it comes to incorporating these programs into the system.

CONSENT TO RELEASE OF GENERAL INFORMATION

I approve and consent to the dean of students' office staff's contact with the off-campus study program adviser, program director, field supervisor, interim instructor, and/or interim course adviser regarding any academic, emotional, medical, or behavioral problem that I may be experiencing at St. Olaf College. I understand that this information will be shared confidentially only with the faculty member responsible for the program for which I have applied, for the purpose of evaluating my qualifications for study on the program specified on this application.

_____

Signature of applicant   Date

_____

Print name   Program

If you have any concerns about this release form, please discuss them with the appropriate dean in the dean of students' office.

PROCEDURAL NOTE ON ABOVE:

When the international and off-campus studies office receives the completed applications:

1. If the above consent form is signed, the student's name will be included in a list sent to the dean of students' office. The appropriate assistant/associate dean will place a check mark after the name of any student about whom there are concerns. The names of those students so checked will be shared with the off-campus study program adviser, program director, field supervisor, interim instructor, and/or interim course adviser. The faculty member will contact the appropriate assistant/associate dean to discuss the concerns.

2. If the above consent form is not signed, the unsigned form will be sent to the dean of students' office. That office will consult with the student to discuss the reasons for a lack of signature. After this discussion, a student may sign the form, in which case the procedure listed in item 1 above is followed. If the student does not sign the form, the off-campus study program adviser, program director, field supervisor, interim course instructor, and/or interim course adviser will be informed that the consent form was unsigned and the faculty member will make the decision whether or not to consider the student's application.

[Source: Adapted from St. Olaf College]

PART II
Principles of Academic Course Design

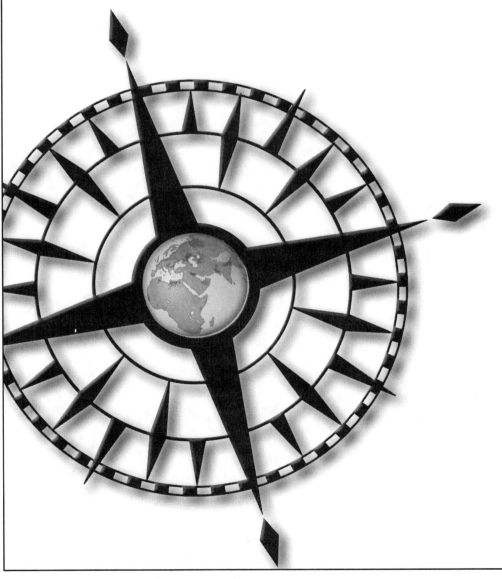

Chapter 5

Program Models

Kathy Tuma

More than 2,000 short-term programs abroad are described in the annual reference guide, *Short-Term Study Abroad*, published by the Institute of International Education. Approximately 60 percent of the programs are sponsored by U.S. accredited colleges and universities. The remaining 40 percent are sponsored by providers (e.g., institutions without U.S. accreditation such as foreign universities and institutes and adult education centers, as well as other U.S.-based and foreign organizations).

Short-term programs are offered year round: during the regular academic calendar, break times, and the summer. Although many programs are developed and administered by the home institution, others are pre-designed programs that enroll students from a number of U.S. colleges and universities.

The type of program that best suits your institution can be determined by a careful review of resources, including the following:

+   Faculty willing and able to teach off-campus courses.
+   An administration that is supportive of faculty proposing off-campus programs.
+   Sufficient staff resources to administer the programs.
+   A student body willing to take advantage of the program offerings.
+   The financial ability of the students and the institution to undertake a specific program.

If you have willing faculty but limited staff resources, consider using a program provider to assist with the planning. If you have students anxious to participate in short-term programs but you lack administrative support, think about sending your students on already existing programs.

At the end of this chapter, you will find a Venn Diagram. Use it as an exercise that may help you decide how to best operate short-term programs on your campus.

The following pages will give you information on various program models. As you will see, there are many ways to design and administer successful short-term programs abroad.

Faculty-Directed Programs

One of the most common short-term models is to offer a course directed by a faculty member from the home institution. Individual faculty and/or academic departments typically propose off-campus courses that expand existing curricular offerings.

In many cases, the idea for such a course comes from the faculty member's own experience. For example, a theater professor returning from sabbatical in London is inspired to develop a course to introduce students to the multitude of theater experiences available there. Or a French department faculty member who recently completed dissertation research in Francophone Africa proposes to take students to this less-traditional region for language study.

In other cases, the faculty member or department recognizes the value of offering a course in a particular location, but does not have contacts in the region. The political science department may wish to offer students the opportunity to study the European Union, but does not have any contacts in Belgium and Luxembourg. The religion department may want to develop a Buddhism course in Thailand, taking advantage of that country's numerous temples and the chance to experience monastic life, but no faculty have been to Asia.

Often, the potential faculty director or international office will have sufficient contacts in the area to arrange the academics and the logistics internally. However, there may be other cases where it will be necessary to employ a program provider for academic resources, logistical needs, or both.

Staffing of programs and payment of salaries can be complicated, and decisions such as those covered in Chapter 3, Administrative Processes, must be considered proactively in order to avoid problems later. The institution must decide if off-campus programs are part of the faculty member's regular course load, count as an overload, or if the salary is to be covered by the institution or by the program fee. The budgets for these programs are usually dependent on sufficient student enrollment, so if a program is canceled, what happens to the staffing plan?

The benefits of a course developed and directed by a member of your own faculty are many:
- The course can be designed to specifically fit the existing curriculum or to fill a gap in the department's offerings.
- The faculty member accompanying the group abroad fully understands the academic expectations of the institution.
- Students have the opportunity to get to know a faculty member in a setting very different from the classroom, and vice versa.
- Increasing the international experience of your students and your faculty leads to an enhanced internationalization of your campus and curriculum.

Partnerships: Customized Program Needs and Program Providers

Many U.S. institutions wish to host their own short-term programs abroad, but do not have the resources or the long-term commitment necessary to set up the on-site facilities. A great option for short-term programs is to work with a program provider to create a customized program for the institution.

The Role of the Program Provider

As fully explained in Chapter 8, Logistics, program provider organizations work with universities to develop programs tailor-made for the needs of that U.S. institution, both predeparture and on-site. Services of program providers can include travel and logistics, on-site support staff, academic support, student services, publicity, enrollment services, orientations, insurance, payment processing, and other services, depending on the organization. Universities are able to select the services they desire when they are designing a program.

A program provider generally has offices in both the United States and overseas. One of the most important elements to remember about the customized program model is that the U.S. institution always retains the identity of its own program. Although there may be other U.S. institutions using a particular program provider overseas, each university designs and administers its program in a way that best suits its students and faculty.

A program provider is useful for universities who may only want assistance with certain sections of a short-term program abroad, to free up the faculty director to focus on teaching, or to coordinate certain aspects of the on-site administration of the program. In any case, it is important to work with a provider that is flexible, in order to provide assistance where it is needed and not be forced into a "package deal."

Direct Enrollment in Predesigned Programs

Universities and colleges are increasingly offering students the opportunity to enroll directly in programs operated by other U.S. or foreign institutions. By encouraging participation in predesigned short-term programs abroad, institutions increase the number of academic fields and geographical locations available to students.

Advantages of this model include the expansion of study abroad opportunities in more countries and academic fields, with differing program lengths and a variety of cost options. Predesigned programs also require a minimum of resources from the sending institution. However, the home institution has little or no influence on the course design and curriculum.

It is important to research the academic credibility of predesigned programs and to advise students when they are selecting a program. Most institutions have policies for students participating in predesigned courses sponsored by a program provider, including a process to approve short-term programs for credit. The transfer of credit, grades, and various forms of financial aid must be considered before the student studies abroad.

A Hybrid Model: Predesigned and Customized Programs

A hybrid model combines a predesigned program with the opportunity for the home institution to influence the program content, course offerings, and curriculum.

Hybrid models offer an option to allow some elements of a short-term program abroad to be modified according to the requirements of the home institution. An academic department may ask that adjustments be made to an existing program to better serve the department's academic and logistical needs. The ideal situation is when the program provider and the institution become partners in developing a customized, hybrid model.

Hybrid models can include several types of cooperation between the program provider and the home institution, such as the following:

♦ The program provider is responsible for the infrastructure but also plays a significant role in the academic program. This includes hiring foreign (local) faculty and making arrangements for the integrated site visits. The home institution provides the students and sometimes may provide a faculty director.

♦ A joint venture where some elements of an existing program are negotiated and adapted to meet the needs of the home institution (e.g., adding specific lectures or site visits). In addition, some courses may be taught jointly by foreign and U.S. faculty.

Like the predesigned model, a hybrid program allows the home institution to save resources, especially staff, but still provides the flexibility to customize a program to take advantage of the academic and cultural resources of a program provider while meeting the academic needs of the sending institution.

Although these kinds of partnerships have few disadvantages, they do take more time than predesigned programs. The direct cost of the hybrid program paid to the provider may appear higher than the cost of independent faculty-directed programs, where the cost is absorbed by the faculty mentor or the international office because they are providing the staffing resources.

When well organized, the hybrid program can combine the advantages of the faculty-directed program (e.g., faculty involvement and faculty development) with the advantages of a predesigned program (e.g., a greater opportunity for cultural immersion, and a reduced responsibility for the home institution to provide a minimum number of students).

Exchange Models

It is possible to develop a short-term program abroad from an exchange agreement. The U.S. institution typically earns one to two credits for each student they have enrolled in a short-term program at a foreign institution, and as a result, credits build to support tuition for incoming semester-long or year-long exchange students.

This type of program is developed to accommodate:
♦ U.S. students who are unprepared linguistically to enroll in the host institution for a semester or year.
♦ U.S. students who are willing and able to participate in a short-term program, but not in a long-term program due to curricular constraints.
♦ A steady supply of international students willing and able to attend the U.S. institution.

The intercultural component of such a program is potentially much richer than with other short-term programs. The bilateral institutional involvement allows students and faculty from both institutions to extend their experiences. Intercultural exchange is not limited to the time that the students are on the host campus, but expands to include time that they may interact with exchange partners on their own campus as well.

In developing a budget for this type of program, you need to consider exchange policies that may already exist, including the following:
♦ Do you need to build in administrative costs for the incoming exchange student?
♦ If the exchange is for tuition only, will this be a problem for incoming students?
♦ How will exchange imbalances be handled?
♦ What will be the cost considerations of slow credit accrual or of not having a regular supply of qualified exchange candidates?

In any type of exchange program it is important to have a written agreement that spells out the obligations of each institution. Such an agreement is particularly important if an exchange arrangement includes a considerable difference in the services provided by each institution.

Ideally, each year the number of outgoing students will balance with the number of incoming students. Try not to build credits too slowly (over more than one year) or you will lose the buying power of the tuition collected.

Although this model offers great benefits to the students and faculty of the participating institutions, it also requires strong faculty and administrative support from both sides. Be sure that such support exists before proceeding.

Consortium Programs

When more than one institution offers short-term programs abroad during the same period in the academic year, they may want to consider forming a consortium in order to share students and faculty directors and increase the number of short-term opportunities.

The structure of the consortium will vary, depending on the culture and involvement of the home institutions. It is important to have a board of directors comprising representatives from each institution. The representatives can be deans, faculty, international directors, and/or administrators. Significant faculty representation will ensure academic quality.

Most successful consortia have a lead institution or organization to facilitate student enrollment and orientation, while each home institution is responsible for faculty recruitment and support, student advising, and other defined details. Most consortia also retain a program provider to organize all logistics and travel and to coordinate marketing.

A consortium model can bring a significant increase in student enrollment with limited use of institutional resources. Like most synchronized efforts, the role of each institution must be clearly defined and formal documentation and contracts must be created and approved by each institution.

Embedded Programs

An embedded program is one where a short-term international experience is included as part of a regular term course. The international component of a course may come during fall or spring break, during interterm break, or in the summer immediately following the end of the regular term. The key is that the international experience is part of the academic requirement of the course.

Ideally, the embedded experience comes at a point during the term that allows the faculty director the opportunity to provide extensive preprogram preparation and postprogram follow-up.

Although an embedded program works in many circumstances, it is particularly well suited to graduate programs and "weekend" colleges whose student bodies are often unable to be away for more than a week or two.

Sample Programs

The following are examples of real short-term programs abroad currently offered by U.S. organizations.

Faculty-Directed Program During Winter Intersession: Bali, Indonesia

At the University of Montana, a professor from the dance department takes students to Bali, Indonesia, during the January intersession. The academic focus of the course is art and its use in everyday culture.

This is a 3-week, 3-credit program that focuses on the art and culture of Bali. It is composed of lectures on a broad range of topics, such as "Balinese Social Structure" and "The Effects of Hinduism on Daily Life," and on several of the individual art forms. Students also receive eight lessons in an art form of their choice, including Batik, shadow puppetry, dance, and traditional flute, among others. There is no foreign language requirement.

—Amy Baty, The University of Montana

MBA Immersion Seminars: Multiple Locations

The Global Immersion Electives (GIEs) provide students in the MBA and Executive MBA Programs at The Kenan-Flagler Business School with an opportunity to engage in short-term experiential learning abroad for academic credit. There are six different GIEs, each of which combines relevant and timely international business issues with nuts-and-bolts discussions of how to do business in targeted countries or regions. The GIEs highlight some of the most dynamic economies in the world. Depending on the expertise of the lead faculty member, a GIE may place a secondary focus on a specific industry or functional area as well. In 2002, the GIE program is scheduled to take Kenan-Flagler MBA and EMBA students to a total of 12 countries on 4 continents. The GIEs begin with predeparture, interdisciplinary lectures on the Kenan-Flagler campus and culminate in a 10-day to 2-week business study tour of the targeted country or region, led by the course professor.

—Amanda McCorkle Laird, The Kenan-Flagler Business School,
The University of North Carolina-Chapel Hill

First and Second Year Seminars: Multiple Locations

Global seminars are 3-week, 3-credit, faculty-directed study abroad programs with no language requirements or prerequisites. These programs are modeled after special on-campus courses developed to help with retention rates among first and second year students. The goals of these courses, matching the goals of the global seminars, are to (1) allow the opportunity for personal interactions between students and professors, and (2) create a community classroom culture. Faculty from all disciplines may apply, but they must use the existing on-site partners of the Global Campus o Study Abroad office to handle the logistical aspects of the programs. On-site partners also handle emergency issues, cultural orientations, and other supplemental aspects such as survival language classes if they are offered. Global seminars offer students an early option for study abroad and allows them to get their feet wet before making a long-term study abroad commitment.

—Amy Greeley, University of Minnesota

Engineering and Liberal Arts Seminars: Multiple Locations

Union College in Schenectady, New York, has two major grants, one from the Christian Johnson Endeavor and the other from the Keck Foundation, to develop and run mini-terms that combine engineering and the liberal arts. The normal pattern is that half of the students are engineers, the other half from the liberal arts discipline (for the most part the social sciences). A team comprising one student from each area is formed, and the team is assigned a project so that they learn to work together from different perspectives. It is, in effect, a double cross-cultural experience. Students can study (dirty) water resources in Brazil, (clean) water resources in Australia, medical technology in Scotland, or electricity in New Zealand.

—William Thomas, Union College

Service Learning Through Teaching: Nhlangano, Swaziland

Ohio University (OU) partners with the Ngwane Teachers' College in Nhlangano, Swaziland, to offer a program that pairs OU students with Ngwane Teachers' College students to team-teach for the final 3 weeks of a Swazi student's teaching practice. The program is entitled "Service Learning Through Teaching in Swaziland," and runs for approximately 5 weeks in the summer. Each OU student has one Swazi teaching partner and usually is responsible for teaching a section of English or math. OU students live with Swazi students in dormitories (though not with their teaching partners). OU sends a designated person (a graduate student or African studies staff/faculty member; it varies each year) with the group to facilitate group discussions, give journal writing assignments, read journals, etc.

—Cathy Huber, Ohio University

Predesigned Program: Thailand

The Council Study Center in Thailand is ideal for students hoping to work in some capacity that will benefit society and the environment or those contemplating joining the Peace Corps or another community-based volunteer program after graduation. The 7-week summer program aims to expose its participants to a broad range of developmental and environmental issues by providing a unique opportunity to meet with the local community in its own environment. Participants study problems and solutions with the people directly involved, such as grassroots political leaders and broad-based people's coalitions, representatives from nongovernmental and governmental organizations, farmer's groups and cooperatives, socially engaged monks, scholars and social critics, authors and journalists, political advocates and human rights activists, and people living with HIV/AIDS. The result of participation in this program is the realization that the problems in Thailand have a global impact and are the responsibility of all citizens of the world.

—Christine Wintersteen, Council International Study Programs

Embedded Program: Cuernavaca, Mexico

Augsburg Weekend College students have the opportunity to register for a course entitled "Mexico: The Church and Social Change in Latin America." This course focuses on the relationship of the church to poverty, political oppression, and social justice in Latin America. It examines the ways in which Christian theology has been used to both justify oppression and injustice as well as to support social justice movements. A distinctive aspect of the class is an 8-day study tour to Cuernavaca, Mexico, with two introductory class sessions prior to the study tour and a single follow-up class session after return from Mexico.

—Regina McGoff, Augsburg College

Understanding the Global and Local: Vietnam

The City College of San Francisco offers a program that focuses on gaining a greater understanding of the Vietnamese and Vietnamese-American perspective and is geared to both students and faculty. The course, "Passage to Vietnam," acquaints participants with several aspects of Vietnam, specifically the people, culture, and landscape of this emerging Southeast Asian country. This is an important alternative, since most often the metaphors associated with Vietnam are those related to war, poverty, and bloody battlefields. The acquired knowledge will enable participants to obtain a deeper understanding of the Southeast Asian community in the United States. Participants will have a chance to interact with Vietnamese faculty, visit historical sites, and acquire knowledge that will help them integrate a Vietnamese perspective into their studies and/or curriculum.

—Jill Heffron, City College of San Francisco

Scholarships for Part-Time Students to Study Abroad

The College of Notre Dame (CND) of Maryland has what may be a unique scholarship program for part-time students interested in taking one of our short-term courses abroad. CND has a significant part-time population in both the undergraduate weekend college and in various graduate programs. We want to provide these students with the same kind of support for study abroad that we provide to our full-time students. Most part-time students could never free themselves up to participate in a semester-long study abroad program, however, many can and do choose a 2-week course abroad. All part-time students who qualify (matriculation, GPA, and completion of some CND credits) earn a tuition scholarship for one course abroad.

—Ann M. Scholz, College of Notre Dame of Maryland

VENN DIAGRAM

Look carefully at the list of program needs. Knowing the situation on your campus, assign each of these responsibilities to one of the circles. This should not be the ideal or the preferred but the reality of who is willing and able to accomplish each of the tasks. Overlap the responsibilities where appropriate. For example, Logistics will likely overlap between International Office and Program Provider. Course schedule may overlap between Program Provider and Faculty. Orientation should fall into all three categories.

Hopefully this exercise will assist you in determining the best means for administering short-term programs at your institution.

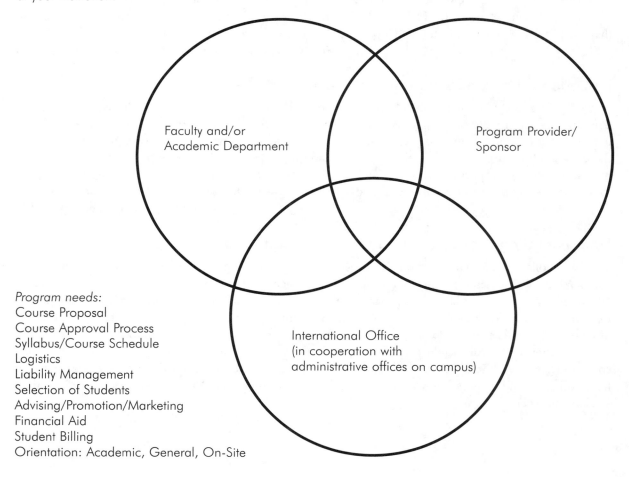

Faculty and/or Academic Department

Program Provider/ Sponsor

International Office (in cooperation with administrative offices on campus)

Program needs:
Course Proposal
Course Approval Process
Syllabus/Course Schedule
Logistics
Liability Management
Selection of Students
Advising/Promotion/Marketing
Financial Aid
Student Billing
Orientation: Academic, General, On-Site

Chapter 6

Designing the Academic Course: Principles and Practicalities

Elise Amel and Anders Uhrskov

Because short-term programs abroad differ from the on-campus teaching experience, this chapter focuses on the components of an academically successful short-term course off-campus. Chapter 14 concentrates on the educator becoming an international educator.

For faculty who are used to meeting students in their classes three times a week and during office hours and are comfortable with the rhythm this brings, it is a challenge to shift gears to short-term programs that are by nature quite intense academically, personally, and physically. The professor moves from having a variety of available resource tools to being the primary resource person who guides students to a different set of tools, often to which faculty and students are not accustomed.

In order for the academic component of short-term programs abroad to be successful, there are several questions that must be considered. What is the perception of such courses on campus? What does it take to teach on the road; what tools are available to design these courses? What is the new landscape of the classroom, and what are the design issues that are so vastly different from on-campus experiences? There are many practical suggestions and possibilities that have been used successfully to design courses that are academically challenging, personally satisfying, and that promote an awareness of cultural diversity for both faculty and students before, during, and after the time spent abroad.

The Academic Image of Short-Term Programs

For students—including academically serious students—short-term study abroad can be perceived as a "term off," a kind of tourism with credit, an experience that is supposed to be not only fun and entertaining, but also academically "lightweight."

It is an unfair reputation, since most short-term programs abroad have a strong academic basis. Therefore, short-term programs that grant credit, particularly those that travel to more than one site, have an image problem to overcome.

Faculty directors can begin to conquer this image problem by creating a detailed description of the academic curriculum of the program, that is, by articulating the intent and expectations, and then making sure those details are carried out. Remember that nothing is more compelling to other faculty and administrators than an excellent track record.

Proposing a Course

Crafting a solid proposal is the first step in creating a positive experience and image. As described in Chapter 3, Administrative Processes, a faculty member may approach the department chair, dean, or international office with the desire to adapt a catalog course to a foreign environment, or to create a new course that takes advantage of the opportunities of an international setting. Most institutions have a procedure whereby a standing committee reviews study abroad programs proposed by the faculty. If a proposal process is in place, written guidelines and examples should be available. Many committees request more detail than they would for an on-campus course proposal. Although faculty may question the need for such detail, academic quality begins as ideas are articulated in writing and a tentative plan is formulated.

Standard academic content issues must be considered, such as learning objectives, readings, and methods of evaluation. However, faculty must also balance these issues with the practical design concerns addressed in Part III, such as feasibility of site, program development timeline, and cost.

Specific course proposal examples are found at the end of this chapter. A basic proposal should contain the following elements:

- A specific description of the short-term program, including:
  - ✓ general and specific learning objectives;
  - ✓ what the students are going to learn (e.g., knowledge, perspectives, skills) in the international environment that they could not learn at home; and
  - ✓ how the program takes advantage of the international environment (e.g., academic and cross-cultural site visits, guest professors, assignments, etc.).

- As with traditional syllabi, listings of required reading, assignments, exams or papers, presentations, academic journals, or field observation reports to be used as the basis for the course grading.

- A day-to-day syllabus, integrating lectures, site visits, readings, assignments, discussions, reflection periods, and field work.

- Specific evaluation and grading criteria with explanations.

- A predeparture component, preparing students for the academic and cultural experience. Depending on the academic calendar, institutional policy, and the unique structure of each short-term program abroad, this may include seminars, orientation meetings, a required course the previous semester, required readings, or online Web assignments.

- A postprogram component, where students are debriefed about their experiences and integrate what they learned abroad into their academic and personal situation back home. Faculty may schedule official seminars that are part of the academic course or more social gatherings such as a photo-swap party or welcome back dinner.

It must be clear to all constituents—colleagues, deans, the registrar, overseas partners, and most importantly, the students—what students will learn and experience, not just what they are going to see or do. By focusing on the academics, these courses can avoid the perception of being a holiday trip or tourist excursion.

Designing Short-Term Courses: Shaping Through Learning Objectives

—*Pamela Nice*

It has been my experience—both as a teacher and as a faculty developer—that defining teaching and learning objectives is the most important factor in course development. When these objectives are clearly and explicitly defined by the instructor, they can help immensely to structure effective assignments and shape the course. Everything is driven by the learning objectives, so the course has a clear focus. This way of approaching course design means that you really need to think deeply about *what you want your students to learn* in your course.

It may be helpful to think of specific knowledge, skills, and attitudes you would like your students to have by the end of your course.[1] The brief duration of most short-term courses is not much time to accomplish your objectives, so you may have to think in terms of *introducing* and *reinforcing* them. Or you may find that you have to throw out some of your objectives as being too ambitious for the length of your course. Ideally, you will want to find a way to integrate texts, performances, presentations by guest speakers, visits to local sites and museums, the students' experiences in the locale, field trips, discussions, and written work to help your students wrestle with specific concepts and skills.

I find it easiest to think of three components of a short-term course: the locale, the content area, and the learning objectives. Thinking of the first two, I start developing my teaching/learning objectives. Which objectives should I focus on, given the duration of the course?

It helps to keep in mind that there are factors particular to these courses that challenge the students' focus. Travel may make them tired or lacking in concentration; accommodations and the local population may provide daily challenges; students may get on each other's nerves (and yours) with the 24-hour a day contact; class on top of a mountain may sound intriguing until you realize that the goats won't leave you alone.

So it is all the more important to keep focused on your objectives. The cardinal rule is **reinforcement**. Make your objectives clear and explicit in
- ✓ the orientation,
- ✓ the syllabus,
- ✓ class lectures or discussions,
- ✓ reflective assignments, and
- ✓ when giving feedback (either verbally or in writing).

Reinforcement is the key to maintaining focus.

An Example from "Encountering Egypt Through the Arts"

I teach a short-term study course abroad in Egypt: *Encountering Egypt Through the Arts*. One of my main teaching/learning objectives is to make students aware of their own personal and cultural lenses when perceiving and interpreting another culture. Most of the students have little awareness of their lenses at the beginning of the course. They also tend to have many stereotypes about Arab cultures, combined with an almost total lack of knowledge about such cultures.

My learning objective: I want to find a way to increase the students' awareness of their own lenses as they perceive and interpret Egyptian culture through its art and through their experiences in the culture.

Introducing the Concept: Syllabus and Orientation

At the orientation, I hand out the course syllabus, which mentions my above objective, among others. Students see it in writing. Then I give them an autoethnography assignment (found in Chapter 15), asking them questions about their personal and cultural lenses. They discuss their answers in small groups, and then we have a whole-class discussion on their answers. The word "lens" appears in the exercise and I write it on the board during our discussions. I draw a diagram showing how our lenses work. Some of the questions with this exercise have to do with how the students—at that time—perceive Egyptian, Arab, or Muslim cultures. We also talk about how the students view their own cultures. Usually, there will be differences in the group due to ethnicity, home regions, or personal backgrounds. We talk about how these aspects of our lives help to create our lenses.

Precourse Worksheets

Before the course begins, the students have some background reading to do on Egyptian history and politics, Islam, and some artists. They also read an Egyptian novel. On their worksheets, I ask them at least two questions about their lenses, or the lens of the writer of a text.

Experiential Learning and Debriefing Sessions

At last, we arrive in Egypt. Experiential learning begins with a vengeance. The young women receive an obviously unexpected amount of attention from men on the streets. We have a debriefing session near the end of the first day. Why do you think you are getting this attention? Through what kind of lens are the men viewing you, do you think? Why? This leads into a discussion of stereotyping of other cultures—both ours and theirs. Their own emotional reactions give palpable evidence that the way we think can lead to hurtful or embarrassing actions that serve to further alienate us from each other.

Content Analysis

At a class session, we view a contemporary Egyptian documentary. The first question I ask the students is, "What is the lens of the filmmaker? How do we know what the lens is—what elements of the form do we look for? How does this influence the focus of the documentary?"

Assessment: Reflective Exercise in Academic Journal and/or Final Paper

During the course, another way I encourage focus is to have the students write an academic journal, some of which is their own reflection, and some of which is in response to questions I give them. At the end of the 3 weeks, I ask the students to reflect on whether their lenses in relation to Egyptian culture and art have changed, and if so, how. They write their last journal entry on this topic.

In this final exercise, as well as in their final papers, I am able to assess how well the students have learned this concept of lenses. I will see if their lenses have changed through the course, and what kind of self-awareness they bring to this process.

This is just one example of how a teaching/learning objective can focus assignments and shape a short-term course.

Covering the Material

When designing a course from learning objectives, teachers often find that they can't "cover" as much material, and see this as a drawback. However, a large body of research on learning suggests that deep learning seldom happens when the teacher lectures or presents material without having students actively engage with it.[2] Active engagement may include, for instance, writing or discussion assignments in which each student expresses concepts in his or her own words, applies concepts, or relates them to previous knowledge. Such activities take time—more time than merely having the teacher "cover" the material.

Likewise, reinforcement of major principles takes time and requires the teacher to make some tough decisions on which objectives are most important. This sort of intentional course design, however, has real benefits for the students' learning, and is much more fulfilling for the teachers—especially when reading final papers!

[1] This approach to course design came from Tom Creed, who was a faculty development consultant for the University of St. Thomas's faculty development program in the early 1990s.

[2] The pedagogical approaches of writing to learn, problem-based learning, learning through inquiry, and collaborative learning, to name a few, are based on the premise that deeper learning occurs through active student engagement with concepts and through practicing certain skills and attitudes.

Teaching on the Road

Although faculty directors may find themselves blissfully removed from the responsibilities of a campus—committee work, administrative duties, and teaching multiple courses—they are likely to experience a loss of the amenities they count on to teach their courses, including:

- computer access;
- access to copiers;
- traditional classrooms, with blackboards and audiovisual equipment;
- research facilities, including libraries;
- ready access to office materials such as books and a hard drive full of exercises, exam questions, and notes; and
- collegial support.

On the other hand, the benefits of off-campus teaching are numerous.

- Because of the relative freedom from campus responsibilities, faculty can take advantage of the organic opportunities that arise in the study locations.
- There is an enhanced opportunity to get to know the current generation of students.
- Students are likely to see the human side of faculty directors as they spend more time with each other.
- The learning experience is based on clear, constant contact with the new cultural milieu, which is visual, auditory, and immediate during every moment of the time spent abroad.
- Students are free from distractions such as work, family obligations, and a thick social calendar, so faculty can plan meetings throughout the day and evenings without losing the attendance of a substantial number of students.

* Depending on the course, there is a greater use of independent and service-learning techniques, which benefit students on site and once they return to traditional classroom settings.
* After teaching abroad, faculty often bring new knowledge, ideas, perspectives, and activities to their on-campus courses.

A short-term course abroad, while academically rigorous, draws its design, its resources, its assignments, and its evaluation from the unique opportunities offered by the program site. Teaching techniques and research methodology all have to be rethought and restructured to make the most of each course that is offered. In the next section, we begin to address these issues in greater depth.

Teaching Techniques

Generally, the basis for evaluation may be broader than a course at the home institution. While there may be fewer lectures, lengthy textbook readings, and traditional research papers required, these can be substituted with techniques that integrate cross-cultural elements, including interviews, academic journals, drawings, photos, cultural artifacts, and oral presentations. Even a local "treasure hunt" for images, monuments, and examples of topics under study can open students' eyes to the rich environment surrounding them.

Regardless of the specific techniques implemented, faculty should consider frequent "prepping" and "processing" opportunities. Often, discussion can be integrated into local culture and customs such as dining together and afternoon tea or coffee. An evening gathering in a lounge can work as well. Suggested questions for processing can be found at the end of this chapter. It is critical to prepare students in advance for what they will see, hear, and experience, and what they should be looking for during excursions. Debriefing, responding to questions and concerns as they arise, and managing student impressions can enhance the overall academic experience.

Research

Research in the traditional sense rarely works on these courses because access to resources can be limited. One way to circumvent these difficulties is to have students prepare their research before departure or after returning from abroad. Other viable alternatives include field observation reports or presentations and academic journals.

Academic Journals

Opinions differ as to the usefulness of the academic journal: some see the journal as a valuable tool for experiential learning; others believe journaling is a useless exercise that is too difficult to grade. It is true that journaling can be ineffective, containing blow-by-blow details of breakfast and the train ride. However, this type of personal journal is likely to result when the journal is simply assigned at the beginning of the course and collected at the end for evaluation without any regular intervention. When managed effectively, journals can reinforce the relevance of course material, reduce students' feelings of being overwhelmed by providing a theme for student experiences, and provide practice enhancing larger, applied assignments, such as those that integrate site visits with theories from class.

Effective management of academic journaling involves clear discussion with students up front regarding expectations as well as providing specific questions and guiding themes as the course progresses. As is true for any condensed course, timely feedback is imperative to getting and keeping students on the right track.

Entries can be short reflective essays. For instance, if students are studying workers from different cultures, faculty might direct them to strike up a conversation with a local while riding the train or eating at a pub. Students might ask about the worker's job, their employer's job policies, and work experience. Students could summarize their findings, then compare and contrast their findings with their own work experience.

Entries can also be integrative. Each course lends itself to some questions that can be prepared in advance of arrival. For example, ask students to apply the components of culture (i.e., values, norms, symbols, etc.) to their experience in a business or with their host family. The questions can also be generated on the spot based on current events and other serendipitous occurrences. Consider the example of having students apply principles of distributive and procedural justice to political decisions and constituent protests. They could evaluate the leadership qualities of figureheads using readings and research articles. Or propose identifying the implications of shiftwork and circadian rhythms on the performance of palace guards.

Additionally, entries can be creative in nature, including drawings, poetry, and short stories.

If a faculty director chooses to use journals as an evaluative tool, it is imperative that students are provided with clear, understandable criteria of how they will be evaluated and graded. Most experienced faculty agree that the more directed you can make the journal assignment, the more reflective and intellectual the work by the student will be. To avoid the "Dear Diary" kind of entry, encourage them to use the journal to:
- describe, interpret, evaluate
- make observations
- raise questions
- note cultural differences
- transcribe interviews
- write down information and facts
- answer questions
- propose solutions
- and reach conclusions.

There are several ways to communicate standards and relieve students' uncertainty regarding journal entries. The best approach is to provide writing samples for students to review. Although time consuming, prompt feedback can also help students to improve their integrative writing skills, and if done well, reduce the gap between faculty and student expectations.

Academic Journal Assignment
"Ireland: Understanding Celtic Spirituality"

You will be required to keep a daily academic journal of your observations and experiences. This will be subject to periodic review and will be submitted for a grade at the end of the course. It will be returned to you. Your journal does not double as your notebook; you should purchase a separate notebook for class and on-site notes.

Purchase a ruled, 8.5" x 11" spiral-bound notebook to use as your journal, in which you will record your observations, experiences, ideas, reactions, and insights. You may even want to include sketches of the sites we visit. Be prepared to devote at least 30 minutes each day to writing in your journal. Date each entry, and note the location (city or site) in which it was made. Note the name and date, or the chronological placement, of each site you discuss in your entries.

The journal is the place for your descriptions of on-site visits: ancient sites, monasteries, churches, stone crosses, museums, cities, and towns; it is also the place to integrate reflections on readings and lectures, comments on the culture of all dimensions, thoughts about history, and conclusions you may have drawn from conversations. Although our time in Ireland is brief, we will become a small community of shared conversation, and what you write in the journal cannot help but be a result of the interaction with others in the group, with your professors, and with people you meet. A journal is not meant so much to be a solitary endeavor as a personal and reflective one. It should be more than just a record of events, and avoid filling it out with a clutter of unrelated facts. You might choose to write a narrative, first-person approach, thus organizing your thoughts chronologically. The journal is not as confidential as a diary, but it is not a notebook of raw material. Your academic journal is your own thoughtful synthesis of your experience.

Grading: To clarify evaluation of this part of your grade,
C – average; student shows some evidence of having participated and having read the material.
B – student who shows a sound and solid grasp of the materials and the variety of experiences, going further in that these are thought out carefully.
A – students who have done all that is expected of B students and have added a substantial amount of clearly articulated imagination and synthesis of ideas. This means that the A student is the one who has fully integrated and internalized, intellectually and experientially, the variety of what we observe, read, and process on this course.

Journal samples will be available for review during the first week.

[Source: Anne King]

Course Design Issues

Contact Hours

As noted in Chapter 3, Administrative Processes, institutional policy must be clear regarding contact hours for study abroad programs. Since these courses take place in the nontraditional classroom, without a structured schedule, it may be more difficult to define the nature and number of contact hours.

The common practice is to define as contact hours any activity in which students are engaged with the learning objectives of the course. This includes lectures by the faculty director or in-country experts, site visits, excursions, discussions, and student presentations.

Site Visits

Although the bus may stop for the spontaneous monument, bazaar, or even an hour at the beach, it is extremely important to the overall structure and academic quality of the short-term program abroad that students are well prepared for each site visit—the site should be introduced beforehand, summarized, and reflected upon after the actual visit.

One excellent method to involve students is to require one to two students to introduce each site visit to the group, explaining the purpose of the visit, what to expect, and something of the historical or cultural background information. This student group, or another, should be charged with formally thanking the hosts on behalf of the group. Following the visit, the faculty director should process and interpret impressions of the site visit with the students in a formal class or informal discussion period.

Some site visits involve a long bus journey. If the bus has a video player and if videos are available in-country, plan to show a movie that is connected to the site or area. For example, show an historic movie describing Berlin in 1933 or 1945 before the students arrive to the Berlin of today. Students may also use the time to read assignments or write journal entries, if motion sickness does not affect them.

Readings

Reading assignments should be carefully chosen and apportioned in amounts that permit them to be read in 1 or 2 hours in the evening, or during free periods of the day. If possible, distribute reading assignments and specially ordered materials at the predeparture orientation, and encourage students to begin reading before they meet at the airport. You can help students stay focused by requiring them to generate discussion questions based on the readings.

Unstructured Time

Unscheduled or "free" time is a complex issue for short-term program design. Too much unscheduled time questions the academic integrity regarding the amount of credit granted, and too little free time compromises the students' ability to learn due to exhaustion and information overload.

Students and faculty need breaks to complete readings and journals, to rest, and to process. How much free time should be built into the program depends on the program model: is it a travel course or is the group based in one place; what are the academic objectives of the course?

Faculty may build-in designed or guided free time. Students are required to choose and attend two to three cultural activities during the week, on their own time, and report back to the group. This allows students to build confidence by traveling to the site on their own, doing their own research, and being held accountable for that time.

Not all students will be anxious to spend every moment exploring the culture. Initially, faculty may have to invite the less-adventurous students to accompany them to a theater performance, museum, or meal. Because they lack the tools of experienced travelers, students should be required to bring a guidebook of the city or country. Faculty may have students identify a "Top Ten" list of things to see and do in each major city from the guidebooks in advance of departure.

Independent Travel

Some faculty design a course where at least one weekend is free, encouraging students to undertake independent travel. This approach builds confidence, can provide a spontaneous educational occasion, and gives members of the group a break from each other. If faculty schedule more than one day off, proactive steps need to be taken to ensure the students' safety. Students should travel in pairs or larger groups, and should submit information such as their destinations and contact numbers, if available, to faculty before departure. Also, faculty should identify expectations, such as being prepared for Monday morning class, as well as review safety guidelines, especially for travel on overnight trains.

Other Suggestions on Course Design

Setting and Achieving Academic Goals

- If prerequisites are identified, they should be appropriate to the course objectives.
- General interest courses are likely to attract higher numbers of students; highly specialized courses may have a much smaller pool of qualified candidates.
- The intellectual challenge of the course, its scope, and the work required of students should correspond to the proposed level of the course.
- The type and amount of work required of students should be compatible with living and traveling conditions.
- Students need to know in advance how they are to procure assigned reading materials (e.g., purchase prior to departure, purchase on site, use local libraries). When students are expected to carry out research projects, faculty should ensure that libraries or other research facilities are available and adequate.
- Pedagogically successful programs usually schedule a short presentation or interactive assignment early in the program. Predeparture readings and/or assignments get students to start engaging before they leave.

Logistics and Travel Planning

- Carefully consider the number of sites visited, their geographical proximity to each other, and the time spent traveling among them.
- Consider the mode of travel, and utilize the opportunities it presents for pedagogy.
- A good case should be made for the amount of travel proposed. Visiting a large number of sites and/or countries does not necessarily make the best course.
- Attempt to balance course lectures, site visits, and unstructured time. Short-term programs abroad can be exhausting, both to faculty and students. Think about jet lag and long bus trips, both of which can add to fatigue.
- Balance the different models of site visits: for example, scheduling visits to three museums in one day will produce tuned-out students by the afternoon.
- Transit makes for good opportunities for faculty to check in with students, find out how they are doing, learn their progress on journals and readings, discover more about their interests and, in general, stay connected with the group.

♦ Successful courses usually provide frequent opportunities for student groups to process their observations and reactions to the cultures they are experiencing. Specific questions are available at the end of this chapter.

Grading Issues

The most consistent "low mark" on short-term course evaluations is "Were grading criteria clear?"

Faculty across the country who teach courses abroad have grappled with the problem: What is different about grading a course taught off-campus from one taught on campus? The challenge is to figure out how to clearly articulate expectations to students, and evaluate how well they meet those expectations.

While evaluation may be based on traditional methods (e.g., quizzes, papers, and exams), off-campus courses may rely more on subjective measures due to their experiential nature. Thus, to reduce this sense of caprice, students require a precise description of how the experiential components of the course will be assessed. It must be clear that it is not the experiential element itself that is graded, but the process of synthesis. Academic journals are an effective tool for synthesis but are particularly challenging to grade because most students are not accustomed to that form of evaluation.

Grade Distribution

Sometimes the best-prepared and most thoroughly designed course can fall short because students are not sure how they will be graded as the course unfolds. Below are two examples of the basic categories faculty have used to grade a course.

In a science course:	Quiz	5%
	Field exercises	40%
	Mid-term	20%
	Seminar participation	15%
	Final	20%
A humanities course:	Attendance	5%
	Participation in group discussion	25%
	Academic journal	30%
	Papers (2 @ 10% each)	20%
	Final essay exam	20%

Each of these faculty directors went to great lengths to explain what they meant by "attendance," "participation," and "academic journal."

Grading Standards

In addition to indicating how much credit each component is worth, faculty should clearly articulate expectations regarding the quality of student work. For instance, the following guidelines lay out various levels of sophistication that can be used to define grades:

A   Demonstrates creativity and integration
B   Demonstrates creativity or integration
C   Demonstrates understanding material
D   Demonstrates confusion
F   No show

Although nontraditional evaluation methods are time consuming for faculty directors and may be initially confusing to students, the final intercultural results are well worth the effort.

Learning Styles

Experiential Learning[1]

A lack of understanding about experiential learning causes an academic image problem. The notion that students can learn anything through travel to another place is grounded in the pedagogical concepts of experiential learning, suggesting "learning is best facilitated in an environment where there is dialectic tension…between immediate concrete experience and analytical detachment."[2] Considered integral to the overall process of educational development, experiential learning is not opposed to traditional notions of learning that emphasize the memorization and recitation of "facts" related to specific topics (book learning), but is more accurately understood as a part of learning that involves grasping the concepts behind those facts within the context of direct experiences with lived relationships with real people and events. In other words, experiential learning does not involve having an experience alone. As an ongoing process, learning through experience requires having a concrete experience followed by some sort of engaged conceptual reflection about that experience, followed by behaviors that utilize those reflections within the context of a new experience, that then generate new ideas about the world, reflection, and so forth.

Service Learning

—*Mike Klein*

"Be the change you wish to see."~ Mohandas Ghandi

At its most basic level, study abroad is about observing: walking the Appian Way, strolling the Louvre, or touring Dachau. Service learning abroad is about observing and getting involved: working on a coffee cooperative in Guatemala, teaching math skills in Tanzania, or building homes in Mexico.

Short-term programs abroad that incorporate service learning add a unique pedagogical and contextual dimension to academic courses. Tapping the idealism of both the college student and academe, service learning can address the educational goals of a course and the social needs of a community. However, if service learning is undertaken without a clear articulation of the academic objectives and an understanding of the community partner, it can be disastrous.

Short-term service learning—whether embedded in a course or encompassing the academic term—should be undertaken when the following factors can be addressed by the faculty director:
- Academic goals overlap significantly with the goals of the community partner or host site. If the match is not an obvious or easy one, look for other partnerships rather than forcing one. Articulating shared goals will help to ensure a positive first-time experience and, if appropriate, a long-term partnership.
- The number of students is easily supported by the work of the community partner. A class of 50 students may overwhelm the community partner and the people they serve; smaller groups of 10 to 20 are generally more manageable. A larger class may be split among several work sites or divided into shifts, alternating classroom time with project time.

[1] Special thanks to Joe Kinsella for this material.

[2] Kolb, David A. (1984). *Experiential Learning: Experiencing as the Source of Learning and Development.* Englewood Cliffs, NJ: Prentice Hall.

- Service-learning projects enhance rather then detract from the work of the community partner. Unlike other pedagogical tools, a service-learning component usually involves vulnerable populations and service providers with scarce resources. Care must be taken by the instructor to respect the needs and limitations of both parties.
- Service learning addresses your institutional mission (i.e., the social mission of a religious institution or community engagement and citizenship in a public institution). Just as study abroad takes more effort than the home campus classroom, service learning requires as much or more attention and commitment. If service learning can be supported within the context of the institutional mission, there may be a greater likelihood of sustainability over the long term.

If your course meets these criteria, then service learning may be an appropriate pedagogical tool.

Service As Text

One way of conceptualizing service learning is to consider the experience as an additional text, one more means of understanding a topic. As with any text, the faculty member will need to preview it in order to present it well. If visiting the site is not possible prior to the start of the course, you might rely on the knowledge and experience of community partners to guide and familiarize you with the site through correspondence and research.

Faculty who use service learning in their courses may be concerned about grading an unpredictable and subjective component of their class. If treated as a text, then service learning can be seen as a didactic experience that is not graded directly. Just as a text is employed to communicate concepts that are in turn graded through an appropriate assessment, so the learning in service learning can be evaluated. By assigning reflective papers, journals, field observations reports, or presentations, the faculty director can assess the students' comprehension of the academic goals without grading students on the more subjective understanding of the entire experience.

Even Better Than Service Learning at Home?

Service learning abroad can also have several advantages over more traditional service-learning models. As international educators know well, travel can have a unifying effect on a class. Students typically develop deeper relationships with classmates than a traditional classroom setting allows. When guided by the faculty director this closeness can lead to a more intentional learning community and more intentional reflection on the issues encountered in service work.

These experiences abroad also allow students to immerse themselves in a struggling community rather than just visiting for several hours each week as they might do at home. Students may become more attuned to the complex issues that underlie their direct service and gain exposure to the personal stories that complement and deepen academic concepts. Service learning abroad can also lead students to a more critical evaluation of local issues when they return home.

The most dramatic benefit of service learning may be the in-depth encounter with the host culture. When students are building a home in the highlands of Guatemala side by side with Mayan laborers they will enter into conversations that are beyond the scope of a classroom interview or presentation. As the indigenous group teaches building techniques to a student in Spanish, the power differential between the "laborer in a developing country" and the "affluent U.S. college student" shifts. Through shared work, the abstractions of global economics, international politics, and intercultural relations are realized—that is, made real—in, for example, the person of Guatemalan farmer Juan Carlos. His lessons in cement block construction may also lead to conversations about scarce resources, differing world views, or Mayan family life. Although the results of such encounters are unpredictable, they offer a cultural exchange rarely found in more structured settings.

Cautionary Notes

Although there are many benefits to service learning abroad, there are pitfalls as well. The following suggestions may help instructors avoid some difficulties associated with service learning:

- Research the integrity of your community partners just as you would any other teaching resource. Ensure that community partners are truly working in concert with the local community and the people they intend to serve.
- Confirm with the community partner that the content and scope of the service project is appropriate to the course and reasonable in relation to the skills and abilities of the students.
- Invest time in preparing students for both the cross-cultural and service aspects of the course. Students will need orientation on working with vulnerable communities or individuals.
- Spend time examining the motivations behind service. Question "do-gooder" attitudes that may do more harm than good. Your service work will not change the world, but it should advance the mission of the community partner.
- Guard against students' temptations to demonize one community and canonize the other when injustices are encountered and examined.

Service-Learning Resources

Check first with the resources on your own campus. There may be colleagues in other disciplines or in cocurricular programs who can offer advice, support, and even connections to long-time community partners.

Campus Compact (www.campuscompact.org)

Most states have local chapters of this national service-learning organization. They offer technical assistance when planning service-learning course components and a vast array of written resources on the subject including monographs, sample syllabi, and educational research.

Breakaway (www.breakaway.org)

This nonprofit organization assists cocurricular programs in site selection, leadership development, and framing the service experience. Their site bank offers a host of community partners and guidance in selecting an appropriate site.

The Response Directory (www.cnvs.org)

Sponsored by the Catholic Network of Volunteer Service, this directory lists over 180 full-time, religiously affiliated volunteer programs. Many of these programs are familiar with linking college students and recent graduates with social service agencies in their communities. Some welcome short-term classes or volunteer groups as part of their mission.

Pedagogy of Place: How to Use Resources Abroad[3]

All short-term programs abroad should make use of on-site learning resources; if not, why take students at all? However, faculty directors use resources overseas with divergent approaches. Some use the site as a backdrop to enhance their own lectures, creating a situation where they are still considered the "expert." Others use the resources the site has to offer while purposely receding into the background, blending as discussant and student.

It is obvious to most that a course should be planned to take advantage of on-site resources. It takes great effort, however, to discover, contact, and confirm these overseas resources. The following is a sampling of possible ways to get started:

Universities and think tanks. Individual researchers are often willing to discuss their topics of expertise with students, though often at a monetary cost. If your travel schedule finds the group at the right place at the right time, some public lectures at universities can be attended for free. Think tanks are often quite forthcoming, though as their notoriety in the media increases, their interest in public education tends to decline.

Governmental and intergovernmental agencies. Though, again, the quality of presentation varies, governmental and intergovernmental agencies can be quite forthcoming and often have the human and material resources to offer enlightening tours and briefings. Like everyone else, these agencies have political interests and an agenda and will see the world through that set of lenses, but that bias can be turned into an occasion for learning about learning.

Nongovernmental organizations. Nongovernmental organizations (NGOs) are presently the most fertile ground when looking for instructional assistance abroad. Their numbers are expanding daily (exploding, really), and they are usually more than happy to discuss issues on their agenda and other topics of passionate interest to them. They clearly see such public education as serving their organizational goals. Access to NGOs is generally quite easy, as their Web sites usually provide direct e-mail communication.

Media. Success with media outlets is a bit variable, as reporters operate under increasing pressure from deadlines and breaking events can derail long-scheduled meetings. Reporters do have their fingers on many issues of the day at the factual level, although they tend to do less well with causes and consequences of problems, global or local.

Museums. The world contains museums for just about everything, from collections of artifacts and official documents, interview transcripts and diaries, to art and film. Entrance to museums can often be gained at reduced or no cost by student groups, and sometimes student groups enjoy privileged treatment. Students can view the public collections or with some prearrangement can often access the archives.

Artistic expressions. Museums, galleries, and musical and theatrical performances are easily accessible, although sometimes at substantial cost. Nevertheless, the arts have no peer in laying bare the issues and tensions of human experience for our consideration.

---

[3] Special thanks to Peter Hovde for this material.

Ordinary people. Contact with local people can range from systematic interviews with people in the street to lengthy and open-ended conversations with people about their lives in their homes or places of work. The Center for Global Education at Augsburg College in Minneapolis, MN, has developed a particularly well-considered pedagogy for such interviews with those on the short end of the globalization stick or on the nub of conflict and violence.[4]

Suggestions for Contacting Local Resources

The easiest method of initiating contact with local resources is to write a letter or e-mail stating something to the effect of, "Our group will be in London from Tuesday, May 1, to Friday, May 4. It would best fit our busy schedule if we could meet in the afternoon of Thursday, May 3. We would like to hear about the role and current concerns of the organization and how they relate to [the topic]."

Remember to attach to the letter the (1) description of the school; (2) description of the study abroad program; and (3) description of the class. Follow up with a gift at the visit, kind words of appreciation at the end of a meeting, and thank you letters on return.

Course Design and the Cross-Cultural Landscape

Cross-Cultural Enrichment and Encounter

Although it is important to plan specific academic experiences ahead of time, some of the most valuable aspects of short-term programs abroad are the cultural encounters that occur while on site. As previously mentioned, while one purpose is to fulfill academic course expectations, an equally valuable purpose is to take advantage of the unique opportunities in the locality of the site, such as history, culture, society, and nature. A political economics course in Paris will obviously include direct academic components, such as government organizations, but could also include a gathering with local English as a Second Language students, a tour of Notre Dame, and major art museums. Much of this can be planned in advance, but there are always spontaneous opportunities so be prepared to take advantage of these situations when they occur.

Faculty must decide whether cross-cultural enrichment activities, particularly those not directly related to the subject matter, will form a part of the student's evaluation. For instance, a London-based business program may include at least one theater performance. However, it is not only attendance that is counted as part of the student evaluation—participation is also required. The faculty director may have a local expert (e.g., a colleague at a university) prepare students before the play and facilitate a discussion following the performance or in the next day's class. Students are expected to include the performance in their academic journal, noting and analyzing any business or cultural themes. This cross-cultural activity, although not directly related to the specific business course objectives, allows students to prepare, experience, and analyze an important characteristic of London culture.

---

[4] See Dan Spencer (1989). "Experiential Education: A Method for Transformation and Liberation." *Global Perspectives* 6 (Spring), pp. 1-2, 8-10, and also Dan Spencer (1988). "Models of Learning in Building a Transformative Education." *Global Perspectives* 6 (Winter), 1-5.

Facilitating the Cross-Cultural Encounter

An important feature of any study abroad program is the cultural encounter between U.S. students and native speakers, guest faculty, or host nationals. Because short-term programs allow less time for cultural immersion, such encounters should be actively incorporated into the course.

For example, at the North Atlantic Treaty Organization (NATO) headquarters in Brussels, Belgium, an outstanding political scholar from Spain receives a group of U.S. students. She reads from a prepared manuscript and her fluent English has a very heavy accent. The students, unfamiliar with prepared, read speeches and listening to foreign nationals, stop listening and start daydreaming. Following her presentation, a relaxed, very personable U.S. NATO representative gives the same students a casual, somewhat superficial briefing. Although the Spanish representative's presentation is informative and complex and of far higher academic quality than the NATO representative's, the U.S. students do not like the Spanish presentation but enjoy the American one much more.

This kind of situation can be avoided by advance preparation in discussing alternative communication styles as well as providing guiding questions, thereby enhancing attention. Your role is to challenge the students to adopt and adapt to new forms of listening and understanding that are culturally different from their own. You must impress upon them the importance of this form of understanding.

Cultural Overload: When to Offer a Taste of Home

Most faculty wish for, and indeed expect, students to culturally engage fully while on site, which usually does not include trips to McDonalds or Starbucks. However, especially in short-term programs abroad, students may be less experienced, lack the confidence to try new things, and be inclined to search out the familiar. If you find your students in the local U.S.-owned fast-food chain, use the opportunity (like cultural encounters) to facilitate discussion and set examples.

There may be moments when students must get a "home fix." For example, a month-long course in Barcelona, Spain, included a scheduled group dinner at the end of the second week. When asked what kind of food they wanted, the students requested Pizza Hut. While this initially appalled the faculty director, the experience allowed the group to literally get a taste of home, and then to plunge back into Catalan culture for the final 2 weeks. In other words, there are moments when it may be appropriate to provide students with the familiar.

Chronic consumption of U.S. fast food, and the attendant and incessant "search" for the recognizable will require you to intervene. One option is to invite the group, or a small group, to come with you to a fabulous local restaurant, allowing you to introduce them to a variety of typical dishes. If they do not speak the local language, spend time with the menu, pointing out familiar foods. Also provide a list of enticing restaurants.

Not all culture-clash situations involve food. You may have students who insist on nonstop shopping, or who use their free time to sit around the hotel and discuss what they miss at home. In such cases, use these opportunities to assign a compare/contrast entry for the students' academic journals. Depending on the course topic, you may direct them to write about ambiance, cuisine, business philosophy, symbols, or customs. Student questions, such as why customers are charged for ketchup in Australia's fast food restaurants, may lead to a fruitful discussion on culture, history, and economics.

Tips on Guiding Students to Cultural and Intellectual Mileposts[5]

Faculty who direct short-term academic programs abroad know full well the challenge of making the most of all their time abroad. We all want students to grow intellectually and personally from the cross-cultural experiences they have. However, it is useful to have an idea of what constitutes "best practices" and what has been successful over the years.

The best short-term courses abroad balance experience with processing the experience. Too many experiences without a context in which to study and reflect on them can leave students overwhelmed and unsure of just what they are supposed to be learning.

What follows are ideas from colleagues in the field that may help you in organizing your short-term course by including regular opportunities for group reflection:

- Every 2 or 3 days the group should be gathered for a 1- or 2-hour reflection session. This is a time for the group members to share any insights, concerns, or questions with each other and with the faculty director. Discussion of readings and site visits may also be combined, to give more structure to the session. These regular sessions and the skill with which they are led are key ingredients in determining whether or not the educational experience will be a transformative one.
- There are many different ways the reflection session can be structured but several guidelines provide essential considerations for these sessions.
  - Every student should have the opportunity to find a voice within the group.
  - The more talkative students need to be reminded to share airtime with others and to cultivate the skill of listening.
  - Although people may disagree with one another, differences should be treated as differing perspectives, not as a contest to see who is right and who is not.
  - The quieter students should be specifically invited to speak, but not forced to do so.
  - When strong feelings emerge it is better to deal with them than to ignore them and let them fester. These feelings may be the result of what students have heard and seen during the day; they may result from intragroup dynamics, or they may be a reaction to some aspect of culture shock.
- If tensions are high in the group, it may be tempting to skip a reflection session. However, an opportunity for reflection can provide a helpful way to redirect the energy of individuals and the group. If a conflict interferes with the group's ability to focus on the program, the conflict needs to be addressed.
- Certain rules, accepted by all members of the group, can provide a positive framework for all group reflections. Some helpful ground rules include speaking and behaving respectfully toward and about all members of the group and all resource people; balancing one's desire to speak with the need to allow others time to speak; making one's needs known so that they can properly be addressed.

Possible Questions to Guide Discussions

Early in the course

? What do you observe as the key elements of this culture that differ from your own?
? What is in your cultural filter that might prompt you to interpret things differently than the people you are meeting here?

---

[5] Special thanks to Adrienne Kaufmann and Ruth Mason for this material.

? What in your background seems similar to what we've encountered here? With whom did you resonate most? Why do you think this is so?

? What criteria might you use to decide if someone is telling the truth?

? Can two people who interpret things quite differently both be telling the truth? Why or why not? Have you experienced examples of this?

? What has surprised you most?

? If you could send home a snapshot from the course, what would it be?

In the middle of the course...

? What are your own definitions of democracy, justice, freedom, peace, art, relaxation, spirituality, etc.? How would the mainstream population here define these words? How are your definitions the same? How do they differ?

? What has been a key moment of insight for you?

? What one word would describe your strongest feeling today?

? What did you observe today?

? How is what you are experiencing here different from what you expected?

? What are the main sectors of society from which you are learning? Do their perspectives align well with your own, or are they quite different? How do their goals and values differ?

? What have you learned about the way the United States is perceived in this society? How have this society's perceptions seemingly been shaped?

? How are the social, economic, political, communication, transportation, education, and health systems working in this society? Where does this country seem strong? Where does it seem weak? Are the same strengths and constraints prevalent in U.S. society?

Near the end of the course...

? Who are the key people shaping the field of study you are engaging in here? Are their roles in this society comparable to identifiable people in the United States who have influence in this discipline?

? What are the key problems with which this society wrestles? Are these the same problems that are prevalent in the United States?

? What signs have you seen of U.S. cooperation with people in this country?

? What is the role of the media in this society? Is it similar to the role of the media in the United States?

? What is the source of economic power in this society?

? What is the role of music, literature, and the arts in this society? How does it compare with the role of these things in the United States?

? What is the role of spirituality and faith in this society? How similar is it to the role of these things in the United States?

? What connections do you see emerging between your life and the lives of the people here? Will that connection be sustained over time?

? What are the strengths of this society as you see it? What do you perceive to be its weaknesses?

? If it is true that "the whole world needs the whole world," what do you see as the gift that the people of this society have to contribute to the world?

Closing reflection...

? What are the three or four most important images or ideas that you will take from this experience? If you were able to put a photograph on the front cover of a leading U.S. magazine, a photograph that would carry a strong message to the people of the United States about this travel experience, what would that photograph be, and what would the caption be?

? What is the main message you want to tell your neighbors, your college peers, and others who may be interested in traveling here?

? What questions or disturbing ideas have not been resolved during your time here?

? What are you taking back with you from this experience? What are you leaving behind?

? What will you do to concretely express your solidarity with the people here when you return home?

roposal for Short-Term Off-Campus Programs

:oposed date:

I. COURSE DESCRIPTION

A. Course title, primary course location(s), faculty director(s) (include department or discipline).
B. Undergraduate or graduate course?
C. Number of credit hours?
D. List any course prerequisites.
E. What is the rationale for choice of course topics, goals, readings, and other elements of the curriculum as they relate to the course location(s)?
F. If English is not the language of the location of the course, will there be a language prerequisite for the course? If not, how will participants carry out their course work and interact with the local population, if applicable?
G. What distribution or general requirements, if any, is this course designed to meet?
H. If the course involves a home stay experience, describe the length of the home stay and the individuals and/or organizations responsible for arranging home stays.

II. INTEGRATED SYLLABUS

Short-term off-campus programs set themselves apart because they attempt to integrate traditional classroom education with experiential learning and site visits. It is very important that you demonstrate how the location and local resources enhance the learning objectives of the course. **Faculty directors should formally identify lectures, readings, site visits, group discussions/reflection times, and cultural activities that are required parts of the course.** As contact hours must be equivalent to those on campus, identify the time spent in these activities. A sample of a previously approved course proposal is available.

The syllabus should include the following items:

A. Course description of 100 to 200 words
B. List the course goals and objectives
C. Required and recommended readings
D. Course evaluation. Be specific with the % of grade for each requirement such as participation and attendance, assignments, exams or papers, presentations, academic journals, or field observation reports that are used as the basis of the course grade.
E. The syllabus must contain the following elements. .Be as specific as possible.
   1. The **length of time** in each location
   2. The various **educational activities** (lecture titles or topics, readings, site visits, group discussions/reflection time, cultural events, etc.). Clearly demonstrate how these activities are linked to the course objectives and location.
   3. Other **culturally orienting activities**.
   4. The length of time spent in these activities. Contact hours, defined as the time when students are engaged in the objectives of the course, must be equivalent to or more than those on campus.
   5. The amount of unstructured time scheduled each day.

III. ENROLLMENT

What are the minimum and maximum numbers of students you will be taking on this course?

IV. TEACHING METHODS

    A. What teaching methods and other pedagogical approaches are used and how do they facilitate the learning process to ensure that the course objectives are met?

    B. Estimate the percentage of the on-site teaching and guiding that you will do yourself. Will you be using guest lecturers? If yes, why and how are they used and how will you integrate them into the course?

    C. If there are two faculty directors:
        1. How will the directors share responsibilities?
        2. What experience do the directors have working together?

II. FACULTY DIRECTOR(S) INFORMATION

    A. What is your training and experience in the course's subject matter (if the course topic is outside your academic discipline, describe what training and experience you have to teach this course.)

    B. Experience in the proposed location(s) and contacts you may have in the host country or countries.

    C. Language(s) and level of proficiency.

    D. Previous experience teaching off-campus courses?

THIS COURSE HAS THE SUPPORT AND APPROVAL OF THE SPONSORING DEPARTMENT.

Faculty director's signature	Date

Department/divisional chair's or program director's signature	Date

[Source: Adapted from the University of St. Thomas.]

Office of Study Abroad
Faculty-Directed Program Proposal

Sponsoring unit _____

Faculty name and title _____

Campus address _____

Telephone, e-mail _____

PROGRAM DESCRIPTION

Program name _____

Program site(s) _____

Duration (in weeks) _____ Dates (approximate) _____

How many faculty members will accompany the group? _____ How many graduate teaching assistants will accompany the group? _____

Which salaries will be paid by the department? _____

Number of credit hours per student: _____ Target student group size (min, max) _____

Courses to be offered: _____

ENROLLMENT and INSTRUCTION – check all that apply

Will KU faculty teach? ☐ NO YES — ☐ Some courses ☐ All courses

Will students enroll in an institution on site? ☐ NO ☐ YES

Name of host institution: _____

☐ The institution is an accredited, degree-granting institution of higher education. Students will receive an official certificate or transcript from the host institution upon completion of courses.

☐ The institution is a local language school or other specialized, nonaccredited institution.

This program is approved by:

Program director _____ Date _____

Department chair _____ Date _____

Academic dean _____ Date _____

Director of study abroad _____ Date _____

Dean of international studies and programs _____ Date _____

Completed form received:

_____

OSA program contact person   Date _____

Program Plan:

Faculty director:

Program dates:

Enrollment and credit:

Location:

Transportation:

Accommodations:

Academic program:

Excursions:

Orientation:

Faculty accommodation:

Safety issues and risk management:

Direct payments made by OSA:

Payments made by the director (all require receipts):

[Source: Adapted from the University of Kansas.]

New Course Proposal
(Please return to the office of the dean)

○ **General education** ○ **Off-campus** ○ **Semester** ○ **Interim** ○ **Summer**

○ **1.00 credit** ○ **.50 credit** ○ **.25 credit** ○ **Graded** ○ **P/N** ○ **Course with writing**
(check all that apply)

Course number and title:

_____

When will the course be offered for the first time?_____

                                         (Term)   (Year)

        Approval is requested for (complete all that apply):

● **General education credit in** _____ _____ ● **Concentration credit in** _____ ● **Major credit in** _____	**Action taken and dates (to be completed by appropriate committees)**

Draft catalog statement (limit to 75 words):

- **All proposals:** Attach (1) the syllabus, or a detailed description of course goals and topics, work required of students, and methods of student evaluation; and (2) a "New Course Rationale."

- **General education proposals:** Attach a "Rationale for General Education Credit."

- **Off-campus proposals:** Attach a "New Course Off-Campus Supplement."

_____   _____
NAME OF PROPOSER (printed or typed)   **Signature and date**

_____   _____
NAME OF DEPARTMENT CHAIR (printed or typed)   **Signature and date**

_____   _____
NAME OF ASSOCIATE DEAN (printed or typed)   **Signature and date**

Updated 11/27/01

New Course Rationale

(Please respond to the following items in the space provided or, if you prefer, on a separate sheet.)

1.   What is the distinctive contribution of this course to the general education and/or major curriculum of your department or program?

2.   What impact will this course have on departmental staffing and teaching assignments? Will other courses in your department be eliminated or taught less often?

3.   What is the anticipated enrollment size for this course, and how did you determine that? What population of students will this course serve?

4.   On what basis did you determine the appropriate level and prerequisites for this course?

5.   In consultation with the collection development librarian and the director of the academic computing center, describe how current library and computing resources would support this course and what additional materials or services might be needed:

6.   How often will this course be offered? On what basis did you determine that?

7.   If this course will come before the faculty as a whole, please provide a CEPC "green sheet" rationale statement:

_____   _____
NAME OF DEPARTMENT CHAIR (printed or typed)   **Signature and date**

Rationale for General Education Credit

(If this course is being proposed for more than one type of general education credit, please attach an additional rationale form for each additional requirement the course is intended to meet.)

1.   General education requirement for which course is proposed:

   _____

2.   Please explain the specific ways this course meets *each* of the guidelines (in order) for the general education requirement listed above. Do not simply allude to the objectives of the course, but fully describe the readings, lectures, writing and speaking assignments, and other instructional features of the course that will further the goals of the guidelines. The content of the syllabus or course outline should be consistent with the claims made in the rationale.

_____

NAME OF PROPOSER (printed or typed)   **Signature and date**

_____

NAME OF DEPARTMENT CHAIR (printed or typed)   **Signature and date**

[Source: Adapted from St. Olaf College]

Appendix O

Off-Campus Supplement
Interim Programs

1. **Itinerary:** Provide an itinerary for the proposed course and include a rationale that relates the itinerary to the academic goals of the course. (See B and C of the Off-Campus Interim Courses section of the IDOCS Academic Policies and Procedures Manual.)

2. **Daily Schedule:** Provide a description of a typical day on-site (include daily schedule, description of traditional academic learning and/or experiential learning activities, and student options for free time). (See B of the Off-Campus Interim Courses section of the IDOCS Academic Policies and Procedures Manual.)

3. **Language Issues:** If English is not the language of the location of the interim course, will there be a language prerequisite for the course? If not, how will participants carry out their course work and interact with the local population? (See B of the Off-Campus Interim Courses section of the IDOCS Academic Policies and Procedures Manual.)

4. **Home Stays:** If the interim involves a home stay experience, describe the length of the home stay, the individuals and/or organizations responsible for arranging home stays, and the criteria used to select host families. (See L of the Off-Campus Interim Courses section of the IDOCS Academic Policies and Procedures Manual.)

5. **Suggested Minimum and Maximum Enrollments:** What are your suggestions for the minimum and maximum numbers of students for this interim? Please provide a rationale for these numbers. (See E of the Off-Campus Interim Courses section of the IDOCS Academic Policies and Procedures Manual.)

6. **Instructor Qualifications:** Provide an account of previous experience in the countries and cultures to be visited (and/or an indication of how you plan to acquire additional knowledge); benefits to your professional development; and previous experience with leading student groups off-campus. Describe your language skills and/or in-country experience if appropriate to the course. (See H of the Off-Campus Interim Courses section of the IDOCS Academic Policies and Procedures Manual.)

Additional signatures certifying approval

Program or concentration   _Signature_

Program or concentration   _Signature_

Program or concentration   _Signature_

[Source: Adapted from St. Olaf College]

Off-Campus Interim Courses

Off-campus Interim courses are central to the institution's global mission. Such courses are designed to capitalize on opportunities unique to the locations where they are taught and to integrate classroom instruction and experiential learning activities into a well-conceived whole. When appropriate for academic and other reasons, affiliations with local academic institutions are encouraged.

Proposals for off-campus Interim courses shall demonstrate the centrality of the course to the college curriculum. Furthermore, they shall provide a rationale for conducting the course off-campus by explaining the significance of the location(s) to the overall educational experience. The proposal and Off-Campus Supplement together shall provide a clear picture of the careful integration of course content and on-site living and learning opportunities.

When preparing an off-campus Interim proposal, please keep in mind the following guidelines developed by the IOS and IDOCS. By following them closely, you will facilitate IDOCS review of your course. IDOCS may request additional information about your course during the review process or request revisions prior to approval.

The Interim Instructor may teach only the approved course during the program. He/she may not modify the focus or level of the approved course. He/she may not supervise independent study/independent research projects.

Proposals (including the Off-Campus Supplement) are due in the Office of the Dean on November 25 of the academic year prior to the year proposed for the course.

A. General guidelines
1. An Interim course that has not been offered during the last 3 years is considered to be a new course. Faculty adapting an on-campus course to an off-campus Interim one must submit a new course proposal with a course number different from that of the on-campus course.
2. Each course shall have a well-defined focus, whether disciplinary or interdisciplinary.
3. Pre-requisites shall be appropriate to course goals.
4. Instructors shall be mindful of how courses fit into departmental or interdisciplinary programs and of how they relate to existing programs in the same geographic area. Faculty members are encouraged to speak to area studies programs and their department chair in advance of submitting a proposal.
5. Instructors shall be mindful also of the intended audience(s), whether majors, non-majors, or both.
6. Instructors who intend their courses to satisfy general education or departmental requirements are encouraged to consult GEC (General Education Committee) and departmental guidelines before submitting proposals and to refer to those guidelines in their proposals.
7. The Interim proposal should provide an accurate and complete summary of all activities associated with the course, including any non-traditional or experiential activities. *(See Appendixes O & P)*

B. Academic guidelines
1. Courses shall have academic integrity and coherence. The relationship between course content and the course location(s) should be articulated clearly. Instructors should give

careful thought to the integration of course readings, lectures, site visits, and independent study and research, and methods of evaluation.

2. Courses shall normally combine experiential learning with more traditional academic learning.

3. The type and amount of work required of students shall be appropriate to the focus and level of the course and compatible with living and traveling conditions. The amount of assigned reading should be similar to what is required in on-campus Interim courses. Students need to know in advance how they are to procure assigned reading materials (by purchase before departure, purchase on site, or the use of libraries). When students are expected to carry out research projects, faculty should ensure that libraries or other research facilities are available and adequate. If English is not the language of the location of the course, careful thought should be given to how students will carry out their course work and interact with local populations.

4. Courses shall have at least twenty class days (not including travel to and from Minneapolis/St. Paul). The time devoted to classroom or course-related-activities shall be at least as much as for on-campus Interim courses, and normally significantly more. Faculty should submit a preliminary daily schedule for both students and faculty that outlines how mornings, afternoons and evenings will be spent.

5. Means of evaluation shall be clearly stated, realistic, adequate and comparable to those used on campus.

C. Itinerary
1. In preparing the itinerary, faculty should balance the academic integrity of the course, the logistics and cost of travel. Faculty are encouraged to consider carefully the number of sites they propose to visit, their geographical proximity to each other, and the time that will be spent traveling between them.
2. Instructors must make a good case for the amount of travel they propose.
3. It is expected that the duration of an off-campus Interim will be 26 days.

D. Course title and draft catalog statement
1. The course title shall reflect the disciplinary or interdisciplinary focus of the course as well as the place in which it is taught.
2. The draft catalog statement shall describe the main theme or focus of the course, its elements (such as readings, lectures, site visits, independent research), and the itinerary. Information about the student work load and assessment should not be included in the catalog statement. Detailed guidelines are available from IOS.

E. Course enrollment
A suggestion for a minimum and maximum number of participants should be prepared and accompanied with a rationale for those numbers.

F. Review of new course proposals
To propose a new off-campus Interim course, faculty need to complete a new course proposal packet along with an International & Off-Campus Studies supplement available from the department chair. Proposals (including tentative program budgets) are due at the Dean's office on November 25 of the academic year prior to the year proposed for the course. A new course proposal (first time offered) requires initial approval of IDOCS for 1 year.

Department chairs are encouraged to arrange 3-1-2 or equivalent teaching loads for all faculty proposing off-campus Interim courses. A member of the faculty will then be able to replace a canceled off-campus Interim course with another course, either during Interim or during Semester II.

G. Interim classes proposed for a second offering (within 3 years of the original offering): The second time an Interim course is proposed, a letter of intent including signatures of appropriate department chairs and associate deans should be submitted to IOS by December 1. By February 15, the following items should be submitted to IOS:
  1. Copy of the original proposal
  2. Major, concentration, and GEC approvals
  3. Copy of the actual syllabus, itinerary, and budget used
  4. A report on the first offering of the class, including a detailed plan for the changes in itinerary, budget, course syllabus, and any other arrangements. If changes in the course warrant, copies of new GEC applications should be attached.

  After an Interim course is approved for the second offering, it is considered an "on-going Interim" (see Section H).

  Department chairs are encouraged to arrange 3-1-2 or equivalent teaching loads for all faculty proposing off-campus Interim courses. A member of the faculty will then be able to replace a canceled off-campus Interim course with another course, either during Interim or during Semester II.

H. Review of on-going Interims
  Instructors proposing off-campus Interim courses already approved by IDOCS as on-going and conducted within the previous 3 years (by themselves or by someone in the same department) need not submit a new course proposal for review by IDOCS. Instead, they should send a letter of intent along with a copy of the most recent course syllabus to IOS by December 1. This letter is indication of the department's intent to offer the course again and should describe any changes instructors intend to make in the course (such as a change in course title, shift in content, the overall structure, sites visited, student work load, grading policy) and a revised budget. This letter is to be signed by the instructor and by the department chair. Signature of the department chair confirms approval of the Interim by the department. IDOCS will coordinate review of off-campus Interim courses with the Office of the Dean of the College.

  Department chairs are encouraged to arrange 3-1-2 or equivalent teaching loads for all faculty proposing off-campus Interim courses. A member of the faculty will then be able to replace a canceled off-campus Interim course with another course, either during Interim or during Semester II.

I. Faculty eligibility
  Any faculty member, with approval of the department chair, may propose an off-campus Interim course to be taught during the second year or a subsequent year on the faculty. Only the person proposing an Interim course shall teach the course. An Interim course instructor shall be familiar with the country(ies) included in the itinerary. Retired faculty members are eligible to serve as off-campus instructors.

J. Teaching load

Normally, Interim courses are taught by an individual faculty member. A team-taught course may be possible contingent upon:

1. Approval of department(s) and Associate Dean(s) with regard to teaching loads. Consideration should be given to on-campus guidelines regarding student enrollment for team-taught courses).
2. Instructional costs not being added to the program costs for either faculty member.
3. The course proposal should address items 1 and 2

K. Off-campus mentoring program

To provide opportunities for faculty to gain experience in leading off-campus programs, January Interims enrolling 20 or more students may include a second faculty member (mentee) who would accompany the Interim group and serve as assistant to the faculty instructor (mentor).

The following guidelines apply:

1. The mentee must not be scheduled to teach during the January Interim. Serving as a mentee does not count as teaching a course, so the mentee will normally have a 3-0-3 teaching load.
2. A faculty member who wishes to be considered for a mentorship position must make their request (in writing) to the Director of International and Off-Campus Studies. The faculty member should *not* contact January off-campus Interim instructors directly. The Director of the Office of International and Off-Campus Studies will conduct the discussions with the possible mentors.
3. The request should include:
   a) A list of January off-campus Interims that the mentee would prefer
   b) A proposal for mentee involvement in a future off-campus study program *following* the mentoring program
   c) The signatures of the mentee's Department Chair and Associate Dean signifying approval of the mentee involvement in the Mentoring Program
4. The faculty instructor (mentor) must have taught at least one off-campus program prior to the start of the mentoring program.
5. All direct program costs (including travel, accommodations, 2 meals per day) for the mentee will be covered by the development fund of International and Off-Campus Studies.
6. A faculty mentee is expected to devote his or her entire effort to the program. Accordingly, family members may not accompany a mentee.
7. Applications should be submitted 1 year prior to the start of the Interim period for which the mentee is applying.

L. Student eligibility

Students who are sophomores, juniors, or seniors in good academic standing may apply for participation in off-campus Interim courses. First-year students in good academic standing may only apply for participation in foreign language Interim courses. Each course instructor shall establish selection criteria for his/her own off-campus Interim course and describe them in application materials. Applications and acceptance deadlines will be provided by IOS by early April and instructors are asked to make every effort to comply with them.

Regular students must register to take the Off-Campus Interim course for credit. Approved Continuing Education students must register for the course but are allowed to audit.

M. Health, safety, and communication (See #4, Off-Campus Supplement form.)
In the interest of the health and safety of participants in off-campus Interim courses, these conditions shall be observed:

1. Interim courses shall only be offered in countries with which the United States has official relations and for which no Department of State Travel Warning has been issued.
2. Instructors shall arrange for means to contact the home campus either at or near the site(s) of proposed courses, and shall have a clear communication link to the campus. Regardless of the location(s) of an Interim course, instructors are encouraged to be prepared to respond to health and safety problems, whether emergency or routine in nature.
3. All Interim courses must comply with College policies about the rental and use of motor vehicles.
4. All home-stays shall be arranged in accordance with IOS best practice guidelines.
5. All private carriers hired to provide required group transportation scheduled during the Interim must provide certification of appropriate insurance coverage.

N. Budgets, fees, and accounts
1. Instructors shall develop budgets in cooperation with IOS. Instructor's salary and benefits are met through the operating budget of the college. Participating students pay a fee for all other Interim expenses.
2. Program budgets are to be submitted with the new course proposal or with the letter of intent. Budgets for off-campus Interim courses that have been taught before shall be updated by the faculty, in cooperation with the staff of IOS, during the month of February.
3. It is expected that off-campus Interims will operate at the cost stated in the off-campus Interims brochure published in April.
4. Pre-course cost adjustments will be made, prior to December 1, if changes in airfare and/or exchange rates result in a difference of greater than 5%. This adjustment can either reduce or increase the cost of an Interim.
5. Post-course refunds to students will be processed according to the following policy: If the fund balance (amount remaining on campus and the amount returned by the instructor) at the end of an Interim is $100 per student or greater, the full amount will be refunded to the student. If the fund balance (amount remaining on campus and the amount returned by the instructor) at the end of the Interim is less than $100 per student, the full amount will be directed to IOS to cover deficits in other Interim budgets and to support Interim program development. This policy encourages Interim instructors to return unused funds to campus rather than handing them out on site; it reduces the expectation of students of a hand-out at the end of Interim; and it eliminates the need for IOS to process small amounts of money.

O. Final report
A final financial report shall be submitted to the director of IOS by Interim grades due date, or earlier. A narrative report should contain detailed information about the academics and logistics of the program and should discuss problems, successes, and make recommendations for future programs. This report is due to the Director of IOS and the instructor's Department Chair by March 1. An Interim that is being offered for a second time, as per Section F, must have the narrative report submitted by Interim grades due date with the financial report.

At the conclusion of the Interim, IOS will ask students to complete a returning student questionnaire about organizational and logistical aspects of the course. IDOCS uses the results in reviewing subsequent Interim proposals.

Faculty are strongly encouraged to ask students to evaluate the academic component. This may be done by administering "gold form" course evaluations processed by the OEIR (Office of Educational and Institutional Research) or by using an instructor-prepared evaluation tailored to the Interim course. Information about course content and the impact of the Interim experience on students' programs of study contributes to the ongoing St. Olaf assessment program.

P. Non-participants accompanying off-campus Interims
    Persons who are neither registered for the Interim course nor members of the immediate family of faculty leading an off-campus Interim, are prohibited from participating unless approval is obtained from the Director of IOS.

    Fees payable to the College will be determined by the Director of IOS for all individuals accompanying an off-campus Interim who are not registered students, registered through the Office of Continuing Education or participating through prior college arrangements *(See Appendix Q)*.

[Source: Adapted from St. Olaf College]

PART III
Program Development and Evaluation

Chapter 7

Feasibility Studies

Allison Keith

The question of feasibility comes into play in the very earliest of stages of short-term program abroad design. Before the proposal is written, you need to evaluate whether a program can get off the ground. Is there a realistic timeline for developing the program? Has the idea been marketed early enough to get the word out to potential participants?

When you look closely at the question of feasibility, all the elements come down to whether the program is marketable. Location, program content, length of program, and time of year ultimately play a part in this question and in whether the program will be a success.

Feasibility Considerations

Location

The choice of program site is a key component. Is the location popular enough with students to interest them, and, more importantly, does the chosen site match the proposed academic content and learning objectives? Are there health or safety concerns related to the site, such as U.S. State Department travel advisories or warnings? Does the program's location allow for only one discipline and group of students, such as learning about agriculture in Argentina, or can the location be used for a general cultural course to open the possibility of participation to a greater number of students.

A note about site visits. It is unusual, and in this day and age irresponsible, not to conduct a site visit before bringing travelers on site. A reconnaissance trip taken by the faculty director can determine if a program's location is feasible. In fact, most institutions require that a faculty director has been on site before developing a new program. Site visits require resources through designated program development funds or budgeting the cost into the program fee.

Time of Year

The timing of a program is crucial to the success of a program as well. Is the program planned for a time when students can be away from on-campus classes, such as summer break or winter intersession? Does this time of year make the program more expensive due to high travel season rates in specific regions? Have you researched major holidays in the country where the program will be held? If everything will be closed for a 3-day national holiday, your group can lose valuable programming time. Are weather conditions favorable to the course's objectives at that time of year? Think about northern and southern hemisphere weather issues: winter or summer, rainy or dry season?

If you are planning an embedded program in the middle of the term, when should it be planned? Are there breaks available so students do not miss other classes? Are part-time graduate students able to travel in the middle of the semester?

Duration

What is the program's duration abroad, and will its length fit with the intended audience? Traditional-age undergraduate students may be able to take 8 weeks, but working graduate students cannot. Does the length of the program limit the number of participants?

Cost

The program fee may be the final component in deciding if a program is feasible. The idea of a full safari on a Tanzania biology course is attractive but can the program be made affordable? If the program fee is excessive, you do not have a program.

Support and Resources

It is essential to make sure that the program has support from the governing bodies (e.g., a senior administrator, department chair, or international office) before it is offered to students. What kinds of resources are required for this program, such as staffing for development and administration? Will faculty directors make their own travel arrangements, or will a program provider be hired for support? Are consortial relationships available to share resources? These questions must be answered before a program is planned.

Program Development Timeline

Timelines vary from institution to institution, but the goal is to plan as far ahead as possible. Following are guidelines for program development. Time estimates are based on a suggested maximum and minimum duration before the program departs.

Campus Support and Program Development I (18–12 months)

A year and a half before departure is an excellent timeframe for developing a new program, including determining program feasibility, making a site visit, deciding on academic content and credit issues, detailing the budget and logistics, and confirming program support on campus. During this time period, faculty directors are chosen and program providers secured. A marketing plan based on audience and objectives should be drafted.

Program Development II (15–6 months)

Program deadlines are established, publicity and recruiting begin, faculty begin training, and itineraries are finalized. Logistical arrangements are confirmed.

Recruiting and Enrollment (8–3 months)

Students are recruited, advised, and selected, and deposits are collected. Coordinate with program providers, travel agencies, and any other organizations so that necessary space is reserved for housing and group flights.

Payment Period (90–60 days)

Collect final payments and begin to pay program providers, airlines, or on-site organizations. At this point, any unused reserved seats must be canceled or penalties will apply.

Predeparture (60–30 days)

Confirm that visas have arrived, if they are required. Orientation, communication from faculty directors, predeparture lectures, and registration take place during this time. Contingency funds are finalized and air tickets are issued.

Departure (3 Hours Before Flight)

When possible, it is helpful to have airport assistance for the group, especially if it is a large group. Last-minute problems will need to be addressed and hopefully solved, such as missing passports or airport closures due to weather.

Return

Submit financial paperwork and final reports. Review evaluations. Hold debriefing sessions with faculty directors, administrators, program providers, and students.

What's Next?

Logistics and financial management planning are imperative to successful short-term program abroad planning. Refer to Chapters 8 and 9 to continue with specific program development issues. Remember to think about what you have time to do, and what you are good at. There are many organizations that can support these other areas.

Chapter 8

Logistics

Sue Jackson and Allison Keith

Travel arrangements—flights, hotels, site visits, meals—make an international course completely different than the on-campus experience. While academic content is informed by the on-site components, thorough logistical planning is key to a successful short-term program abroad.

It is most helpful for the faculty directing short-term programs to be familiar with the countries, cultures, and sites where they are taking students, and most institutions require it. Often, even the most experienced faculty encounter surprises, and the more familiar they are with the terrain and customs of their destination, the more easily they are able to keep order in the group or situation, and to offer a quality academic experience.

In order to plan the logistical components of a short-term program abroad, the following questions must be answered. These answers will also inform the specifics of setting a budget, as covered in Chapter 9, Financial Matters.

How is the group traveling from point of departure to destination, and within country?

✓ Plane

✓ Train

✓ Bus

✓ Ferry

✓ Taxi

✓ Host families providing transportation

✓ Faculty-driven vehicles

✓ Other

Where does the program originate?

This may sound like an odd question, but it is sometimes a good idea for a program to begin from a major hub airport, especially after a major holiday or vacation, when students may be at home and not on campus. For example, the institution may be in Colorado Springs, CO, which has an airport, but the program may depart from Denver, CO. This often reduces the cost and gives students a little more flexibility.

Where will the group be staying?

✓ Hotel

✓ Hostel

✓ Home stay

✓ University residence halls

✓ Conference facilities

✓ Self-catering flats

✓ Guest farm

✓ Bed and breakfast

What meals are included?

- ♦ Do accommodations provide meals as part of the cost?
- ♦ Will there be group meals? How many?
- ♦ Where will students take their independent meals?
- ♦ Will a meal allowance be budgeted in the program fee to cover independent meals, or will students be expected to bring additional money?

Is classroom space required?

- ♦ Do the accommodations have meeting space?
- ♦ Will classrooms be needed every day?
- ♦ If renting a classroom, is there a charge? If yes, make sure it is included in the budget.

Note: If your group will be staying at a hotel, the bar may seem to be an appealing, laid-back place to hold a class session. However, most groups find it difficult to listen inside a bar, and ultimately find such a location distracting.

Do participants need a passport?

- ♦ If yes, it is important to encourage students and faculty to apply for their passports as soon as possible.
- ♦ Do not assume that students know the process for applying for a passport—tell them what they need to do.
- ♦ If your campus is not in close proximity to a passport application location, consider inviting an official to your campus to process applications. They are often happy to spend an afternoon processing a large number of applications.

Does the country or countries to be visited require a visa?

If so, you should:
(a) provide *extremely* detailed information to students about what a visa is and how they should apply for one, or
(b) have students submit their completed documents to the international office and process the applications all together.

Option B gives you the peace of mind of knowing that each student has the necessary documentation. It takes more time up front but can save countless hours later if a student shows up at the airport without the needed visa.

Are particular inoculations or medications required or recommended?

If so, please refer to the recommendations in Chapter 16, Safeguards for Short-Term Programs.

A Note about International Students

You may have degree-seeking international students applying for a study abroad program. Although they may already be "studying abroad" from their home nations, they provide an invaluable point of view to the academic and cultural experience.

Remember, students who are not U.S. citizens may need to apply for a visa in order to enter the country where the program is to take place.

International students should be reminded to check with their on-campus advisers to confirm that their paperwork has been completed in order to re-enter the United States.

Does the program require a translator or guide?

If yes, make sure to emphasize to the tour operator that this is an academic course, not a tour. Send a copy of the syllabus before arrival, and have very explicit guidelines articulating that faculty directors will be testing and evaluating students, and your expectations for the guide.

Are emergency procedures clear?

Do the faculty director and students know whom to notify (e.g., home institution and individual family members)?

Do all participants have adequate health and travel insurance?

Will the International Student Identification Card be required to supplement personal insurance?

Before planning begins, first decide if arrangements will be made in-house or by a program provider. The following pages will assist in making that determination.

Working with a Program Provider
When Is the Assistance of a Program Provider Needed?

Program providers can provide local knowledge and resources when an institution wishes to have support abroad, and are able to assist with both the development stage of the program and curriculum planning. The options are flexible as to what services are needed, depending on the length of program, the desired support, and details that need to be arranged.

Many U.S. institutions hire program providers for short-term programs abroad for budgetary reasons. They realize that by sharing the resources of a program provider with other schools, they are actually able to lower the cost of the students' program fee. For example, instead of being forced to rent a classroom for an entire day when it is only needed for a couple of hours, schools can split the hours up through the coordination of a program provider and only pay for what they use. Institutions sometimes find it much easier to pay one invoice to a program provider in U.S. dollars than to worry about making foreign payments for student housing, academic needs such as language instruction or classroom space, and guides at museums.

Program providers are also able to assist with publicity on a program, and this can be very helpful for new programs or for schools that need to look nationally to fill their programs. They also have an established network and can easily get the word out concerning new programs that are open to participants from other schools.

Range of Services

Each short-term program abroad will have different needs, based on academic and logistical structure, and program providers can offer a range of services to support the specific needs of a program.

Contracts

Program providers should always present a written agreement or contract. This written document will make it clear to everyone, including an accompanying faculty member, what services will be provided both before departure and on site.

With all negotiated relationships, every travel and academic transaction must be in writing.

Be sure that faculty directors go overseas with copies, or originals if possible, of all contracts and correspondence.

Predeparture
- ✓ Program design, including budget
- ✓ Curriculum development
- ✓ Internship placements
- ✓ Orientations
- ✓ Publicity materials

Transportation
- ✓ Airfare for students and faculty
- ✓ Arrival and departure airport transfer
- ✓ City bus/metro passes

Accommodations
- ✓ Accommodations and meal plans
- ✓ Student and faculty housing placement
- ✓ Meal allowances
- ✓ Special meals

Academics/Classrooms
- ✓ Local institution arrangements, classes or classroom space
- ✓ Select local adjunct faculty to be approved by U.S. institution
- ✓ Remuneration of local adjunct faculty
- ✓ Academic support and supervision
- ✓ Faculty office and equipment
- ✓ Classroom scheduling
- ✓ Equipment coordination
- ✓ Guest lecturers
- ✓ Library access
- ✓ Computer and Internet access for students and faculty

Visits/Excursions/Cultural Activities
- ✓ Excursion and activities planning
- ✓ Museum passes
- ✓ Bus coordination
- ✓ Guides
- ✓ Coordination of cultural activities

Services
- ✓ Liability insurance
- ✓ Payment collection (direct payment from students or one invoice to school)
- ✓ Insurance for students and faculty

On-Site
- ✓ Student advising
- ✓ Health and safety implementation
- ✓ Student handbooks
- ✓ Access for students to local clubs
- ✓ Assistance with independent travel
- ✓ Management of program funds
- ✓ Facilitation of internships, site visits, etc.
- ✓ Communication with U.S. institution
- ✓ Administrative support for faculty and program coordinator
- ✓ Student evaluations
- ✓ Evaluation visits from U.S. administrators

Does Using a Program Provider Cost More?

Whether using a program provider will cost more will vary depending on what services are negotiated and how important the administrator considers the additional support, both predeparture and on site. A program provider is always willing to put together a proposal detailing the services included and a final cost for the services. This request for proposal must happen in the early phase of program development. With budget figures in hand, it is much easier to decide what is best for students and faculty, as well as the administrator or faculty director.

What Can Be Expected from a Program Provider?

Some institutions require a program provider for liability and financial security reasons. Program providers should have financial stability, good contacts, and references.

Other important services offered by program providers are health and safety planning and implementation. Many U.S. institutions use program providers because of this support.

When searching for a program provider, look for one who has a positive philosophy of education abroad compatible with the philosophy of your institution. They should have solid experience with academic programs and understand the importance of this focus on short-term programs abroad.

Program providers should also have a strong network of resources, including housing, airlines, and potential academics on site to assist institutions in developing their programs and making them a success. Constant upgrading of facilities and program resources will show that a program provider understands the link between academic quality and the facilities available to students and faculty. Program providers should always be willing to research new program opportunities, and to keep abreast of new locations, museums, or excursions that might add to the academic content of a program.

Institutions can expect flexibility and accessibility from a program provider. Both parties should collaborate to create a program tailored to their respective needs. Budget flexibility is important, should circumstances arise such as low student enrollment or additional academic needs.

A program provider needs to be able to cooperate with faculty, staff, students, and parents and must be accessible through 24-hour emergency lines. Some program providers offer predeparture and on-site orientations.

What Do Program Providers Expect from Short-Term Program Administrators?

Most importantly, there must be a cooperative agreement between the program provider and the U.S. institution. Information must be shared before, during, and after the program. This constant communication and support means that the program provider's U.S. office almost becomes an extension of the international office. If an international office is small or understaffed, this connection with the program provider can prove crucial in the school's ability to operate a greater number of programs.

How Can I Find a Reliable Program Provider?

At writing there is no centralized list of program providers for U.S. institutions. A good method is to ask colleagues for advice and recommendations. References are the best way to find out about a program provider, what type of programs they are experienced in administering, and whether their philosophy fits with the sponsoring institution's goal for its short-term programs abroad.

Other Study Abroad Organizations

Full-service program providers are not the only travel organizations that support short-term programs abroad. The following independent organizations may be hired to coordinate travel logistics; some may be hired by program providers to facilitate travel.

Travel Arranger

Travel arrangers are most often travel agencies that may or may not specialize in student travel. They may specialize in a particular area of the world or in a particular theme (e.g., choir performances for a group of musical students). The agencies may or may not be local.

Tour Operator

Tour operators manage the travel logistics of a program. They are either based on site or they use a series of subcontractors to provide travel services such as accommodations, guides, transfers, transportation, special events, meals, etc. Tour operators may have offices in the United States and other countries and they may be headquartered anywhere in the world.

On-Site Program Service Agents

Service agents provide specific services for study abroad programs in a specific area of the world. Examples include home-stay providers, apartment rental agencies, guest lecture providers, internship providers, and classroom rental organizations.

Making Your Own Arrangements

This section will expand on the checklist from the previous section and will provide some hints on how arrangements can be made without using a program provider. The better the communication and understanding of mutual expectation between the international office and the faculty directing the program, the more smoothly the operation will run, and the fewer cracks there will be into which details can fall.

Air Travel

Most programs require some air travel and airline tickets will often be a substantial part of the program cost. It is imperative that careful research be conducted on the best transaction method for these tickets. Institutional policy or a limited budget may necessitate the purchase of the least-expensive tickets, even if the route is inconvenient with multiple stops and early departure times. However, a program is sometimes better served by a more direct schedule with fewer possibilities of flight delays and missed connections. This can allow the students and faculty director to arrive on site less jet-lagged and ready to begin the program. In all cases, good stewardship of student dollars should be a strong consideration in making arrangements.

Designated Travel Agents

Some institutions have designated travel agents with whom the international office or faculty director must work, even if there are cheaper or more convenient airline tickets elsewhere. In this situation, the administrator should be well acquainted with the practices of the travel agent in terms of how far in advance to make reservations, pay deposits, and purchase the tickets. Benefits of this kind of arrangement include potential flexibility in terms of changing the names of participants, adding or canceling travelers, and an established payment system within the institution.

Finding a Reliable Travel Agent

If your institution allows you to work with any travel agent, consider the following:

* Confirm that the agency is a member of the American Society of Travel Agents
* Confirm that the person you work with has taken Certified Travel Counselor training.
* Ask for references, particularly from other educational institutions. Call the references. It is important to know that your travel agent is willing and able to accommodate special requests and will be patient with student changes.
* Make sure that the agent is used to working with groups and will negotiate with the group desks of appropriate airlines. An agent who simply quotes you a rate from the computer is not doing his or her job.
* If the agent is local, ask if he or she is willing to meet the group at the airport on departure day to do a group check-in.
* Make sure there is good follow-up once the group has departed—out of sight should not mean out of mind. The agent needs to keep you informed of any changes to the return schedule and should be available to provide assistance in the case of missed flights, etc.

Making Airline Reservations

You should have at least three quotes for an itinerary—from a local travel agent, a major national student travel company, and a consolidator—and you may want to check with an airline group desk, too. Before asking for quotes, the departure and return dates should be set and the group size defined, as airlines have different criteria for what constitutes a group rate. Some airlines or companies may issue a certain number of free tickets per group.

Airline Reservations

When making airline arrangements, consider the following:

* Are there free tickets available with group reservations?
* What is the service charge per ticket?
* Is there 24-hour access to change flight arrangements?
* Will flight deviations be supported?

Flight deviations

Flight deviations are any change from the group itinerary, such as a student staying after the course return to travel independently; there is usually a charge.

As when working with program providers, initial contact with a travel agent should be made very early in the program development process. Whenever possible, try to be flexible in program dates to allow the travel agent to research the best fares.

Check to see if there are other services that come packaged with a group booking, such as a night at a hotel.

Be aware of minimum numbers for group bookings; if your group is not likely to reach the needed size, make other arrangements.

Ticket Fees

Many travel agents charge a fee for each ticket issued. If you must use a designated travel agent who charges a fee, there is no option but to pay the fee and build the cost into the program budget. If you have the flexibility to use other travel agents, you will have to decide whether the convenience of working with a particular agency that charges a fee outweighs the savings acquired by finding an agency that does not, but which may not be as convenient in other areas. Try to negotiate a fee waiver or reduction for your group.

Airline Deposits

Most airlines require deposits when contracts are finalized. Since this is usually well before student monies are collected, the deposit will have to be covered by bridge funding. Check your institution's policies.

Some airline group desks, in order to offer competitive prices, ask for a significant sum up front, to be refunded once the group has departed. Once again, bridge funding will be necessary for this kind of arrangement. Most airlines will refund the seat deposit after departure.

Cancellations/Refunds

You should consider cancellation and refund policies when reserving tickets. The contract with the airline will outline its policies and important deadlines.

Other Forms of Transportation

Rail

If traveling by train, tickets may be purchased from the agent who facilitated the airline reservations. Consider seat reservations if your group is large or the travel distance is long.

Airport Transfers

An airport transfer needs to be arranged from the airport to the accommodation site. It is often most efficient to arrange this through an on-site tour operator or bus company. The faculty director or your travel agent may be able to suggest someone to work with. If not, ask someone at the accommodation site to make a recommendation.

Renting Vehicles

Some courses require group travel by rented vehicles, or a faculty director will hire a car for on-site use. Again, the faculty director or your travel agent may be able to suggest someone to work with. Check to see if your institution has an arrangement with a major rental company. Since many rental companies are international, you may be able to take advantage of institutional discounts.

If there is more than one faculty member with a group, or if there is a teaching assistant assigned to the group, you may wish to plan for one of the group leaders to arrive in the host country a day or two before the rest of the group to get over jet lag, arrange for rentals, and generally be refreshed when the bedraggled but excited group arrives.

Accommodations

It is important to know the faculty director's expectations in terms of accommodations. Often, when taking a group of students to a familiar place, a faculty director is willing to use his or her host-country contacts to make accommodation arrangements. Deposits are often requested, and, like airline deposits, bridge funds need to be secured until student fees are collected.

Location Is Important

- Sometimes a faculty director knows of general areas for accommodations, such as Bloomsbury in London, but does not have specific hotels identified. Consult a travel agent, the Internet, travel books, or personal or professional networks to identify accommodations in a specific area.
- As with travel arrangements, the least expensive accommodations are not always the best ones. A centrally located hotel may cost more up front but can save in time and travel.
- Always try to negotiate a group rate. Ask for a free room for group leaders. If the price quoted is too high, ask for a reduced rate. Hotels want to fill their rooms and are often willing to negotiate.
- Some hotels are reluctant to take student groups. You may have to reassure the hotel that you have carefully screened your students and discussed with them the need for respectful behavior.

Payments for Airline Tickets and Accommodations

Airline and accommodations payments can usually be made by credit card. Be sure to clarify whether a corporate or institutional card is available, or if the faculty director or international office staff must use their personal credit cards and be immediately reimbursed. As covered in Chapter 4, Internal Support Systems: It Takes a Campus to Run a Study Abroad Program, work with the appropriate campus office to obtain a credit card in the institution's name, as it provides another layer of liability between the faculty and on-site organizations. If a deposit is required and it is not possible to use a credit card, funds will have to be sent from your campus. Again, use your partnership with your business office to do this efficiently.

Meals

Before you can complete your program budget (See Chapter 9, Financial Matters) you need to determine the meal plan for your group.
- Which meals will be included in the cost of accommodations?
- Can arrangements be made for special banquets or group meals, either for lunch or dinner? Who will make those arrangements?
- Is the cost of all other meals built into the budget so the faculty can disburse funds to students to buy their own meals, or must students bring additional funds to buy meals?

Many experienced faculty directors will attest that there is nothing worse than a horde of hungry students. Be sure to take into account arrival times and the number of hours spent on buses, and do whatever is necessary to ensure that food is available at appropriate times. If the group will be arriving in the host country or city too late to get to a restaurant, ask the hotel if a late meal can be arranged. If it will be difficult to exchange money before the next mealtime, arrange and prepay for a group meal.

In some countries, extra precautions need to be made to ensure students do not eat unsafe food. Confirm that the faculty director knows which foods are safe and where such food can be obtained. If the water supply is not drinkable, bottled water should be included in the budget.

In-Country Tour Offices

It is recommended that programs begin with an orientation tour of a city or region, and many cities have offices where such tours can be booked. Tourist offices can also be valuable resources for other information, too, such as restaurants, local entertainment, reputable vehicle rental agencies, English-speaking doctors, and so on.

Guided Tours

Often faculty directors want to schedule guided tours to specific destinations, the theater, and museums, or plan other excursions that support the academic and cultural learning goals of the course. Advance reservations should be made for tours. Museum entry fees are usually paid on site. Theater tickets may be purchased in advance. Arrangements can usually be made through e-mail or a Web site.

Sensible Things to Do

It is always a good idea to make two copies of all passports and airline tickets. One set should be sent with the faculty director and the other should remain in the international office. Replacing lost documents is greatly facilitated if copies are available.

Working with Graduate Students

Although most short-term programs abroad are developed for undergraduate students, these programs are ideal for graduate students, especially those who are working adults.

Although program development logistics and academic structure are similar, working with graduate students may differ in a number of ways.

Airline Tickets

Many short-term graduate courses do not include group airline tickets, especially to European destinations. Students may be located in different cities, want to combine business travel, or extend their stay for personal travel.

Travel-Savvy Students

Graduate students tend to be more travel savvy than their younger colleagues. Many have traveled for business and personal holidays, and they may have higher expectations of hotel and bus quality. They may also request a single hotel room, so be sure that you have cost information for a "single supplement."

Flexibility

Graduate students may need more flexibility built into a study abroad program (e.g., can they skip a group dinner to deal with a work or family situation). Instead of standard billing statements, they may request a detailed budget and billing statement for tuition reimbursement by their employer.

Communication

Communication rarely occurs in person, with students relying heavily on e-mail and phone contact. For this reason, it is important that your printed and electronic information are accurate, and they may need to be more specific than for undergraduate students.

Travel Companions

A student may request to bring a travel companion (e.g., spouse, partner, guests) with the intent that the companion will share the student's accommodations and enjoy the cultural sites while the student takes part in the academic course. If a program allows travel companions, carefully define in advance the limits and expectations related to the companion's participation in the program.

Chapter 9

Financial Matters

Sue Jackson

<u>Setting the Budget</u>

The purpose of a budget is to ensure sufficient funds for a program's needs. There are several budget models and this chapter will help you decide which one is the best for your program.

First, who will create the budget? Will it be the faculty director, the program provider, the international office, or all of these in consultation with each other? Collaboration is the most common, with the faculty director or program provider identifying costs and the institution advising and applying policy.

What Expenses Are Covered in a Program Fee?

The most basic formula is as follows:

$$\text{Faculty director expenses} + \text{direct student expenses} = \text{program fee.}$$

Rarely is it this simple.

Faculty Director's Expenses

When calculating the director's expenses, it must be determined which expenses will be covered by the institution, and which will need to be supported by the program budget. In some cases, faculty salaries are paid by the institution, because the course is part of a faculty member's load and is therefore not an extra responsibility. However, the faculty director may spend significant time creating the program—over and above normal teaching and course preparation time. Is this considered extra work that should be compensated? In other cases, the course is an overload for the faculty member. Will the administration pick up the extra cost, or will the faculty director's salary and expenses have to be budgeted into the program fee? As demonstrated in Chapter 3, Administrative Processes, these policies must be clarified before the budget can be finalized.

In most cases, the faculty director's out-of-pocket expenses, such as airfare, ground transportation, accommodation, meal allowance, and group theater tickets and museum entry fees, need to be included in the program budget. Budget meal allowances according to the program site; London will be more expensive than Accra.

Direct Student Expenses

It is important for the international office to have consistent guidelines, policies, and if necessary, limitations, for which items can be included in a program budget. If your institution offers a number of programs, it is imperative that there is budgeting consistency since students often use cost in choosing a program. Not only do students need to accurately compare costs, but faculty need to function under the same guidelines.

Tuition

Will tuition be charged? If so, does it need to be included in the program fee? If tuition is an extra cost, will the students be billed separately for tuition and the cost of the program, or can it be billed as one fee? Is there a separate tuition rate for a study abroad program, or is it the same per-credit tuition charged by the institution?

As examined in Chapter 7, Feasibility Studies, the academic calendar and timing of short-term programs have a significant impact on the budget. For example, if an institution has a January term that is part of a faculty director's teaching load, and tuition is already covered in a comprehensive fee, an international office need only charge for the direct costs of the program. However, if a program is to take place in the summer, which typically is not part of a faculty director's teaching load, and salary must be budgeted, the program will necessarily be more expensive. These kinds of factors can help in deciding when a program should take place.

Tuition Models

There are a number of tuition models used in short-term programs abroad.

Full tuition revenue. In this model, full tuition from study abroad courses is retained by the international office. Faculty salaries are supported by the tuition collected; faculty expenses and direct out-of-pocket expenses are paid in the program fee.

Partial access to tuition revenue. The off-campus program is allowed access to a percentage of the tuition dollars. Like the full tuition revenue model, salaries and faculty and academic expenses are covered by tuition; students' direct out-of-pocket expenses are paid in the program fee.

No tuition charged. Faculty salary, all expenses, and direct out-of-pocket expenses are paid in the program fee. A percentage of the program fee may be added to cover indirect costs and is kept at the institution.

Outsourcing. If your institution is using a program provider, students pay all direct expenses to the external organization, and tuition is collected to cover the faculty director's salary and other institutional expenses.

Administrative Fees

Many international offices charge administrative fees in addition to a program fee. This money is usually used to cover administrative costs. A standard fee may be charged for all programs, or there may be different fees for different programs, depending on the amount of administrative work.

Travel and On-Site Costs

Expenses to be considered include:

- airfare
- accommodations
- meals (how many)
- in-country transportation (metro passes, tour buses, train tickets)
- airport transfers
- required group events (museum entry fees, excursions, theater tickets, guide fees)
- guest lecture fees
- classroom costs
- visas.

Textbooks

Decide if textbooks should be included in the program cost or purchased separately by students.

International Student Identity Card

If the International Student Identity Card is required, should the cost be budgeted into the program fee?

What Is Not Included in the Program Fee?

In consultation with the faculty director, it should be determined what will be included in the budget and what will not, and this must be made clear to students. Rarely included in the program fee are passport costs, inoculations and medications, host family gifts, spending money, and costs of identified meals. It is useful to give the students guidelines for how much spending money to bring.

Setting the Budget Specifics

Fixed Versus Variable Costs

The distinction between fixed and variable costs should be borne in mind when the budget is created. Fixed costs are those that will not vary based on the number of students, such as airline tickets, theater tickets, and meal allowance. Variable costs are dependent upon the number of participants. For example, if you pay a guest lecturer $200, in a 10-student program each student must contribute $20; in a 20-student program each student must contribute $10.

Minimum and Maximum Numbers

The determination of minimum and maximum participant numbers in a course is, again, a collaborative decision between the faculty director and the administrator. Determine whether there are institutional guidelines or limits that must be considered.

In many cases, the minimum and maximum numbers are determined by physical limitations. A studio art course may only have studio space for a limited number of students; a historical survey course may be able to take large numbers of students.

Because each program will have a number of variable expenses, the size of a group will affect the budget. For example, if you plan to rent a bus, how many people (plus their luggage) will fit on the vehicle? What are the implications if you have to rent an additional vehicle? Is it financially worthwhile for a small group to travel in a large vehicle if a smaller vehicle is not available?

During the planning stages, it can be helpful to make more than one budget, with each budget based on a different number of participants. This will help the faculty director and administrator decide on optimal participant numbers.

A sample budget form can be found at the end of this chapter.

Cancellation Policy

It is important for every organization involved with short-term programs to have a policy about when to cancel a program based on low enrollment. Ideally, the policy should allow for some budget modifications to be made to accommodate a lower number of students, provided those modifications do not compromise the academic integrity of the program.

Audit Policy

You should be clear about how academic credit relates to the course. Most programs will be approved for a certain amount of credit and participants will pay for and receive that amount. The issue becomes more complicated if students wish to audit the course (i.e., participate without earning credit). Your institution should have an established policy that outlines whether audits are possible and, if they are, what audit fees will be charged.

An important factor to bear in mind is the nonprofit status of educational institutions. This may be jeopardized if the administrator makes arrangements for "nonstudents" to participate in a program (i.e., participants are not receiving credit). The Internal Revenue Service can interpret such arrangements as the institution performing travel agent-like services for the nonstudent and tax may be assessed to the institution. There are various ways to avoid this situation and an audit fee is one way. If it appears that there will be nonstudents on a program, it is advisable to speak to your institution's financial comptroller to understand how the situation should be handled.

Cost Changes and Contingency Funds

Since programs are planned and budgets set significantly in advance of the departure date, it may be difficult to know the exact price of certain budget items, given the fluid state of currencies and travel costs. If you are worried that variable costs and exchange rates may affect your program, it is wise to have a contingency plan in place, depending on your institution's budgeting systems. Possibilities include the following:

- The institution may be willing to provide extra funding for excess costs that occurred since the program fee was advertised.
- Create a policy that allows the administrator to share unanticipated cost increases with students. You might consider a percentage policy: if costs increase less than 5 percent or 10 percent (or whatever your institution will allow), the institution will absorb the increase; if costs increase more than the agreed upon percentage, any increase over that percentage will be passed on to the student.
- Advertise the program fee based on a number of students, such as $3,200 for 15 participants.
- If your institution is unwilling or unable to absorb any cost increases, then you need to build a contingency fund into any budget that would be able to take care of shortfalls due to cost increases or other emergencies.

Keep in mind that few currencies fluctuate significantly, so a 5 percent margin of error would usually cover any shortfall. Because these programs usually do not exceed 8 weeks in length, it is unlikely that costs would escalate to such an extent that the program would be in real financial difficulty. Currency fluctuations can also work to your advantage. If the U.S. dollar is suddenly able to buy more at the program's destination, the director has the enjoyable task of deciding whether to add extra programming, give money back to the students, or retain the funds for other programs.

What If There Is Money Left Over at the End of the Program?

It is important to know *before* the program departs what will happen to unused funds. You may choose to:
- retain the money to support future programs
- contribute to a contingency fund to cover emergencies or overages
- use funds for program development and site visits
- refund money to the students.

Your institution needs to have a refund policy in place. Some institutions allow faculty directors to refund money directly to students on site. If this should occur, students must sign a receipt indicating that they have received funds. The receipt is an important document for program account reconciliation. The faculty director should also keep a small amount in case other unanticipated bills need to be paid or contingency funds are needed on the way home.

Some institutions require refunds to be made after the program has ended and all accounts have been tallied. You may wish to consider some guidelines so that you do not end up processing very small refunds to large numbers of students. This may be more work for you and your accounting office than it is worth.

Whose Money Is It?

This seemingly innocent question bears further scrutiny because there could be more than one answer. If tuition has been included in the price of the program, then that portion of the money ultimately belongs to the institution. The remaining funds once belonged to the students and have been entrusted to the institution for stewardship, to provide certain services. It is always incumbent on the international office and on the faculty directing the program to make the most judicious use of these funds. It is not appropriate, for example, for the director to augment his or her library out of student funds, on the grounds that the books are necessary for course preparation. The faculty director's department should cover such expenses. Neither should the faculty director use student funds to upgrade personal meals or accommodations. Also, if items like cell phones or Palm Pilots are purchased for the program, they are the institution's property and should be kept in the international office when not in use.

Sample Refund Policy from a Private, Liberal Arts College

If the remaining balance in a program budget exceeds $100 per student, that amount is refunded to the students. The refund will be credited to the students' comprehensive fee account after it is determined that all program expenses have been covered.

If the remaining balance in a program budget is less than $100 per student, no money will be refunded to students. It will be moved to a contingency account that can be used to cover emergencies or deficits in other programs.

[Source: St. Olaf College]

The finances of every program should be audited once that program is complete, and any person should be able to look at the accounting and be satisfied that the money was judiciously spent.

Who Makes Financial Decisions?

As discussed previously, it is important to have institutional policies and guidelines to assist faculty directors in making financial decisions on site. But as is often the case, policies and guidelines will not cover every eventuality. Faculty should be trained to distinguish between those decisions they can make themselves and those that require consultation with the international office or administrator of the program.

Collecting and Disbursing Monies

As discussed in Chapter 4, Internal Support Systems, it is essential to have a good relationship with your accounts department or business office. It is also wise to have a good relationship with the financial aid office. Students may count on loans, grants, and scholarships to fund a portion of their program fee, and systems need to be in place to move money into program accounts.

Accounting Procedures

Work with your accounts department well in advance of the program's start date to determine when and to whom students will pay their fees and how payments should be made. Whenever possible, try to make your needs fit into their systems and follow their specific procedures.

Accounts will need to be created; tracking income and expenses will be much easier if you can create a separate account for each program.

Ideally, the business office or student accounts office will be responsible for bills and payments. If this is the case, be sure that the appropriate office has complete and accurate information on which students to bill, how much they should be billed, and when billing should occur. You must also define whether tuition is billed separately, and how the institution wants tuition dollars to be administered. If it becomes the responsibility of the international office to collect program fees, be sure that you have a good procedure for crediting payments as well as a safe place to keep payments.

Student Deposits

Most study abroad programs require that student pay an application fee, a deposit, or both, to hold their place in a program.

Requiring an application fee, particularly if it is nonrefundable, can help to confirm the serious intent of the student. A second deposit, paid by the student after acceptance to the program, can be used to cover advance payments to airlines, accommodations, etc.

How Are Students Billed for a Program?

Students may be billed for their program fee by the institution's account office (similar to an on-campus course), by the international office, or by an external program provider. Although many international offices historically handled the collection of program fees, many are creating procedures to have whichever office is responsible for on-campus billing handle the study abroad billing as well. Not only can financial aid then be applied through normal procedures, but also this adds to the perception that this is a course rather than a trip.

How to Pay for Services

It is best to pay for as many services as possible before the course departs, including airfare, accommodations, train tickets, on-site transportation, classroom expenses, and even prepaid theater tickets. Bank drafts in the host country's currency may be ordered to pay guest lecturers directly. Travel agencies, hotels, and tour companies providing buses and guides should be able to bill the administrator directly. These bills can be paid in advance by credit card, institutional check, foreign draft, or wire transfer.

Prepayment reduces the amount of cash the faculty director must carry, as well as saves valuable time otherwise used paying bills. If you are using a program provider or travel agent, pay them in a lump sum at least 6 weeks before departure so that they can use the funds to pay travel expenses.

Institutional Credit or Debit Card Programs

If your institution has such a program, consider having credit cards issued in the faculty director's name charged directly to either an institutional account or a local bank account. The card can be used to pay expenses in advance of departure as well as on site.

Foreign Currency Drafts or Wire Transfers

It is often useful to pay for services in advance with foreign currency drafts or wire transfers. Your institution's business office will probably have a preferred method of doing this. Also see Chapter 4, Internal Support Systems.

On-Site Payments

In some cases, the charge for goods or services will need to be paid on site and the director will need to carry funds to cover these expenses. Funds are usually given to directors in the form of a travel advance. If the arranged credit or debit card has ATM capability, funds may be drawn and many faculty consider this to be easiest when cash machines are readily available. However, it is risky to rely solely on ATMs; the faculty director must have access to other funds. It may be most convenient to carry travelers' checks that can be exchanged at local banks or other agencies. Consider negotiating with your organization's bank to waive traveler's check fees.

It is important to understand the financial situations in the country or countries to be visited. The director of a course in a major European city may find an abundance of functioning cash machines. The director of a course in a remote location may have no access at all to an ATM. Some countries have very specific currency restrictions and limitations (e.g., Cuba, where neither U.S. credit cards nor travelers' checks can be used). In such cases, careful research must be done to determine the most effective and safest way for managing funds.

Tracking Expenses

It is standard operating procedure to document every expense so that the program's accounts can be reconciled upon return. There are various ways to track expenses, including tracking expenses on a laptop computer or Palm Pilot™ or using an expense report form (see Expense Journal Sample, at the end of this chapter).

Receipts

Faculty directors must be trained to keep all receipts, just like other business expenses. Encourage directors to have some system for organizing receipts. Since the receipts are often printed in another language and reflect a different currency, it can be helpful to keep all receipts for the same country (if the program covers multiple countries) in separate envelopes or zippered bags. The administrator or program provider usually keeps prepaid receipts to document expenditures and to reconcile the final audit.

"Nondetail" Faculty Directors

A faculty director's organizational and detail-oriented strengths and weaknesses may not be known to you if you are working with him or her for the first time. If you have identified the faculty director's weaknesses, however, there are preventive measures you can put in place. Encourage the faculty director to have a teaching assistant, staff member, or other faculty member who is accompanying the program manage the finances. You can also develop expense record sheets as well as income/expense reports that not only help the director track expenses but also document how much money is budgeted for each line. See samples of these forms at the end of this chapter.

Reporting Deadlines

Faculty directors should be given a deadline by which financial reports and return of unused funds must be submitted to the international or business office. The deadline should be no more than 3 weeks after the end of the program. This gives the administrator the opportunity to check the reports and clarify any discrepancies before important details are forgotten.

Short-Term Study Abroad Budget

Course title: _____ **Term/Year:___**

The following costs will be included in the per student course charge for the above course based on a minimum target enrollment of _____ X students.

Part I		Per student	Total cost
A. Director/leadership expenses	Comments		
Transportation - air		$0	$0
Transportation - rail		$0	$0
Local transportation		$0	$0
Accommodations: Location 1	$ x ___ days	$0	$0
Location 2	$ x ___ days	$0	$0
Meal allowance		$0	$0
Gratuities/tips		$0	$0
Events: tickets, admissions, excursions, other		$0	$0
Personal incidentals		$0	$0
Stipend/salary (if applicable)		$0	$0
Vaccinations		$0	$0
International Teacher ID Card		$0	$0
Total faculty director/leadership expenses		$0	$0
B. Direct student expenses		**Per student**	**Total cost**
Transportation - air		$0	
Airport departure taxes (if applicable)		$0	
Transportation - motorcoach		$0	$0
Transportation - rail		$0	$0
Local transportation		$0	
Accommodations: Location 1	$ x ___ days	$0	
Location 2	$ x ___ days	$0	
Group meals		$0	
Classroom rental		$0	$0
Guest lecturers		$0	$0
Events: tickets, admissions, excursions, other		$0	
Indirect funds or emergency funds (5-10%)		$0	
Orientation costs		$0	
Administrative fee		$0	
Group funds		$0	
Total student expenses		$0	
Total expense billed to student (Parts A and B)		$0	

Part II: Additional student expenses		Per student	Advertised program fee:
Passport		$0	_____
Books		$0	
Vaccinations		$0	Final program fee:
Total additional expenses		$0	

[Source: St. Olaf College]

Expense Journal Sample

Date	Paid to	Type of expense (hotel) taxi, dinner)	"Business" purpose	Foreign currency amount	Currency conversion rate	U.S. dollar amount	Account and object code (see key below)	Receipt
__/__/__								Yes No
__/__/__								Yes No
__/__/__								Yes No
__/__/__								Yes No
__/__/__								Yes No
__/__/__								Yes No
__/__/__								Yes No
__/__/__								Yes No
__/__/__								Yes No
__/__/__								Yes No
__/__/__								Yes No
__/__/__								Yes No
__/__/__								Yes No
__/__/__								Yes No
__/__/__								Yes No
__/__/__								Yes No
__/__/__								Yes No
__/__/__								Yes No
__/__/__								Yes No
__/__/__								Yes No
__/__/__								Yes No
__/__/__								Yes No
__/__/__								Yes No
__/__/__								Yes No
__/__/__								Yes No
__/__/__								Yes No
__/__/__								Yes No

6510 - Air travel   6530 - Lodging   6590 - Other travel expenses

6520 - Ground transportation   6540 - Meals

[Source: University of St. Thomas.]

Sample Income/Expense Report for Australia

INCOME: 25 students @ $4,600 each = $115,000.00

EXPENSES:	Paid by administrator	Carried by faculty director
Flights ($2,605 x 26)	67,730.00	
Y on the Park, Sydney	4,305.76	
Sydney Opera House		
Tour CC	142.00	
Play CC	714.44	
Kingsford Smith Transport	265.41	
Curtin University	10,096.00	
Center for Aboriginal Studies		1,326.00
Guest lectures		500.00
Mercure Inn	1,470.97	
Goldenlines (Kalgoorlie Bus)	344.52	
Ayers Rock Resort	1,275.70	
Territory Rent-a-car – CC	200.00	
ATT Kings – transfers	219.47	
Park Hyatt – CC	900.00	
City Center Hotel	961.23	
Scenic travel	702.03	
Food ($525 x 26)		13,650.00
Entrance fees ($125 x 26)		3,250.00
Perth Transportation ($100 x 26)		2,600.00
Other Perth buses		600.00
Group incidentals ($85 x 26)		2,210.00
Textbooks	778.70	
T-shirts	316.34	
Personal incidentals		350.00
TOTALS	90,422.57	24,486.00

Prepaid expenses:	$90,422.57	
On-site expenses:	$24,486.00	
	$114,897.56	
TOTAL INCOME:	$115,000.00	
TOTAL EXPENSES:	$114,908.57	
BALANCE	$91.43	

[Source: St. Olaf College.]

Chapter 10

Marketing and Promotion

Kathy Tuma

You cannot have a short-term program without students, and most study abroad courses require some attention to promotion in order to recruit students. The goal may be to create so much anticipation that a marketing plan is not needed. Until then, utilize your faculty director's expertise and enthusiasm to promote the program to students.

Step 1: Know Your Students

The first step in your marketing plan should be an analysis of your student body. There are three types of students:

Type One: The "When Do We Leave?" Student
This student is ready to travel anywhere, anytime. She or he is first in line to receive new brochures and applications and has deposit money in hand.

Type Two: The "I Could Be Convinced" Student
This student may have thought about study abroad but needs a push to make the commitment.

Type Three: The "I've Got All I Can Do To Keep Up On Campus" Student
With this type of student, the challenge is to remove obstacles, whether real or perceived, and show that study abroad (or more specifically, short-term study abroad) is an option.

If you have a campus full of Type One students, you may stop reading and go on to the next chapter. If, like most institutions, many of your students fall into the Type Two and Type Three categories, read on.

There are several reasons students fall into the Type Two or Type Three category.

First generation or at-risk students. For these students, the decision to attend college was a major one. They may have had to struggle with high school guidance counselors, college admissions counselors, or even their own families for the chance to attend college. Simply being on campus is a major achievement.

First-time travelers. Study abroad can seem too adventurous for students who have never had a passport or traveled outside the country. They may be reluctant to take the risk.

Nontraditional students. These are the students with full-time jobs and/or a family. They barely keep their heads above water with all of the responsibilities in their lives and study abroad does not seem like even a remote possibility.

Double/triple majors. These students have a carefully planned schedule and they have ruled out study abroad because a semester- or year-long program would jeopardize their progress toward graduation.

Students with disabilities. Although there are many good opportunities for students with disabilities to study abroad for a longer duration, they may be unwilling to take the chance without first having had the opportunity to prove themselves on a shorter program.

Step 2: Advising

Study abroad advising, in the traditional sense (an adviser and student in discussion regarding goals, type of program, etc.) rarely occurs with students opting for short-term programs abroad. The process of choosing a short-term program is very different from that of choosing to go abroad for a semester or year. Students opt for this type of program because the program goes to a place they have always wanted to see, because it fulfills a needed graduation requirement, or perhaps because their best friend has applied. Students think they do not need to consider the more serious issues that are prevalent in the selection of a semester- or year-long program.

For short-term programs, the quality of the written materials presenting the courses available or specific course descriptions is very important.

Because students often make their choices casually and because we do not have the opportunity to assist them in their program selection, it becomes crucial to provide a careful and thoughtful orientation program. More information about this follows in Chapter 15, Orientation and Reentry.

Step 3: The Marketing Approach

The first thing you need to do to promote your courses is to make short-term study abroad **unassailably academic**. That is, nothing about these programs should seem like a trip or a vacation or a junket. They should be marketed as a valuable part of the curriculum, as an opportunity for a student to continue and enhance his or her studies by going beyond the classroom.

Encourage faculty directors to shape the courses in such a way that they will fulfill general and/or major/minor requirements. As much as we wish students would study abroad purely for the joy of learning, we know that they are much more likely to participate in a program that meets an academic requirement.

As long as a course is unassailably academic and developed with an audience in mind, there is nothing wrong with promoting the more exciting aspects of study abroad. The places you can go, the people you can meet, and the things you can learn—these are the essence of short-term programs abroad and they should be promoted shamelessly. Who would not be tempted to leave a Minnesota campus in January to study the literature of the Caribbean? Why not get political science students excited about attending a meeting of the British Parliament?

Step 4: Informing Students

The mechanisms for getting information to students about your programs will vary depending on your institution. Following are a number of suggestions; it is up to you to determine which will work best for your school. If you are not sure, talk with your campus communication or publication director. She or he should be able to give you good advice about what works well in your situation.

Printed Information

Brochures and Catalogs

If you offer a selection of short-term programs abroad during a specific term, such as summer or January intersession, list these courses in one printed brochure. Include general application, selection, payment, and cancellation information. Arrange the course listings by geographic region or by discipline and include:

- ✓ brief course description
- ✓ name of faculty director(s)
- ✓ prerequisites
- ✓ cost

- ✓ maximum enrollment
- ✓ requirements that the course fulfills (e.g., "counts toward Art History major/minor," or "fulfills Area A of core curriculum")

Course Descriptions

Consider creating a course description for each short-term program abroad. These 1- to 2-page narratives give students additional information to help them make appropriate decisions and allow faculty directors to set academic and travel expectations. Include the following topics:

- Location(s) and dates, including departure and return dates. Give students an idea of how much travel is required.
- Description of academic course: learning objectives, integration of sites, prerequisites, and evaluation methods. What will students learn?
- Program structure: what to expect during the program. What will a typical day be like?
- Faculty director information: brief biography and previous international experience.
- Housing and meals. Where will students live? What will they eat?
- Cost. What does the program fee cover?
- Information on how to apply.

Place the brochures at various locations around campus, including:
- ✓ near the registrar's office;
- ✓ in appropriate academic department offices;
- ✓ in residence hall lobbies; and
- ✓ in other appropriate offices (e.g., the women's center for a course that counts toward Women's Studies majors and minors).

Other methods of getting the word out about your short-term programs abroad include the following:
- Student newspaper. Ask the student newspaper to run articles promoting your programs.
- Department newsletters. Include information about specific short-term courses abroad in departmental newsletters.
- Posters. Put posters on visible bulletin boards around campus.
- Tabling. Set up tables in prominent locations and ask past program participants to hand out printed information to interested students.

◆ Intercampus mail. Send course descriptions to specific majors and minors, to specific student clubs (e.g., the Pre-Law Club may be very interested in a "Law in London" course), and to academic counselors and faculty academic advisers.

Message Centers

Is there is a place on your campus where students regularly look for announcements—perhaps an electronic message board in the cafeteria? If so, be sure to post information about your short-term programs there.

Electronic Information

◆ Put information about courses, application procedures, deadlines, etc., on your office Web site.
◆ Ask the faculty director to put information about the course on his or her departmental Web site. Encourage the faculty director to highlight the information, not just list it along with all of the on-campus departmental offerings.
◆ Set up and use an office e-mail address to which students can direct inquiries, and make sure that someone in your office checks it regularly and responds to all inquiries.
◆ Some office on your campus has the ability to send an e-mail to all matriculated students—most likely it is the registrar's office. Ask a staff member from this office to send an announcement to all students as you approach your application deadline. The following paragraph is a sample:

INTERIM 2003 OPEN HOUSE

The Open House for the January 2003 international and domestic off-campus interims will be held in the Black and Gold Ballroom from 4:30 p.m. to 6:30 p.m. on Wednesday, September 12. Faculty instructors for the courses will be available to answer questions about the interims and assist students in completing application forms.

The DEADLINE for applications for the 2003 off-campus interims is October 5. Some interims are already closed based on registrations completed last spring. Please consult the International Office for up-to-date information on open and closed courses.

Call x1234 or stop in at the international office if you have questions.

E-mail Aliases

Find out if your institution creates an e-mail alias for each course. If so, use those aliases to send e-mail messages about programs that may be of interest to students taking certain classes. For example, you could send information about an anthropology program in Guatemala to all of the students currently registered for Cultural Anthropology.

Open Houses

Arrange at least one Open House at which you promote all of your short-term programs abroad. Ask faculty directors to be present and invite past participants, if they are available. Faculty can bring photos, maps, and souvenirs from the location; play some regional music; or put on a slide show or Power Point presentation. Encourage the faculty to be creative.

Ask students to sign lists expressing interest in particular programs. These interest lists can be used to help recruit students later, should the need arise.

Class Visits

Encourage faculty directors to visit classes that would be natural feeders to the short-term course abroad. If the course gives fourth level French credit, talk with the students currently in the third level classes.

Miscellaneous Tips for Marketing Your Program

Application Process

Make the application process for your short-term programs abroad as user friendly as possible. The Type One student will be happy to complete an 18-page form; the Type Three student may give up on page 3. Make your instructions clear and concise and ask only for the information you really need; if you want students to print an unofficial transcript from the Web, tell them how to do it. Do not compromise your selection standards but do your best not to put up any roadblocks.

Admissions Office

Encourage your admissions office to include information about your programs in their publicity materials. The programs can be great recruitment tools for the institution and can give you a good head start on marketing.

Language

Choose and use your language carefully. Do not make reference to "trips" or "tours." Emphasize that your programs are academic programs and/or courses.

The Surprise

You may be surprised to find that those reluctant students—the Type Two and Type Three students—come back from their experiences as Type One students. They return with a newfound confidence in themselves and their ability to study in another culture and will often apply for other short-term or even semester- or year-long programs.

Conclusion

One last piece of advice—never get so carried away with your marketing that you promise things you cannot deliver. Nothing will destroy the reputation of a program more quickly than unhappy returned student participants. Market your programs reasonably and honestly and deliver what you promise. This will create a pool of satisfied customers—and they are the best marketing tools of all!

Chapter 11

Student Selection and Enrollment

Sarah E. Spencer

The short-term program has been approved and developed, and the budget is in place. Now you are ready to select and enroll students!

As the number of short-term programs abroad has increased in the last decade, so have the systems that enroll students in these courses. In the past, "first-come, first-deposit-down," was enough to get a student on a program. Now, many students must submit application dossiers, write essays, and sit for full interviews.

As with most aspects of short-term programming, agreeing on the requirements and systems before marketing to the students and clearly articulating the selection criteria and other enrollment pieces will reduce your organization's liability, limit questions from confused students, and create a better experience for all.

Why Do You Need a Selection Process?

If you are a faculty member without an international office to support your program, or if you are an administrator without oversight of a short-term program, everything tells you to forgo the selection process. You know the students, the faculty director does not want the hassle, and there is little time to recruit students. However, you should have a process to select students even if you are directing only one course or administrating multiple programs. Why?

+ A selection process ensures seriousness among the students because they cannot take their participation for granted. This reinforces the academic quality of the program.
+ The process articulates the policies and procedures of the program and the institution before the student applies.
+ A selection process creates a system where the best-qualified and best mix of students can be assembled.
+ By following a clear enrollment procedure, students can be treated fairly and uniformly.
+ If you are administering more than one program abroad, it is important to have an efficient system that is endorsed by your organization and works to manage future program growth.

The short-term application and approval timeframe also ensures time to enroll enough participants and finalize logistics. For example, if your program departs June 1, and as of April 15 you have four students enrolled, will you be able to make the budget work? Can you maintain your group airline reservations, which require a minimum of ten seats?

Admissions Processes

Before designing enrollment materials such as an application, course description, or policies and procedures, you need to determine what kind of admissions process will be in effect.

Admission by Selection

Students submit a full application dossier, which is reviewed by the faculty director or a selection committee. The review occurs after all application dossiers have been submitted and produces the best balance of students, but it is the most time consuming.

Deadlines must be set and adhered to because students will be submitting materials. This system works well if you must select from a large pool of applicants.

Admission by "Rolling" Procedures

Rolling admission, or "first-come, first-money-down," was common for short-term programs when first developed. This process allows the faculty director to immediately accept students and know how many students have been recruited. If you are operating in a consortium, rolling admission is logistically straightforward when distance and different institutions make communication a challenge.

However, rolling admission with minimal eligibility requirements may create a perception of "sign-the check; go-on-the-course," without any serious thought from the student. Be aware of this as you develop application and recruiting materials. You can never eliminate the student who chooses a course based solely on geographic locale or weather, but with emphasis on course content and with academic expectations clearly defined before a student applies, you may be able to reduce the number of students who should be going on spring break, not study abroad.

Admission by Seniority

For oversubscribed or popular short-term programs abroad, the least time consuming process is admission by seniority. By following the official registration list used by your institution, students are enrolled as they would be for an on-campus course.

This process eliminates much of the work, and creates an equitable system exactly like the one used on campus. However, it is a "blind" selection, and faculty directors give up their authority to select students for an overseas experience.

In summary, you will find that institutions offering short-term programs are moving toward admission by selection. This process allows faculty directors to get to know students and to discuss the motivations and goals for the students' study abroad experience. It also helps to weed out students with potential behavior problems and allows students to ask questions about the program and the process.

Eligibility Requirements and Selection Criteria

Student Eligibility

Before planning any study abroad program, eligibility requirements must be outlined and consistently adhered to. Most programs set these requirements to ensure that nondeserving students (i.e., those on disciplinary probation or not academically qualified) are not accepted. The following may be considered:

- Institutional/organizational policies (e.g., students currently on academic or disciplinary/conduct probation may not be able to study abroad).
- Grade point average (GPA) minimums: your institution may require a minimum GPA to study abroad, or there may be differences in the GPAs required to participate in short-term and longer-term study abroad. Many institutions require students to maintain a minimum GPA of 2.0, with higher GPAs required for upper-level courses.
- Course prerequisites.
- Other policies set by the administrative office or faculty director.

Criteria for Selection

To reduce liability and to articulate to students how they will be selected—similar to an academic course where criteria are documented on how students will be evaluated—selection criteria must be published and used. Criteria may include:

- academic preparation and strength;
- sense of maturity, responsibility, and citizenship;
- ability to describe how the study abroad experience will apply to academic and personal goals; and
- knowledge of proposed destination and culture; applicants should be prepared to provide some factual information from both historical and current perspectives.

It is important to develop an admissions process in which the selection criteria can be applied.

The Application and Approval Process

The goal of a defined application and approval process is to collect information necessary to screen applications and the personal and academic information necessary to administer the program, such as the student's emergency contact. You also want to collect any permissions required

> Regardless of what process and materials you use, require students to submit complete application dossiers!

to access records, waive Family Education Rights and Privacy Act (FERPA) rights, and have students agree to your policies and procedures. This process also streamlines short-term programs into the semester- and year-long study abroad procedures that already exist on your campus.

Before designing application materials, the eligibility and selection criteria and the admissions procedures must be identified. Once the criteria and procedures are in place, application materials must be created and you must determine who will collect the materials. Materials may include the following:

Application/information sheet.
- Provides necessary student information, emergency contact information, and data required for statistical analysis.
- Serves as a contract between the student and the organization. The student's signature allows administrators to access disciplinary records and bill student accounts for the program fee.
- Allows you to check whether the student has a passport, and if the student is a non-U.S. citizen, allows you to take steps to get any necessary visas.

◆ Gives permission to register students, if applicable.
◆ Contains FERPA waiver.

See the sample "Application for Short-Term Study Abroad" at the end of this chapter.

Policies and procedures. The policies and procedures document defines what information the student should be responsible for before he or she applies for a program and the administrative procedures required after the student is accepted. Possible topics include:

◆ Philosophy of short-term programs abroad
◆ Policies for student participation
◆ Academic information
    Course credit
    Grading
    Program evaluation
    Taking courses pass/fail
    Registration information
    Auditing courses
    Nondegree students
◆ Enrollment information
    Application dates
    How to apply
    Wait-list students
    Confirmation of courses
    Transferring between courses
    FERPA and study abroad
◆ Financial Matters
    Program costs
    Comprehensive program fee
    Exclusions
    Administrative fee
    Payment schedules
    Cancellation and refunds
    Financial aid
◆ Health and safety concerns
    Proof of sufficient insurance
    Insurance coverage abroad
    Student Identification Card
    Required and recommended immunizations
◆ Orientation information
◆ Travel information
    Flight deviations
    Visas
◆ Passport information

FERPA and Study Abroad

Many administrators ignore the Family Education Rights and Privacy Act (FERPA) of 1974, as amended, which affords students the right to authorize the release of education information to third parties. You will want to make a decision, in consultation with your FERPA expert (registrar, legal counsel) if you will request that students waive their FERPA rights before they study abroad. Such a statement might read:

(Administrator) requests that students authorize the release of education information to third parties by signing the application for "Short-Term Study Abroad." Students sign to the following statement and direct questions to the international education office:

I understand that the Family Education Rights and Privacy Act of 1974 (FERPA), as amended, affords students the right to authorize the release of education information to third parties. I also understand that studying abroad may involve circumstances which require (administrator) to release certain information to third parties, but for which it may be difficult to obtain my prior written permission. For these reasons, I herewith authorize university officials to release my education information to parties who, in their judgment, have an interest in the study abroad contemplated by this document provided that those officials, in their judgment, are acting in my interests as well. This authorization is valid from the time I submit this signed document through a period of one semester after my program abroad ends.

Consortium application. If you are working with other institutions, the consortium should have one form that all students must complete.

Transcript (unofficial or official). The transcript allows for GPA verification and review of previous coursework. Students may be able to print an unofficial transcript from their institution's Web site.

Budget form. The budget form provides the financial aid office with required information for applying for additional financial aid.

Application fee or deposit. This fee or deposit is required to hold a place in the program, confirm the serious intent of the student, and be used to cover advance logistical payments.

Essay or personal statement. Topic suggestions include (1) why the student wishes to participate in the study abroad program, and (2) the student's academic goals for the program and how do these academic goals fit with his or her professional and personal goals?

Application checklist. If you manage multiple programs or wish to communicate clearly regarding application materials an application checklist will be helpful.

Sample Application Checklist

- Download application forms using Adobe Acrobat Reader. Print and keep "Short-Term Policies and Procedures," which contains important information such as cancellation fees and passport information.
- Submit application materials to (<u>administrator or faculty director</u>). Incomplete application dossiers will not be accepted.

All courses require the following:

a. **Short-Term Application.**
b. **Study Abroad Agreement.** Parent signature required on page 2, if student is considered a dependant for income tax purposes. Submit **one copy** with your application and keep one for your records.
c. **Unofficial Transcript.**
d. **Receipt for $350 Deposit.** Use the attached <u>deposit voucher</u> when making your $350 payment to the business office.
e. **Two ID Photos.** These photos are not for your passport! You are responsible for applying for your passport.
f. **Essay.**
g. **Course-Specific Materials.**
h. **Interview.** The faculty director will review application materials; not all applicants are guaranteed an interview.

Interview Guidelines

If students are interviewed, the following guidelines should be adhered to:

- It is important that interviews are conducted in an unbiased manner, in order to give each student an equal opportunity.
- Interviews should be conducted with at least one other person. Possible committee members may include codirectors, other faculty directors, past student participants, or other appropriate faculty or staff.

- Students should be initially screened for academic and disciplinary probations and other prerequisites. Other application materials may be used to determine whether a student is selected for an interview.

Printed Materials Versus the Web

Current technology is constantly changing and many organizations are replacing application materials once available solely on paper with the Web as a 24-hour office for students. Web-based applications may require students to submit information electronically by inputting information into Web forms or may provide downloadable application materials such as an Adobe Portable Document Format file (.pdf file) that is printed, filled out, and submitted to the identified office or person.

There are many advantages to using the Web, including:
- increased flexibility in updating application materials;
- student access to application materials after office hours;
- shifting away paper and printing costs from the administrative office;
- marketing of related programs via students visiting your Web site;
- reduced phone time for staff (when enrollment procedures are clearly documented); and
- visibility for your organization's international programs via a Web presence.

The disadvantages, if you see them as disadvantages, are few. You should have a dedicated Web manager who will devote time to learn and then apply the necessary technology. Ideally you would choose someone who is familiar with the processes and programs in your office, so that you do not lose control of the Web site if someone else decides that it is not a priority.

- If you do not have a Web-dedicated employee, staff will be diverted from other activities.
- Communication that usually is verbal must be carefully transcribed for Web readership, again requiring staff time.
- Updating the Web content becomes a daily activity.
- Updating computer software and hardware is expensive.
- Training of staff can be expensive and time consuming.

Approving Students to Study Abroad

After the faculty director has accepted a student, and the student has been approved to study abroad by the administrator, the following steps may occur:

- Letter of acceptance, covering:
    - ✓ cancellation policy;
    - ✓ reminder of the academic/travel fusion and challenge of this kind of course;
    - ✓ status of passport;
    - ✓ orientation information;
    - ✓ required paperwork;
    - ✓ financial aid information and contact information;
    - ✓ travel logistics, including flight deviations;
    - ✓ billing and final payment information; and
    - ✓ registration and grading (pass/fail).

◆ Medical report. Provides personal health and insurance information to be reviewed by the faculty director. This information cannot be collected **before** a student is accepted to the program. See the example Short-Term Study Abroad Medical Report at the end of Chapter 16.

◆ Study abroad agreement or liability waiver. See examples in Chapter 16, Safeguards for Short-Term Programs.

◆ Other forms. These may include the Parental Waiver, host family information (if the program includes a home stay), registration materials, International Student Identity Card application, etc.

Faculty directors receive copies of emergency contact information, the signed liability waiver or agreement, and the medical report.

Application for Short-term Study Abroad
Undergraduate and Graduate Courses

Name as it will appear on passport (Last, First, Middle)			Social Security #	

Mail #	E-mail Address (School e-mail only)	Local Phone # ( )	Birthdate (Mo/Day/Year)	Sex ☐ Female ☐ Male

Response to the following is voluntary. Please check one to describe yourself. This information is used for general study abroad statisics.
Ethnicity/Race: ☐ American Indian/Alaskan Native ☐ African-American ☐ White, Non-Hispanic ☐ Multiracial
☐ Asian-American or Pacific Islander ☐ Hispanic-American ☐ Do not know

Course/Program Title	Academic term you plan to participate FA JT SP SU Yr _____

Local Address	City	State	Zip Code

Academic Status
☐ Undergrad Day ☐ School for Continuing Studies ☐ Graduate ☐ Non-Degree ☐ Other Institution _____

Present Year in School? 1 2 3 4 GRAD n/a	Year While Abroad 1 2 3 4 GRAD n/a	Academic major #1	Major #2	Minor #1	Minor #2	Cum. GPA

Name of Emergency Contact	Home Phone ( )	Work Phone ( )

Street Address	City	State	Zip Code

Are you a U.S. Citizen? ☐ Yes ☐ No	U.S. passport number and expiration date ☐ Do not have one yet	If you are a holder of a non-U.S. passport, which country is it from?

Where did you first hear about Study Abroad?	What foreign countries have you visited and for how long?

If you have a disability and require special on-site accommodations, you are strongly encouraged to contact the Enhancement Program or Specialized Services as soon as possible.

Your signature verifies the following:
1. I have completed the necessary prerequisites to enroll in this course.
2. Study Abroad programs require that applicants and participants are in good academic and disciplinary standing at the university, and I authorize the staff of (administrator) access to my academic and disciplinary records.
3. I authorize (administrator) to register me, upon acceptance, for the above listed study abroad course/program.
4. I authorize (administrator) to bill my student account. I understand that all cancellations must be submitted in writing.
5. I have read, understood and will abide to the terms of the *Policies & Procedures*, included with this application.
6. I understand that the Family Education Rights and Privacy Act of 1974 (FERPA), as amended, affords students the right to authorize the release of education information to third parties. I also understand that studying abroad may involve circumstances which require the institution to release certain information to third parties, but for which it may be difficult to obtain my prior written permission. For these reasons, I herewith authorize university officials to release my education information to parties who, in their judgment, have an interest in the study abroad contemplated by this document provided that those officials, in their judgment, are acting in my interests as well. This authorization is valid from the time I submit this signed document to International Education through a period of one semester after my program ends abroad.

Signature of Applicant	Date of Signature

Signature of Faculty Director	Date of Signature

This application must be completed and returned to _____

OFFICE USE ONLY
Apply Date _____
Received By _____

Attach photos here

[Source: Adapted from University of St. Thomas]

Chapter 12

"It Changed My Life": Strategies for Assessing Student Learning

Patrick Quade

"It changed my life." This conclusion to an off-campus study experience often stands as the total validation of the academic program for students. Students do experience transformations through their immersion in off-campus study programs and we all have witnessed an increase in their intellectual abilities through the structured academic, experiential learning offered on these great programs. However, students, study abroad professionals, and even faculty often find it difficult to quantify or document this growth. Often the distinctions between academic progress and personal growth through experiential learning become blurred.

The character of Tom in Tennessee Williams' play, *The Glass Menagerie*, states early on in the play, "Yes, I have tricks in my pocket, I have things up my sleeve. But I am the opposite of a stage magician. He gives you illusion that has the appearance of truth. I give you truth in the pleasant disguise of illusion."[1] A premise for assessment of any kind should have as its goal the capacity to distinguish truth from illusion, especially in the "It changed my life" statement. All of us want our students to discover the truth, not the illusion. This chapter is intended to provide students, faculty, and off-campus study professionals with a process for developing strategies that will strengthen methods for assessing the various values and documenting the success of short-term programs abroad. The approach is complete with exercises and sample materials to provide the reader with both a theoretical basis and practical implementation suggestions to assist the student, faculty member, and international office in developing a workable strategy for assessing student learning and program quality.

As professionals involved in study abroad, we have an obligation to provide our students and our colleagues with the opportunity and the tools to quantify, reflect, and document all of the possible outcomes from the increasingly popular (and increasingly expensive) off-campus opportunities. We need to develop and employ a comprehensive strategy and efficient methods to assess student learning in all dimensions of the academic and intercultural experience and not be satisfied with superficial and often anecdotal sentiments of student satisfaction with off-campus study programs. The existing research base to begin the development of this task has the capacity to provide a foundation for us today. Institutions are genuinely interested in developing instruments for the assessment of the experiential cultural growth and development that claims to be so transformational for our students. The reader is encouraged to consult the listserv of the Section on U.S. Students Abroad (SECUSSA-L) and the NAFSA archives for a wide range of documents and current research pertaining to assessment for off-campus study programs.

---

[1] Williams, Tennessee (1945). "The Glass Menagerie," in *Six Modern American Plays* (Act I). New York: Random House.

Four interconnected dimensions for those involved in short-term programs abroad are (1) the academic core, (2) development of intercultural competence, (3) logistics involved in all parts of the program, and (4) assessment of program quality. These four core areas each suggest differing sets of objectives, strategies, instruments, and possible outcomes. For the purposes of this chapter, the writer makes the following assumptions:

- The short-term program is designed around a specific academic course offered by a home-institution faculty member.
- The short-term program is between 3 and 5 weeks in duration, although not necessarily all of that time is spent in the off-campus environment.
- The program site is a significant factor for the academic discipline examined by the students and faculty member. The same course could not be offered in an on-campus environment. The site for the program may be international or domestic.
- The students will have substantive predeparture and reentry sessions connected with the program.
- Structured experiential learning is among the primary pedagogical styles used in the course.
- In addition to assessing individual learning, the individuals involved in the short-term programs are also interested in overall program quality.

A legitimate element in designing a strategy of assessment is to equip the faculty member with a profile for each student in the group so that the goals and standards used to assess student learning take into account those factors of individual characteristics that will influence assignments and measures needed to reflect individual differences. The following listing indicates those specific details that you may wish to consider when looking at any of the elements in the assessment strategy:

- ✓ Gender
- ✓ Year in college
- ✓ Age
- ✓ Previous experience abroad
- ✓ Previous experience in this particular country
- ✓ Previous academic work related to this off-campus study opportunity
- ✓ Internship opportunity
- ✓ Course fulfilling major requirement
- ✓ Course fulfilling general education requirement
- ✓ Elective credit
- ✓ Island program
- ✓ Immersion program
- ✓ Site details
- ✓ Home-stay opportunity
- ✓ Orientation, reentry
- ✓ Language base
- ✓ Additional opportunities (field trips, interactive opportunities)

Of course, the faculty member must also determine who will assess the students and whether the students will assess themselves or be assessed. Consider the following options:
- Student self-evaluation
- Faculty (on-site) evaluation

♦ Faculty on-campus evaluation of student progress
♦ Student portfolio

Let's begin by looking at a brief essay that appeared on the SECUSSA electronic sampling results Web site, authored by Donald Rubin and Richard Sutton at the University of Georgia and quoted in the spring 2001 edition of *International Educator* magazine:

Assessing Student Learning Outcomes from Study Abroad

Study abroad can be one of the most powerful experiences in a student's education. International educators know from observation, example, anecdote, and personal involvement that living and learning in another country can exert profound influence on an individual. Research and evaluation studies over the past three decades have closely examined effects of such international exposure on students. Although the results of those studies are by no means unequivocal, existing research literature warrants the conclusion that studying abroad can enhance many affective or attitudinal outcomes such as students' ethno-relativism, global-mindedness, and sense of self-efficacy.

We are on less firm ground in documenting the effects of study abroad on students' learning outcomes. How have a student's knowledge, thinking skills, and processing abilities improved as a result of studying overseas? Here, the efforts to assess what students have learned face many of the same challenges international educators confront in trying to demonstrate the learning outcomes of general education, the core curriculum, or liberal studies. Those in the field believe intuitively (and in most cases are convinced absolutely) that there are definite learning outcomes associated with successful completion, yet it is difficult to clearly articulate expectations, find ways to measure the achievement by students, and identify factors that influence success or failure.

The centrality of study abroad to undergraduate education will be greatly strengthened when educators can document more effectively its impact on students' academic success, mastery of knowledge, powers of reasoning, critical thinking skills, and intellectual capacity—that is, when educators can show that a veteran of study abroad is not just more well-rounded but also better educated. This evidence can have particular relevance among constituencies who have viewed the overseas experience as, at best, a marginal supplement to academic endeavors. If study abroad can be shown to add meaningful value to the core goals of postsecondary learning, it will cease being a choice that only one percent of U.S. students make. Rather, it will become an integral part of college to which every serious student aspires.

Those in the field of international education believe the field will benefit from new research studies that focus on student learning outcomes. Several such studies are underway, incorporating a variety of design elements that can shed light on different aspects of the learning process abroad. For example, the University System of Georgia has recently initiated a multi-year learning outcomes assessment that incorporates analyses of students transcripts as well as self-reported learning. It compares study abroad participants' knowledge before and after the overseas experiences, and it also compares participants with non-participants. Detailed information about academic, logistical, and co-curricular aspects of programs can then be correlated with learning outcomes. Research designs such as this will hopefully yield substantive knowledge about the impact of study abroad on student learning outcomes that will advance debate on, and advocacy for, the value of international education.[2]

---

[2] Rubin, Donald L. and Richard Sutton (Spring 2001-Volume X, Number 2). Assessing Student Learning Outcomes from Study Abroad, *International Educator*, NAFSA: Association of International Educators, Washington, D.C., 31-32. Used by permission.

The Academic Core

Prior to beginning the task of looking at the first dimension, the core academic experience, it will be helpful to place the learning to be measured in context. One of the most effective tools for this purpose is the Teaching/Learning Goals Inventory developed by Thomas A. Angelo and K. Patricia Cross, and published in *Classroom Assessment Techniques*.[3] The inventory appears at the end of this chapter. The inventory takes a few minutes for the faculty member to complete, but the results enable the faculty member to take a particular course and examine it from the perspective of what he or she truly hopes students will learn. This process gives the faculty member the overarching standards from which to assess student learning.

The faculty member competent in the specific subject area, familiar with the potential to develop that area on site and equipped with a well-defined set of instructional goals along with an accurate profile of students, is prepared to design the short-term study program. This preparation will enable the instructor to structure the course to assist students in developing specific cognitive skills such as creative thinking, comparative models, or systems approaches. Or perhaps the goals will focus more specifically in regard to cross-cultural skills such as cross-cultural communication and awareness of new values and perspectives coupled with critical examination of the host country and the student's own culture. Of course, the professor will detail the specific knowledge and academic skills in his or her field and aid the students in coming to new insights and understanding.

The process of defining instructional goals should not ignore specific knowledge about the host country's human and natural geography, government, societal norms, and value systems.

The following list provides some specific assessment tools to measure instructional goals in addition to specific academic objectives of the course. Again, with gratitude to Thomas Angelo and Patricia Cross and used by permission.

- Create an annotated bibliography.
- Create a brochure or poster.
- Create a budget with full rationale.
- Create a case study or analysis.
- Create a cognitive map, web, or diagram.
- Write a contemplative essay.
- Engage in a debate.
- Create a diary of a fictional or historical character.
- Write an article for publication.
- Create a flowchart.
- Engage in a group discussion.
- Create an instructional manual.
- Write a letter to the editor.
- Create a lesson plan to teach others.
- Create a multimedia presentation.
- Prepare a research proposal for a grant agency.
- Develop a review of the literature.
- Develop a summit conference within the class.
- Prepare a term paper.
- Create a work of art, architecture, or sculpture.
- Use traditional techniques of:
  - ✓ an essay exam,
  - ✓ a multiple choice exam,
  - ✓ a series of quizzes,
  - ✓ a matching test, or
  - ✓ a term paper.
- Deliver an oral report.
- Develop a project associated with the learning.

---

[3] Angelo, T. A. and Cross, K. P. (1993). *Classroom Assessment Techniques*. San Francisco: Jossey-Bass. Used by permission.

At this point in preparing a short-term course abroad, the academic, cross-cultural, and student learning goals will benefit from a conscientious approach using the pedagogy of the experiential learning model. The reader is referred to Chapter 15, Orientation and Reentry, Academic, for a discussion of Dr. David Kolb's model for developing a quality experiential learning program.

The faculty member armed with theory of experiential learning, their personal, course-specific results from the teaching/learning goals inventory, and a keen awareness of the students enrolled in the course is prepared to design his or her own course goals, assignments, and assessment tools that will make it possible to measure both the capacity for learning and the actual learning that has taken place on an off-campus study program. The end result is to enable the faculty member to assess just what a student *knows* and is able to *do* at the end of a course.

Of course, this more elaborate approach can be augmented with the regular course/faculty evaluation forms used on most college and university campuses (see the "Course/Faculty Evaluation Form" at the end of this chapter). The goal, remember, is to determine the academic competency of the student learning in the off-campus environment.

Development of Intercultural Competence

The second major dimension to examine is that of intercultural competency. Janet and Milton Bennett and Mitchell Hammer have conducted the major influence in this area of research and assessment and the author uses their model of intercultural competence as the standard resource in this area. In addition to the academic skills acquired in a short-term program abroad, another essential core of our efforts is the desire to provide the student with the opportunity to gain intercultural competency, enabling the student to understand other cultures and his or her own. It is in this area more than any other that we need to provide students with accessible tools and assessment techniques to assist them in reaching a clear understanding of their personal growth and development. It is primarily in coming to grips with their own level of intercultural competency that the truth will replace the illusion of how the short-term study experience actually changed their lives.

I quote extensively from the Bennett's work (with their permission) first published in 1986, to provide the reader with the background theory and practical aspects of the Developmental Model of Intercultural Sensitivity (DMIS) (See the Bennett Model at the end of this chapter).

The first reading is from an article entitled "Intercultural Communication: A Current Perspective" by Milton Bennett, which appeared in *Basic Concepts of Intercultural Communication* published by Intercultural Press, Inc.

When people anticipate doing something cultural of an evening, their thoughts turn to art, literature, drama, classical music, or dance. In other words, they plan to participate in one of the institutions of culture-behavior that has become routinized into a particular form. I refer to this aspect of culture as "Culture writ large," with a capital "C." The more academic term that is used by most writers is objective culture . Other examples of objective culture might include social, economic, political, and linguistic systems—the kinds of things that usually are included in area studies or history courses. The study of these institutions constitutes much of the curriculum in both international and multicultural education. For instance, courses in Japanese culture or African American culture are likely to focus on the history, political structure, and arts of the groups. While this is valuable information, it is limited in its utility to the face-to-face concerns of intercultural communication. One can know a lot about the history of a culture and still not be able to communicate with an actual person from that culture. Understanding objective culture may create knowledge, but it doesn't necessarily generate competence.

The less obvious aspect of culture is its subjective side—what we can call "culture writ small." Subjective culture refers to the psychological features that define a group of people-their everyday thinking and behavior—rather than to the institutions they have created. A good working definition of subjective culture is the learned and shared patterns of beliefs, behaviors, and values of groups of interacting people. Understanding subjective cultures—one's own and others'—is more likely to lead to intercultural competence.

Of course, social reality is constructed of both large and small "c," aspects of culture; people learn how to behave through socialization into the institutions of the culture, which leads them to behave in ways that perpetuate those same institutions. As noted above, traditional international and multicultural education tends to focus only on the objective mode of this process; in contrast, intercultural communication focuses almost exclusively on the subjective mode. For instance, interculturalists are concerned with language use in cross-cultural relationships, rather than in linguistic structure. They study how language is modified or supplanted by culturally defined nonverbal behavior, how cultural patterns of thinking are expressed in particular communication styles, and how reality is defined and judged through cultural assumptions and values. In the following pages, examples in each of these areas will illustrate how understanding subjective culture can aid in the development of skills in cultural adaptation and intercultural communication.

Levels of Culture

The definition of subjective culture also provides a base for defining "diversity" in a way that includes both international and domestic cultures at different levels of abstraction. National groups such as Japanese, Mexican, and U.S. American and pan-national ethnic groups such as Arab and Zulu are cultures at a high level of abstraction—the qualities that adhere to most (but not all) members of the culture are very general, and the group includes a lot of diversity. At this level of abstraction we can only point to general differences in patterns of thinking and behaving between cultures. For instance, we might observe that U.S. American culture is more characterized by individualism than is Japanese culture, which is more collectivist.

While cultural difference at a high level of abstraction provides a rich base for analyzing national cultural behavior, there are significant group and individual differences within each national group that are concealed at this level. These differences provide a diversifying force that balances the unifying force of national culture.

At a lower level of abstraction, more specific groups such as ethnicities can be described in cultural terms. In the United States, some of these groups are African American, Asian American, American Indian, Hispanic/Latino American, and European American. People in these groups may share many of the broad national culture patterns while differing significantly in the more specific patterns of their respective ethnicities. It should be noted that in terms of subjective culture, ethnicity is a cultural rather than a genetic heritage; dark skin and other Negroid features may make one "black," but that person has not necessarily experienced African American enculturation. Most black people in the world are not American in any sense. Similarly, "whites" are not necessarily European American, although in the

United States it is difficult for them to escape being socialized in the patterns that are currently dominant in U.S. American society.

Other categories of subjective cultural diversity usually include gender, regionality, socioeconomic class, physical ability, sexual orientation, religion, organization, and vocation. The concept can embrace other long-term groupings such as single parents or avid sports fans, as long as the groups maintain the clear patterns of behavior and thinking of an "identity group." By definition, individuals do not have different cultures; the term for patterns of individual behavior is "personality."

Stereotypes and Generalizations

Whenever the topic of cultural difference is discussed, the allegation of stereotyping usually is not far behind. For instance, if cultural patterns of men and women are being compared, someone may well offer that she is a woman and doesn't act that way at all.

Stereotypes arise when we act as if all members of a culture or group share the same characteristics. Stereotypes can be attached to any assumed indicator of group membership, such as race, religion, ethnicity, age, or gender, as well as national culture. The characteristics that are assumedly shared by members of the group may be respected by the observer, in which case it is a positive stereotype. In the more likely case that the characteristics are disrespected, it is a negative stereotype. Stereotypes of both kinds are problematic in intercultural communication for several obvious reasons. One is that they may give us a false sense of understanding our communication partners. Whether the stereotype is positive or negative, it is usually only partially correct. Additionally, stereotypes may become self-fulfilling prophecies, where we observe others in selective ways that confirm our prejudice.

Despite the problems with stereotypes, it is necessary in intercultural communication to make cultural generalizations. Without any kind of supposition or hypothesis about the cultural differences we may encounter in an intercultural situation, we may fall prey to naive individualism, where we assume that every person is acting in some completely unique way. Or we may rely inordinately on "common sense" to direct our communication behavior. Common sense is, of course, common only to a particular culture. Its application outside of one's own culture is usually ethnocentric.

Cultural generalizations can be made while avoiding stereotypes by maintaining the idea of preponderance of belief. Nearly all possible beliefs are represented in all cultures at all times, but each different culture has a preference for some beliefs over others. The description of this preference, derived from large-group research, is a cultural generalization. Of course, individuals can be found in any culture who hold beliefs similar to people in a different culture. There just aren't so many of them—they don't represent the preponderance of people who hold beliefs closer to the norm or "central tendency" of the group.

Deductive stereotypes occur when we assume that abstract cultural generalizations apply to every single individual in the culture. While it is appropriate to generalize that U.S. Americans as a group are more individualistic than Japanese, it is stereotyping to assume that every American is strongly individualistic; the person with whom you are communicating may be a deviant. Cultural generalizations should be used tentatively as working hypotheses that need to be tested in each case; sometimes they work very well, sometimes they need to be modified, and sometimes they don't apply to the particular case at all. The idea is to derive the benefit of recognizing cultural patterns without experiencing too much "hardening of the categories."

Generalizing from too small a sample may generate an inductive stereotype. For example, we may inappropriately assume some general knowledge about Mexican culture based on having met one or a few Mexicans. This assumption is particularly troublesome, since initial cross-cultural contacts may often be conducted by people who are deviant in their own cultures. ("Typical" members of the culture would more likely associate only with their cultural compatriots—how they stay typical.) So generalizing cultural patterns from any one person's behavior (including your own) in cross-cultural contact is likely to be both stereotypical and inaccurate.[4]

In a paper presented at the Diversity Symposium in Boston, MA, in June 2001, Janet and Milton Bennett offered useful definitions for terms associated with culture, ethnicity, and race. Again, the extensive quotation below aids the reader in framing the context for working with the DMIS.

Like other authors preceding us, we have a disciplinary perspective which informs our work in diversity and which, in our case, emerges from the social science field of intercultural communication, the study of face-to-face interactions between people who are culturally different. Since intercultural communication draws heavily on psychology, anthropology, and sociology, it is inherently interdisciplinary. While none of us has a panacea for all the complexities of diversity, intercultural communication brings a particularly useful emphasis on the development of intercultural competence. In general terms, intercultural competence is the ability to communicate effectively in cross-cultural situations and to relate appropriately in a variety of cultural contexts. Developing this kind of competence is usually a primary goal of diversity initiatives in organizations, where it is assumed to contribute to effective recruitment and retention of members of underrepresented groups, management of a diverse workforce, productivity of multicultural teams, marketing across cultures, and to the development of a climate of respect for diversity in the organization.

Based on this subjective culture perspective, diversity is defined as cultural differences in values, beliefs, and behaviors learned and shared by groups of interacting people defined by nationality, ethnicity, gender, age, physical characteristics, sexual orientation, economic status, education, profession, religion, organizational affiliation, and any other grouping that generates identifiable patterns.

While the definition of subjective culture is fairly standard among diversity professionals, it does stimulate a variety of other questions about the meaning of culture. The first of these questions immediately arises from reading the above list: Where's race in this configuration? Two of the most challenging issues in diversity work are overcoming the idea that race is culture and overcoming racism itself. The latter issue will be examined later in this paper, but the definitional foundation of culture must be clarified, and the distinction between culture and race must be established.

The outdated view that biological characteristics somehow define the way people behave, think, and interact has now been thoroughly discredited by the recent genome studies. People do not behave the way they do primarily because of race, but rather because of cultural factors.

While this brief foundation cannot begin to address the power and complexity of race issues, it is vital for the diversity professional to recognize the distinction between self-identification and that designated by others. This self-identification may be entirely different from the designation given to the individual

---

[4] Bennett, Milton J. (1998) "Intercultural Communication: A Current Perspective," in *Basic Concepts of Intercultural Communication.* Selected Readings, edited by Milton J. Bennett. Yarmouth, ME, Intercultural Press, Inc., 3-8.

by observers. Diversity professionals must consistently attend to both the individual's self-perception and worldview on racial (and cultural) matters and to those likely designations assigned by others. Confusing the two is not wise.

Finally, just because race is not culture does not mean that the impact of color and white privilege can somehow be left out of diversity training. Our worldviews are heavily structured by our experience of culture, but they are also formed by our experience of color. The distinction between these two kinds of experience does not elevate one above the other; in fact, it is a necessary first step in the difficult task of minimizing the incidence of racism and privilege while simultaneously maximizing the appreciation of diversity.[5]

Milton Bennett first published his model of intercultural sensitivity in an article appearing in *Education for the Intercultural Experience* edited by Michael Paige.[6] This model is the core of intercultural competency assessment. The reader is encouraged to examine the model in its entirety in the original article. The reader will be well served in finding practical definitions, implications, and suggestions for development steps. As an additional step, I would encourage a representative from your institution to participate in the Intercultural Communication Institute Intercultural Development Inventory (IDI) Seminar to become certified to administer the IDI to students and faculty at your institution. This instrument is an ideal way to aid individuals in understanding their personal status and issues related to intercultural competency. The inventory is an excellent tool to use as a before-and-after measure for students prior to and following their participation in an off-campus program.

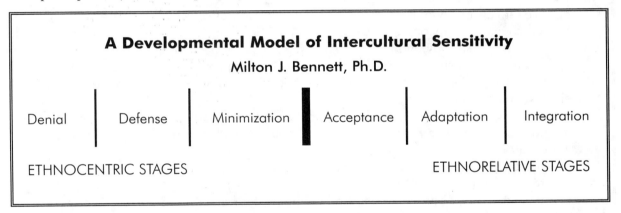

A Developmental Model of Intercultural Sensitivity
Milton J. Bennett, Ph.D.

| Denial | Defense | Minimization | Acceptance | Adaptation | Integration |

ETHNOCENTRIC STAGES   ETHNORELATIVE STAGES

Logistics

The third dimension is the logistics. The earlier chapters in this book provide models and examples for the planning and implementation of the myriad of details necessary to support short-term program abroad. Assessment models for this dimension are abundant, as most institutions already use an instrument that solicits information from the student regarding the nonacademic aspects of the off-campus study program. It is understood that although these elements are technically "nonacademic," they do play a crucial role in the overall success of the program. The reader is referred to the "International and Off-Campus Studies

---

5 Bennett, Janet M. and Bennett, Milton J. Developing Intercultural Sensitivity: An Integrative Approach to Global and Domestic Diversity. Paper presented at the Diversity Symposium, June 28-29, 2001, Boston, MA, 5–10.

6 Bennett, Milton J. (1993) "Towards Ethnorelativism: A Developmental Model of Intercultural Sensitivity." *Education for the Intercultural Experience*, edited by R. Michael Paige. 2nd edition. Yarmouth, ME, Intercultural Press, Inc.

Returning Student Evaluation" and the "Returning Student Questionnaire" found at the end of this chapter. Each of these instruments gets at slightly different aspects of an off-campus program.

Assessment of Program Quality

The final dimension in designing an assessment strategy for off-campus study is program review. The reader is encouraged to take advantage of existing documents that assist in program review from sources such as NAFSA: Association of International Educators and the Council on International Educational Exchange (CIEE). The reader is also referred to The Institute for the International Education of Students (IES) Model Assessment Practice. The Off-Campus Study Program Evaluation/Review in this chapter may also prove to be helpful.

Off-Campus Study Program Evaluation/Review

The criteria used to evaluate and review off-campus programs is based on information provided by (1) student feedback using formal evaluation instruments and oral debriefing sessions following the program, (2) faculty member written report and oral debriefing on faculty-led programs, and when appropriate, (3) the host evaluation and summary report.

Items that are included from the various information providers are:
1. The specific objectives of the course
2. The academic character of the course
   a) academic viability of host institution (accreditation status), when appropriate
   b) full course description, syllabus
   c) student course evaluations
   d) description of nature of instruction and types of learning experiences (lecture, seminar, field trips, experiential learning components, associated cultural events-theater, museum, etc.)
   e) curriculum vitae of instructor(s) in course
   f) how the course relates to general education, graduation and major requirements
   g) how the course integrates with the on-campus curriculum (prior to and following the program).
   h) the role of language learning in the program
3. Program staffing on site
   a) qualifications of administrators, staff members, tour agents and guides
   b) method of selection of home-stay families (if appropriate)
   c) opportunities for cultural immersion
   d) how are students prepared to understand and engage the culture and what opportunities are there to reflect on that cultural understanding
4. Health and safety issues
   a) specific health concerns, access to English speaking medical care
   b) insurance statements of coverage for any transportation carriers
   c) specific safety concerns of program site and methods used to manage risk
5. Enrollment patterns over past 3 years.
6. Program cost
7. How the course fits into geographic distribution compared with all other programs
8. Academic discipline(s) represented in the program
9. Student recruitment, selection, orientation, and reentry issues
10. Documentation of all details of course including examples of student work

[Source: Adapted from St. Olaf College]

Reporting of Conclusions

From these various sources the individual or individuals charged with the responsibility for assessing short-term programs abroad must formulate a case for the value of the program and develop the necessary documentation to validate the analysis of the information and data. This information should then be made available to a campus-based off-campus policy committee or the individuals and/or groups having the capacity for making necessary changes for the improvement of study abroad opportunities.

We should also remember that the long-term effects of study abroad represent an important dimension that has not been addressed in this chapter. The implications of the study abroad program for a student 5, 10, and more years after the experience can be substantial.

And finally, the ultimate value of implementing this strategy is to provide substantive assessment for students, faculty, and the institution and provide legitimate supporting data affirming the student's statement that the short-term off-campus study program did indeed, "CHANGE MY LIFE!"

Teaching/Learning Goals Inventory

Purpose: The Teaching/Learning Goals Inventory is an assessment of instructional goals. Its purpose is threefold: (1) to help teachers become more aware of what they want students to accomplish on off-campus study programs; (2) to help determine assessment techniques to assess how well students are achieving their learning goals; and (3) to provide a starting point for discussions of teaching and learning goals among colleagues.

Directions: Please select one short-term course in which you are currently involved. Respond to each item on the inventory in relation to that particular course. (Your responses might be quite different if you were asked about your overall teaching and learning goals, for example, or the appropriate instructional goals for your discipline.)

Title of the specific course you are focusing on:

_____

Rate the importance of each of the 51 goals listed below to the specific course you have selected. Assess each goal's importance to what you deliberately aim to have students accomplish, rather than the goal's general worthiness or overall importance to your institution's mission. There are no "right" or "wrong" answers; only personally more or less accurate ones.

For each goal, circle only one response on the 1-to-5 rating scale. You may want to read quickly through all 51 goals before rating their relative importance.

In relation to the program or course you are focusing on, indicate whether each goal you rate is:

(5)	*Essential*	A goal you always/nearly always try to achieve
(4)	*Very important*	A goal you often try to achieve
(3)	*Important*	A goal you sometimes try to achieve
(2)	*Unimportant*	A goal you rarely try to achieve
(1)	*Not applicable*	A goal you never try to achieve

PART I

Rate the importance of each goal to what you aim to have students accomplish in the course.
(Note: Only 5 items out of the 51 items can have a "5" [essential] rank.)

		5	4	3	2	1
1.	Develop ability to apply principles and generalizations already learned to new problems and situations	5	4	3	2	1
2.	Develop analytic skills	5	4	3	2	1
3.	Develop problem-solving skills	5	4	3	2	1
4.	Develop ability to draw reasonable inferences from observations	5	4	3	2	1
5.	Develop ability to synthesize and integrate information and ideas	5	4	3	2	1
6.	Develop ability to think holistically: to see the whole as well as the parts	5	4	3	2	1
7.	Develop ability to think creatively	5	4	3	2	1
8.	Develop ability to distinguish between fact and opinion	5	4	3	2	1
9.	Improve skill at paying attention	5	4	3	2	1
10.	Develop ability to concentrate	5	4	3	2	1
11.	Improve memory skills	5	4	3	2	1
12.	Improve listening skills	5	4	3	2	1
13.	Improve speaking skills	5	4	3	2	1
14.	Improve reading skills	5	4	3	2	1
15.	Improve writing skills	5	4	3	2	1
16.	Develop appropriate study skills, strategies, and habits	5	4	3	2	1

17. Improve mathematical skills	5	4	3	2	1
18. Learn terms and facts of this subject	5	4	3	2	1
19. Learn concepts and theories in this subject	5	4	3	2	1
20. Develop skill in using materials, tools, and/or technology central to this subject	5	4	3	2	1
21. Learn to understand perspectives and values of subject	5	4	3	2	1
22. Prepare for transfer or graduate study	5	4	3	2	1
23. Learn techniques and methods used to gain new knowledge in this subject	5	4	3	2	1
24. Learn to evaluate methods and materials in this subject	5	4	3	2	1
25. Learn to appreciate important contributions to this subject	5	4	3	2	1
26. Develop an appreciation of the liberal arts and sciences	5	4	3	2	1
27. Develop an openness to new ideas	5	4	3	2	1
28. Develop an informed concern about contemporary social issues	5	4	3	2	1
29. Develop a commitment to exercise the rights and responsibilities of citizenship	5	4	3	2	1
30. Develop a lifelong love of learning	5	4	3	2	1
31. Develop aesthetic appreciation	5	4	3	2	1
32. Develop an informed historical perspective	5	4	3	2	1
33. Develop an informed understanding of the role of science and technology	5	4	3	2	1
34. Develop an informed appreciation of other cultures	5	4	3	2	1
35. Develop capacity to make informed ethical choices	5	4	3	2	1
36. Develop ability to work productively with others	5	4	3	2	1
37. Develop management skills	5	4	3	2	1
38. Develop leadership skills	5	4	3	2	1
39. Develop a commitment to accurate work	5	4	3	2	1
40. Improve ability to follow directions, instructions, and plans	5	4	3	2	1
41. Improve ability to organize and use time effectively	5	4	3	2	1
42. Develop a commitment to personal achievement	5	4	3	2	1
43. Develop ability to perform skillfully	5	4	3	2	1
44. Cultivate a sense of responsibility for one's own behavior	5	4	3	2	1
45. Improve self-esteem/self-confidence	5	4	3	2	1
46. Develop a commitment to one's own values	5	4	3	2	1
47. Develop respect for others	5	4	3	2	1
48. Cultivate emotional health and well-being	5	4	3	2	1
49. Cultivate an active commitment to honesty	5	4	3	2	1
50. Develop capacity to think for one's self	5	4	3	2	1
51. Develop capacity to make wise decisions	5	4	3	2	1

In general, how do you see your primary role as a facilitator of short-term programs abroad? (Although more than one statement may apply, please circle only one.)

1. Teaching students facts and principles of the subject matter
2. Providing a role model for students
3. Helping students develop higher-order thinking skills
4. Preparing students for jobs/careers
5. Fostering student development and personal growth
6. Helping students develop basic learning skills

(Teaching/Learning Goals Inventory Continued)

PART II

Cluster number and name	Goals included in cluster	Total number of "essential" goals in each cluster	Cluster ranked– from 1st to 6th by number of "essential" goals
I Higher-order thinking skills	1-8	_____	_____
II Basic academic success skills	9-17	_____	_____
III Discipline-specific knowledge and skills	18-25	_____	_____
IV Liberal arts and academic values	26-35	_____	_____
V Work and career preparation	36-43	_____	_____
VI Personal development	44-51	_____	_____

PART III

Compute your cluster scores (average item ratings by cluster) using the following worksheet.

Cluster number and name	Goals included	Sum of ratings given to goals in that cluster	Divide C by this number	Your cluster scores
I Higher-order thinking skills	1-8	_____	8	_____
II Basic academic success skills	9-17	_____	9	_____
III Discipline-specific knowledge and skills	18-25	_____	8	_____
IV Liberal arts and academic values	26-35	_____	10	_____
V Work and career preparation	36-43	_____	8	_____
VI Personal development	44-51	_____	8	_____

[Source: Adapted, with permission, from Angelo, T. A. and Cross, K. P. (1993). *Classroom Assessment Techniques.* San Francisco: Jossey-Bass]

International and Off-Campus Studies Returning Student Evaluation

We are asking you to assist in the planning of future programs by completing this questionnaire. Please let us know any positive or negative aspects of the interim and how we can improve our assistance to you.

Thank you very much for your help.

_____
(Name of short-term study program)

_____   _____
(Department and course number)   (Instructor's name)

A) PERSONAL INFORMATION

1. What is your sex?   2. What is your age?   3. What is your class?

a. Female   a. 19   a. Sophomore
b. Male   b. 20   b. Junior
                       c. 21   c. Senior
                       d. 22   d. Special
                       e. Other: ___

4. What is your race: _____ 5. Major: _____
             (optional)

B) TRAVEL ARRANGEMENTS

1. Travel arrangements were generally:

	Excellent	Good	Fair	Poor
a. Air	1	2	3	4
b. Train	1	2	3	4
c. Bus	1	2	3	4
d. Van	1	2	3	4

Comments:

2. Accommodations were:

	Excellent	Good	Fair	Poor
a.	1	2	3	4
b.	1	2	3	4
c.	1	2	3	4
d.	1	2	3	4
e.	1	2	3	4
f.	1	2	3	4
g.	1	2	3	4
h.	1	2	3	4
i.	1	2	3	4

3. Program Itinerary

a. Places visited	1	2	3	4
b. Time spent in each place	1	2	3	4

Please list places you wish to comment on separately:

	Adequate	Too short	Too long
a._____	1	2	3
b._____	1	2	3
c._____	1	2	3
d._____	1	2	3
e._____	1	2	3

4. Were there any problems with visas ?
    (if applicable)

5. Do you plan on taking another off-campus program?

	International	Domestic
a. Interim	1	2
b. Semester or year program	1	2

C) GENERAL EVALUATION

1. There are many reasons why people study off-campus. We would like to know how important each of the following reasons was in influencing your decision.

	Extremely important	Somewhat important	Not important
a. To support academic goals	1	2	3
b. To explore career options	1	2	3
c. To heighten interest in community service	1	2	3
d. To broaden knowledge of specific geographical and cultural areas	1	2	3
e. To gain another perspective on the U.S.	1	2	3
f. To become acquainted with students from other places	1	2	3

2. Which of the above really happened on the interim?   Circle: a   b   c   d   e   f
       (Circle all that apply)

(International and Off-Campus Studies Returning Student Evaluation Continued)

3. Which one of the above reasons (a - f) was the most important influence in your decision to study off-campus?   Circle one: a b c d e f

	Exceptionally well	Reasonably well	Poorly
4. How well did this form of learning (experiential/ academic) suit you?	1	2	3
5. How well did the experience contribute to your understanding of the cultures involved?	1	2	3
6. How well did the academic and cultural experiences complement one another?	1	2	3

	Enough	Too Much	Too little
7. Opportunities for activities outside the curriculum (independent sight-seeing, local contacts, cultural functions):	1	2	3
8. Did study off-campus offer you resources which would not have been available if you had remained on campus during interim?	1	2	3

9. Would you recommend this course to a friend? Why or why not?

D) PREDEPARTURE INFORMATION AND ORIENTATION

	Excellent	Good	Fair	Poor	Did not attend
1. The orientation meetings with the interim instructor were:	1	2	3	4	5
2. Interim evening orientation:	1	2	3	4	5
3. Application assistance from the office of international and off-campus studies:	1	2	3	4	5
4. Availability of information concerning travel arrangements and accommodations	1	2	3	4	5

Comments:

5. Orientation materials (if provided) 1 2 3 4 5

a. If orientation materials were not provided, what should have been provided?

E) Miscellaneous

1. Is there anything necessary for your interim which was not provided?

    a. Yes b. No

Comments:

2. If you went on a domestic interim, did you do so because an international interim was too expensive?

    a. Yes b. No

3. How much did you spend in addition to the required program costs?

    a. Less than $500 b. $500-1000 c. $1000-$1500 d. more than $1500

4. Was the interim worth the cost?

    a. Yes b. No

Comments:

[Source: Adapted from St. Olaf College]

Returning Student Questionnaire

We are interested in maintaining high-quality international studies programs and in finding ways to improve them. An important way of doing this is to learn how the program affected individual student participants. Your responses to this questionnaire will allow you to reflect on the impact your study abroad experience had on you as well as provide insights that will help ensure that those who follow you will have as positive an experience as possible. Your responses will remain confidential. Your student number is included for research purposes only. Thank you.

International program: _____ Major: _____

Sex: 1 Male   Class: 1 Sophomore   Student number: _____
    2 Female   2 Junior   (Used for research purposes only.)
                   3 Senior
                   4 Special student

1. There are many reasons why students study abroad. We would like to know how important each of the following reasons was in influencing your decision to study abroad.

	Extremely important	Very important	Somewhat important	Not important
1) To support academic goals in your major.	1	2	3	4
2) To add diversity to your academic program	1	2	3	4
3) To explore options for your future.	1	2	3	4
4) To broaden your knowledge of specific geographical and cultural areas.	1	2	3	4
5) To gain another perspective on the U.S.	1	2	3	4
6) To gain a sense of self-confidence/ independence.	1	2	3	4
7) To take advantage of an opportunity to travel and see new places.	1	2	3	4

2. Which of the above (1-7) really happened on the the program?

(Circle ALL that apply.)
1 2 3 4 5 6 7

3. Which one of the above reasons (1-7) was most important influence in your decision study abroad?
(Circle ONE.)
1 2 3 4 5 6 7

Has your experience abroad:	Very much	Some-what	Little or not at all
4. Enhanced your foreign language skills?	1	2	3
5. Influenced your future plans?	1	2	3
6. Influenced a change in your lifestyle?	1	2	3
7. Altered your world view?	1	2	3
8. Increased your understanding of the U.S.?	1	2	3
9. Increased your feelings of self-confidence?	1	2	3
10. Increased your world political awareness?	1	2	3
11. Caused you to seriously consider living and/or working in another country?	1	2	3
12. Increased your desire to travel abroad?	1	2	3

13.	Increased your understanding of your self?	1	2	3
14.	Increased your ability to cope with and adapt to new and different situations?	1	2	3
15.	Altered your values, priorities, and goals?	1	2	3
16.	Heightened your interest in community service?	1	2	3
17.	Increased your knowledge of the country(ies) in which you studied?	1	2	3
18.	Increased your sensitivity to and understanding of news reports in the U.S. from countries you visited?	1	2	3
19.	Increased your appreciation for the study of foreign languages?	1	2	3
20.	Altered your academic direction?	1	2	3

		Exceptionally well	Reasonably well	Not very well	Poorly
21.	How well did the study abroad program contribute to your understanding of the culture(s) involved?	1	2	3	4
22.	How well did the academic components of your program and your own cultural interactions complement one another?	1	2	3	4
23.	How well did the program structure (e.g., organization, schedule, and activities) contribute to enhancing your experience?	1	2	3	4
24.	In retrospect, how well prepared were you for your study abroad experience?	1	2	3	4

		Excellent	Good	Fair	Poor
25.	PROGRAM ASSISTANCE. Please evaluate the following:				
1)	International and Off-Campus Studies catalog and other written information about programs	1	2	3	4
2)	Advising from International/Off-Campus Studies prior to application	1	2	3	4
3)	Applications and application process	1	2	3	4
4)	Selection process/interview	1	2	3	4
5)	Financial information	1	2	3	4
6)	Predeparture assistance from International/Off-Campus Studies	1	2	3	4
7)	Orientation	1	2	3	4

26. FINANCES.
    1) How much did you spend in addition to the required program costs?
        a. Less than $500   b. $500-$1,000   c. $1,000-$1,500   d. $1,500-$2,000   e. More than $2,000
    2) How much spending money would you recommend participants on this program take?
    _____

27. Would you recommend your program to other students? a. Yes   b. Maybe   c. No
    Why or why not?

28. What is the most important thing you have learned from this experience?

29. What should we do to incorporate a greater international perspective in <u>on-campus</u> courses?

[Source: Adapted from St. Olaf College]

Course/Faculty Evaluation Form

THE STUDENT

1. Class:
First year
Sophomore
Junior
Senior
Special

2. Gender:
a) Female
b) Male

3. How does this course fit into your academic program?
a) General or distribution requirements
b) Major/concentration requirement or elective
c) Elective (not in major or concentration)
d) Unsure
e) Other (specify: _____)

4. How much interest did you have in the subject matter before taking taking this course?
a) Almost none
b) Little
c) A fair amount
d) Much
e) An exceptional amount

5. Compared to other courses you have taken on-campus, the amount of effort you put in was:
a) Much less in this course
b) Somewhat less
c) About the same
d) Somewhat more
e) Much more in this course

6. Compared to other courses you have taken on-campus, the amount you learned was:
a) Much less in this course
b) Somewhat less
c) About the same
d) Somewhat more
e) Much more in this course

THE COURSE

	SD	D	DS	AS	A	SA	DK/DA
7. The course had clear objectives.	1	2	3	4	5	6	
8. The assigned reading material was helpful in meeting course objectives.	1	2	3	4	5	6	
9. The classroom sessions (lectures, discussions, etc.) and reading material worked well to complement one another.	1	2	3	4	5	6	
10. The assignments or papers made a significant contribution to learning in this course.	1	2	3	4	5	6	
11. The examinations reflected the important aspects in the course.	1	2	3	4	5	6	
12. The evaluation of students' work was fair and impartial.	1	2	3	4	5	6	
13. Students felt free to ask questions, disagree, and express their ideas in this course.	1	2	3	4	5	6	
14. The course provided a stimulating atmosphere for critical and independent thinking.	1	2	3	4	5	6	
15. The course stimulated my interest in the subject.	1	2	3	4	5	6	
16. The course material was well organized.	1	2	3	4	5	6	

THE INSTRUCTOR

17. Was skillful in helping students understand difficult topics.	1	2	3	4	5	6
18. Showed a genuine interest in students.	1	2	3	4	5	6
19. Provided helpful feedback on written work, when assigned.	1	2	3	4	5	6
20. Was sufficiently available for office hours and appointments.	1	2	3	4	5	6
21. Kept students adequately informed of their progress.	1	2	3	4	5	6
22. Returned written work with reasonable promptness.	1	2	3	4	5	6
23. Related the subject to other disciplines when appropriate.	1	2	3	4	5	6
24. Was effective in eliciting good classroom discussions.	1	2	3	4	5	6
25. Treated students with respect.	1	2	3	4	5	6
26. Provided an equitable learning environment for men and women.	1	2	3	4	5	6

OVERALL

	Excellent	Poor	Fair	Good	Very Good
27. How would you rate this instructor's teaching effectiveness?					
28. How would you rate this course overall?					

ADDITIONAL QUESTIONS

(Response options provided for up to 28 additional questions supplied by the course instructor.)

OPEN-ENDED ITEMS

What were the strengths of this instructor or course?

What suggestions do you have for improvements? (You may wish to discuss those items for which you darkened a disagree response on the reverse side.)

[Source: Adapted from St. Olaf College]

PART IV
Preparing to Travel

Chapter 13

The Role of the Faculty Director

Susan MacNally

Classroom teaching does not in itself prepare a faculty member for successfully directing a study abroad program. In addition to the role of teacher, the faculty director dons several hats. As the title "director" implies, there are administrative duties such as logistics, enrollment, and financial matters. The director is likely to encounter difficult and ambiguous situations requiring skills of leadership, interpretation, decision-making, and diplomacy that are rarely if ever faced in the classroom. Finally, by definition of "abroad" the program is removed—at least geographically—from support systems found back home; from university rules, policies, offices, and personnel; from colleagues and the home culture. On top of all this, the faculty director is working with students who are adjusting physically and emotionally to the new site, their group, and the culture they have come to learn about.

Preparing faculty directors includes advising them of the job duties and providing resources to help them think outside "the box" of the classroom and to consider course material in relation to the variables of time, activities, cultural learning, and student goals. Preparation encompasses training faculty in administrative procedures such as enrollment changes, bookkeeping, and protocol for student discipline. It is about helping faculty understand their role as intercultural guide and to recognize patterns of cultural adjustment in students. A faculty director must be able to uphold and implement institutional policies and positions on issues of discipline, alcohol, student privacy, and student health. Preparation involves coaching faculty to maintain a role of authority, establish a positive relationship with students, recognize potential problems, and resolve behavioral issues effectively. Finally, preparation is about ensuring that faculty directors understand and rely on the support systems on site and at the home campus that will help distribute the burden of all of these responsibilities.

The responsibilities are awesome, but the faculty director does not have to shoulder them all alone. Safety, responsibility, and liability concerns prompt us to advocate a model where the faculty director and the program are firmly connected to institutional and on-site support. Common sense tells us that the more responsibilities piled on one person, the greater the chances are for something to go wrong. Faculty preparation is as much about defining the institutional role as it is about defining the additional responsibilities the director must assume.

A good faculty preparation program will consist of establishing the director's responsibilities to the students and to the institution, grounding these responsibilities to support structures at the home institution and on site, and offering opportunities for faculty to develop skills to meet the challenges of directorship effectively.

Teaching Short-Term Off-Campus Courses: An Overview

William Hoffa

Teaching a diverse group of students in a foreign setting represents a huge challenge that you will likely find at times to be both time consuming and frustrating. No one should enter this work with the anticipation of accomplishing much scholarly research overseas—which, except in the rarest of circumstances, must be subordinated to prescribed teaching and administrative duties. Many personal and professional satisfactions, however, will come with the successful implementation of the program and the knowledge that the lives of U.S. students have been significantly enriched through the experience. In sum, although you will have to balance a wide variety of responsibilities and roles—teacher, intermediary, adviser, program administrator, and advocate for students—this enlarged faculty role brings with it ample additional rewards and gratifications from students, parents, your faculty counterparts, and your home institution. Faculty members who have directed past programs are almost universal in commenting on the unique professional development and personal rewards of living, traveling, and learning with students far from home, as well as the enhancement of their teaching on campus.

In his article, "It's Like Wearing All the Hats"[1] John C. O'Neal, professor of French and director of the Hamilton College Junior Year in France provides an insightful account of the demands of directing an overseas program. Professor O'Neal, serving his fourth year as director of the Hamilton program, likens the overseas experience to being college president and dean and academic adviser and lecturer and psychological counselor and accountant and even, in some cases, repairman. This perceptive article describes these multiple roles as a series of constantly shifting responsibilities for which adequate prior training is likely to be minimal and on-the-spot problem-solving ability, critical. Although some of what O'Neal says applies only to year-long, branch-campus programs, in point of fact, no matter how long or short the overseas experience, leadership demands remain surprisingly congruent whatever the length, location, or curricular focus.

As faculty director, you are the curricular *architect* of the program. Beyond this, you serve as *liaison*, *coordinator*, and *facilitator* among the many different constituencies and components of the program: home campus, students, on-site facilities, host families, the local and national government overseas, and last but not least, the host culture. What any given faculty member does obviously depends largely on the nature and purpose, the design and structure of the particular program she or he is directing.

Once overseas, you assume full *administrative* and *academic* responsibility for the integrity of the program, as well as *personal* responsibility for the well being of all students. You are the *legal representative* of your home institution for the period of the program. You may be asked to contact your home campus at intervals—by whatever means (e-mail, fax, phone)—with

---

[1] John C. O'Neal, "It's Like Wearing All the Hats" *ACADEME*, Sept./Oct. 1995

program updates, though many on-site decisions are inevitably left to your own judgment. As an administrator, you are responsible for the overall direction of the on-site program. Your on-site administrative responsibilities necessarily begin well before arrival. Housing assignments, special dietary arrangements, health issues, special needs accommodations—all must be dealt with well in advance of arrival.

Above all, you are responsible for the academic quality of the program and must be willing to assure those who need to know that the expectations of both participants and your home campus are being met. Your on-site supervision assures that academic quality comparable with home institution standards is being maintained. This may require extensive and structured student contact. You might schedule frequent one-on-one sessions with students, offer optional times for consultation, or set up optional or mandatory group discussions to process what has been read or seen. The daily schedule of teaching, student advising, and making logistical contacts with host organizations and individuals is likely to be rigorous and demanding.

Directing a study abroad program for participants who most likely have limited experience in a new culture provides a range of challenges that go far beyond what might be required at home. Participants will see you as a resource person who can alleviate the initial confusion and disorientation that confronts them and then guide them along the paths of new knowledge and cultural integration. It is very important to understand the variety of motivations that encourage students to study overseas; not all will be as purely academic as faculty would prefer. Indeed, the desire to "get away" from the academic pressures of the home campus may be as fundamental as a student's desire to test him- or herself in a new and "foreign" environment. Successful teaching and advising must acknowledge this complexity of student hopes and desires, providing counsel that balances the twin academic and experiential bases of international education.

You will need to be skilled in *diplomacy*, *logistics*, and *group dynamics*. You will invariably be asked to be a *cultural interpreter* and *analyst*, helping students understand what is going on and how it relates (or doesn't relate) to things back home. Unless there is someone else on the local scene who really knows the host country's social, cultural, and academic fabric, you must be prepared to take on the role of explaining it to students. Above all, you must be prepared to be a cheerful and supportive *friend-in-need* to students, not simply an authority figure. Whatever is prescribed and expected, chance and circumstance often rise up to demand yet additional imperatives and responsibilities.

Experience shows that the most successful faculty directors are those with the physical stamina to manage long hours and a high level of interaction with students and local contacts, the patience and good humor to deal with frequent frustrations, and the knowledge and independence to function well in a culture not their own. Fundamental to all of the above, you need to be an eager and committed *teacher* who knows how what you are teaching relates both to the home campus and to the culture of the host country. In sum, you are responsible for providing reasonable access to opportunities for both successful academic and personal experiences.

Due to the sensitive nature in acting as both advocate for the students and liaison among the distinct program components, you must exercise caution in personal matters concerning individual students. This is especially true during periods of emotional stress that some students may experience as they undergo cultural shock and learn strategies for adapting to a new cultural setting. Conversations with individual students must be regarded as confidential. Matters of particular concern are the violation of trust or privacy of students through the unauthorized sharing or disclosure of information; any act that can be interpreted as sexual harassment; or any discriminatory act reflecting prejudice based on sex, age, race, sexual orientation, or religious belief.

As faculty director, you are expected to behave as a trustworthy representative of your home institution abroad, and be conscious of what this implies. Dignity, decorum, tact, and discretion must be the rule in both public behavior and private handling of individual problems. Few faculty would consciously cause problems through careless words or acts, by a misplaced sense of humor, or by a cross remark in pressured situations, but this can sometimes happen under the pressures of the moment.

You must work to develop and maintain rapport with the group, but a certain social distance should be maintained as well. The ideal combination is "a heart of gold and a will of iron," as one past director said, in the face of unreasonable complaints and attempts by students to ignore program regulations. You should work to avoid the perception that you have favorites with the group; do not reveal a personal dislike for any participant or on-site staff member. Be professional.

Your role in the face of any student problems is *to work with the student to find a solution, no matter how long it takes*. In addressing physical and mental health issues, a rule of thumb is not to assume that problems that persist for more than 3 days will eventually go away by themselves. Keep on top of the situation from the beginning to prevent escalation and a potential crisis. Finally, if a student expresses a wish to return home, listen carefully and empathetically, offering coping strategies and other suggestions. If the student persists, despite your efforts to help in the adaptation process, let the student make travel plans to leave. Often this serves as enough of an outlet for the student's frustration and she or he may decide to reconsider things.

We hope the preceding paragraphs have not frightened you away from teaching abroad, but have given you a realistic picture of what *may* happen while abroad. In sum, your home campus provides faculty with an opportunity to work with students from other institutions, and to get to know this generation of students beyond the classroom.

Defining Responsibilities

The Job Description

Every program, depending on its design, will have different responsibilities in the job description. Every faculty member approaches directing a study abroad program with a slightly different schema of what such a task entails. Some have directed programs at other institutions and have a model in mind. Others draw from their experiences as a student abroad, or even as a parent of a student abroad. A written job description will help to avoid the confusion and frustration bound to erupt when the institution and faculty director find that their schemas do not match. Although every program may have a different set of specific tasks for the director, the institution as a whole can develop a document written in general terms that addresses the institutional expectations of all faculty directors.

Keep It Simple

The faculty director's general job description should focus on broad areas of responsibility not encountered in the classroom or of heightened importance while leading a group abroad. Grouping responsibilities under different "hats" will help faculty (and administrators) develop a clear, organized picture of the job. Several key roles are outlined in the Sample Faculty Director Job Description at the end of this chapter. In addition, the administrative responsibility lists in Chapter 3, Administrative Processes, will provide fodder for defining the job.

Get Approval

Since the faculty director responsibilities cross academic, administrative, and student life branches of the institution, these offices should be involved in approving the job description. A bonus of involving various offices in the approval is that it raises consciousness about the complexity of the job. The resulting official job description can be an effective tool with which to advocate for additional compensation and recognition.

Faculty Contracts

Many institutions are moving in the direction of requiring faculty to sign contracts acknowledging responsibilities such as participating in promotional events, attending faculty and student orientations, or filing accounting and a report by the due date. See the Cover Letter and Contract example at the end of the chapter.

Key Roles

There are several areas of responsibilities that are difficult to reduce and therefore should be addressed in the faculty director's job description. These responsibilities form the focus of faculty preparation informational tools and training.

The **developer and recruiter** roles require an investment of time and energy before the program begins. As a developer, the faculty director addresses the academic side of programming, integrating site and curriculum as well as logistics and financial planning. The director must be involved in the planning stages to be able to take on administrative and financial responsibilities on site. Faculty involvement in recruiting is essential. There is no more effective recruiter than a faculty director who is excited about his or her program. Not only does the faculty director represent the fundamental value of the program, academic credit, he or she is the guide to a new experience. Students need to have the opportunity to interact with the person who will lead them in this venture.

The roles of **administrator and financial manager** are perhaps the most clear-cut. On site, the director may have to confirm logistical arrangements, make payments, manage discretionary funds, keep books, and handle enrollment changes. There may be specific state or institutional rules to follow that have dire consequences if broken.

The director acts as the **institutional representative** to the students and to the host culture, as the head guest and colleague. She or he establishes and maintains institutional relationships with the counterparts, hosts, and providers that make the program happen. In addition, she or he governs how participants behave. The faculty director must facilitate administrative processes, uphold institutional policies, and be willing to implement disciplinary sanctions. Finally, the director is the communication link back to the home institution.

The role of **adviser/facilitator** to students involves establishing a leadership role and positive group dynamic, preparing students before departure, providing assistance and referrals when a student is in need, and intervening when appropriate. Skillful advisers/facilitators are often able to prevent issues from becoming problems. Whether or not culture is an academic focus of the program, the faculty director is also the intercultural facilitator; she or he is the liaison between home and host cultures.

Faculty preparation is all about avoiding as many crises as possible, but faculty directors may still find themselves in the role of **crisis manager**. Some crises cannot be prevented, and at that point the institution and the students rely heavily on the director for strength, level-headedness, direction, communication, and good judgment.

Tools to Prepare Faculty

Preparing faculty for directing a program abroad is not unlike preparing students for studying abroad. Students have different questions and need different types of information at various stages of their journey: program selection, application, predeparture orientation (critical and colloquial), on site, and on return to the home campus. The faculty director's journey is analogous: program idea and development, recruitment/admission/selection of participants, faculty and student orientation, on-site management, and reporting and debriefing on return.

Before Proposal

The job description is an important component of defining the faculty director's responsibilities, but it will not give the prospective director a clear idea of how much work, how much support, and what kinds of tasks will be required of him or her. A couple of additional tools will give more shape to the job:

- A division of labor chart describing division of the workload between the faculty director and institutional offices (see "Program Development and Administrative Responsibilities" in Chapter 3, Administrative Processes).
- A timeline that spans program development to the final report and debriefing upon return (See Chapter 7, Feasibility Studies).

Sample Faculty Director Job Description
University of Utah International Center Director's Manual

I. RESPONSIBILITIES
Academic Counseling
It is the director's role to provide academic advice to participants, ensuring that the academic experience is appropriate to a university-level study and learning experience. The director's assistance to students should be continuous throughout the program.

Personal Assistance
The director will act as a resource to participants who may need assistance with personal, emotional, financial, and health problems that may arise during the program. The director acts as the liaison among participants and the appropriate local agencies that provide assistance in these areas.

Activities
The director is expected to organize (as appropriate) activities that will enhance participants' learning experience. Excursions, field trips, and cultural events are examples of activities that may be organized.

Institutional Liaison
The director serves as the liaison between the participants and the university. It is the director's primary responsibility to inform the international center of any emergency situation that may arise during the program, including participant behavior problems. Discretionary judgment is assumed on the part of the director in these matters.

II. BUDGET AND FINANCES
The director is responsible for the management of the group's funds during the program. The director will meet with the international center's finance officer prior to departure to review the program budget, including expense allowances, payments abroad, and institutional accounting requirements. A complete budget report will be required from the director at the end of the program.

III. LIABILITY AND INDEMNIFICATION
The director and all program assistants approved by the university are considered the legal representatives of the university. As such, they are entitled to the same liability protection given to all university representatives. Legal representation will be provided for the director and assistant(s) in all matters related to the program if required.

IV. CRISIS MANAGEMENT AND EMERGENCY RESPONSE
It is the responsibility of the director to be prepared to respond appropriately to any emergency situation that might arise during the program. The director's first responsibility will be to attend to the safety of participants and to determine whether or not there is a threat. If it is determined that there is potential risk to the participants, the director will notify the international center at the university as soon as possible, informing the office about any action taken to minimize or eliminate that risk.

[Source: Adapted, with permission, from University of Utah]

The program proposal samples and guidelines for starting a new program found in Chapter 3, Administrative Processes, are instruments that will give you an idea of the program structure in academic and cultural contexts, as well as policy issues. To round out the picture, the prospective director should be given information on compensation, workload adjustment, and the contract for employment.

Faculty Handbook

Once the program is defined, implementation begins (think of a student applying for a program). This stage is heavy on procedures. A well-designed handbook and/or Web site can be referred to when questions arise. See the samples, Director's Handbook Table of Contents and the Handbook for Faculty Teaching Short-Term Off-Campus Programs, found at the end of this chapter. Because not everyone will read about procedures, redundancy can be built in by sending reminders to faculty via e-mail. A reference to the source (handbook or Web site) should always be included. Self-explanatory forms are helpful; people don't expect to have to read instructions. The one method to avoid at this stage is a meeting to explain all the procedures (e.g., budget guidelines, meeting minimums, acceptance procedures, confirming student participation, deadlines, and enrollment). Procedural information is not easily grasped in lecture format. Those who remain awake through such a meeting may well resent having attended.

> **Guidelines for Setting Program Rules:**
>
> 1. Keep them short and simple. Be sure they are necessary to protect participants and program goals.
> 2. State rules in behavioral terms.
> 3. Rules must be enforceable.
> 4. Director must enforce the rules.

Faculty Orientation

After students have been accepted to a program, they are ready to receive the low-down about their responsibilities as participants. Likewise, once a group is formed, faculty directors will be ready to review and discuss the nitty gritty of the responsibilities laid out in their job descriptions and the institutional policies they will use as guides. Faculty orientation usually follows student selection but precedes student orientation, and you may consider having more than one, as shown on the Agenda for Faculty Director's Meeting at the end of this chapter. This informational need is very difficult to meet by text alone. Opportunity for discussion and consultation with administrative representatives from general counsel, counseling services, the offices of academic deans, and student life is important to answer questions as well as to demonstrate institutional support. In addition to covering concepts such as "in loco parentis," the session should explore examples of the kind of decisions faculty directors face.

Guidelines for Faculty Orientations
* Include representatives from other campus offices.
* Require attendance.
  * ✓ Support from the administration and deans is necessary.
  * ✓ Seasoned pros come as mentors.
* Encourage administrators to attend or participate.
  * ✓ Invite the study abroad or international committee, deans, and chairs.
  * ✓ Administrators who attend show their support of faculty and will better understand the value of the directors' work.

- Keep it short.
    - ✓ Faculty are busy.
    - ✓ Focus on topics that can't easily be covered another way, such as in print or during a one-on-one appointment.
    - ✓ Schedule time for questions at the end so those in a hurry can leave.
- Provide real-life examples.
    - ✓ Include examples of behavioral, academic, mental health, and alcohol problems.
- Provide reference material.

Linking Director Responsibilities to Support

This section will look at possible forms of support for the various roles directors play, in terms of (1) informational tools, (2) predeparture training, and (3) on-site assistance. Note that the roles of developer/recruiter and administrator/financial manager are detailed in written form (handbook) whereas institutional representative, adviser/facilitator, and crisis manager rely on interactive training (faculty orientation) for effective preparation.

If faculty are working by themselves, it is still critical that institutional support be defined before departure. Know what offices you can rely on for assistance and know what liability coverage is provided (See Chapter 4, Internal Support Systems). Faculty members working without much support from the home institution, in particular, should consider using a program provider.

Developer/Recruiter

Tools:
- Samples of program plans, itineraries, syllabi.
- Resources for development—overseas institutions, providers, contacts, environmental information.
- Promotional materials and events.
- Marketing plan.
- Cheat sheet of points to cover in class visits.

Training:
- Work with experienced faculty mentors.
- Hold a program development workshop.

Assistance:
- Faculty colleagues can help spread the word and offer further contacts for program development.
- Department can offer development and recruitment assistance.

Administrator/Financial Manager

Tools:
- The faculty handbook or Web site is one of the most effective tools to inform directors about procedural responsibilities.
- Clear rules and simple forms for financial management and enrollment procedures; guidelines should be concise enough to take overseas.
- Timeline for critical due dates.
- Records of correspondence with on-site providers.
- Coded budget to take overseas, showing what is to be paid on site and what has been prepaid.

Training:
* Lectures about administrative procedures are ineffective; use other means to disseminate the information.
* Try e-mail reminders that refer to the handbook or Web site documents.

Assistance:
* Make prepayments to reduce financial burden on site.
* Use on-site providers to handle arrangements and payments.

For more detailed information about financial forms and systems, refer to Chapter 9, Financial Matters.

Institutional Representative

Tools:
* Copies of important policies, particularly the student code of conduct available via Web site or in print, to take along;
* Scenarios and case studies to use as discussion start points to illustrate the type of situations that crop up, the type of decisions that must be made, how policies are implemented, how sanctions might be imposed, and when it is appropriate to dismiss a participant.

Training:
* Orientation session with representatives from general counsel, student life, offices of the academic deans.
* Explanation of institutional policies as they relate to study abroad, including the student code of conduct (academic and nonacademic), additional rules for study abroad participants, alcohol and drug abuse, sexual harassment, crime reporting, etc.
* Discussion of the institutional interpretation of concepts such as "in loco parentis," due process, and legislation such as the Family Educational Rights and Privacy Act and the Americans with Disabilities Act.
* Discussion of faculty scenarios and case studies, especially with respect to behavioral/academic grounds for dismissal.

Assistance:
* Easy access to consultation with home offices while abroad, either directly or through the international office.

Adviser/Facilitator

Tools:
* Tips and topics for holding a program orientation and assembling orientation materials.
* Concise counseling guidelines for recognizing signs of trouble, knowing when to assist, how to intervene.
* Ice-breaker suggestions for building group cohesion.

Training:
* Involve the counseling center.
* Cover leadership topics such as developing a positive group dynamic, encouraging students to set individual goals, managing behavioral problems, maintaining authority while being friendly, preserving participant confidentiality, overseeing program time and free time.
* Discuss providing assistance to students in need: recognizing signs of emotional or mental health problems, when and how to assist or, if necessary, intervene.

- Intercultural session (facilitators from the multicultural center, communications department, international center) to discuss cultural passage of students, physical and emotional ranges and fluctuations, how to guide participants in cross-cultural learning.
- Best practices sessions with experienced faculty.

Assistance:

- Control ratio of students to staff.
- Send a new director as an understudy to an experienced director.
- Identify on-site counseling resources.
- Identify an on-site intercultural facilitator.
- Ensure easy access to home institution offices for consultation.

Crisis Manager

(For more detailed information, see Chapter 16: Safeguards for Short-Term Programs.)
Tools:

- Local emergency numbers: medical, emergency evacuation services, legal, police, consulate, housing.
- Concise emergency procedures on site, including when to call home.
- Emergency documentation form.
- Emergency numbers to home institution: key offices and contacts.
- Tips sheet for emergencies.
- Student emergency contact information.

Training:

- Discuss types of emergencies: student, personal, program, natural disaster, political/social.
- Discuss locating on-site resources: contacts, agencies, facilities.
- Discuss when to notify the home institution.

Assistance:

- Ensure easy access to home institution offices for consultation.
- Contact available resources on site: people, agencies, facilities.

Offering Opportunities to Build Skills

Each faculty director has his or her own strengths and weaknesses. Likewise, each program has the need for different levels of involvement in the key roles listed above. For instance, there are charismatic faculty member who have to do little more than walk into a classroom to get a full slate of applicants. Others may have trouble conveying their excitement about the program to students, or perhaps they are addressing a much smaller pool of students. Faculty who are great teachers and directors but who are not detail oriented might be better off using a program provider to reduce logistical and financial duties on site. Be realistic when laying out the job in relation to the program

Group Dynamics and Student Expectations

1. Establish these at orientation with students.
2. The director sets a tone—put a positive spin on the program rules.
3. Establish concern for individual student experience by checking in occasionally with students and being available for private consultation.
4. The director sets student expectations. Identify the goals and objectives of program and motivate students to be adult learners.

design. It is worth spending time with a prospective director in the early stages to draw out his or her strengths and to anticipate areas where a bit more training and support is needed.

Written materials such as a handbook and related forms and documents provide critical information. Skills directors rely on are not, however, best acquired by simply reading about them. Providing opportunities to build leadership skills is a key part of your preparation program. This will be more fully covered in Chapter 14, If You Cross Over the Sea…Program Leadership for Intercultural Development.

Some ideas for skill-building opportunities include:
- pairing new directors with experienced mentors during development and planning;
- round table discussions with representatives of counseling, general counsel, or student life;
- best practices sessions with experienced faculty;
- leadership training through the human resources department;
- site-integrative teaching methods workshops with the curriculum development center or education faculty; and
- e-mail listservs, especially those that offer a forum for discussion.

It is extra work to organize and promote these added opportunities, but there are bonuses. Offering such programming for faculty underscores institutional support, recognizes the complexity of the director's job, enhances the confidence directors have in the organizing office, and most importantly, builds a cadre of faculty director colleagues who can support one another in their journeys on the path of directing study abroad programs.

Example of Faculty Contract Cover Letter

Cover Letter
Dear

I am pleased to inform you that your course has been approved. We look forward to the prospect of an exciting and academically rewarding opportunity for the participating students.

Following this letter you will find a list of policies established for short-term courses abroad. This list constitutes the general terms of your contract. If you accept the appointment and the terms outlined, please sign and return the original and one copy to the international office. The third copy is for your own records.

Sincerely,

Contract: Policies for Directing a Short-Term Program Off Campus

1.   The January term is to be treated as a discrete unit of study for which course instructors may not require preparatory work prior to the end of the Fall term or summary work after the beginning of the Spring term. You may, however, list required readings on the promotional literature.

     The faculty director will have the opportunity to screen and select all applicants for their course. The application process and timetable for screening is as follows:

3.   During February, each director will meet to discuss and plan the detailed itineraries and travel arrangements.

4.   The faculty director must prepare the following material for the promotion of the course. The information must be sent no later than February 10. A sample is enclosed.
     a.   Course description
     b.   Indication of grading basis (A, B, C, D, F, or S/U)
     c.   List of prerequisites (considering the possibility of a student with special needs participating in your course, you must outline any physical demands here)
     d.   Autobiographical sketch
     e.   Recent photograph
     Faculty directors must also be involved in the promotion of their courses throughout the recruiting season (April–October).

5.   Each course directed by a single faculty member is based on enrollment of 15 students. Each course led by two faculty members is based on enrollment of 25 students. If fewer than that number enroll, the feasibility of rearranging the program for a smaller group will be negotiated. Since the course instructor's expenses are prorated among the paying participants, a minimum enrollment is necessary to contain costs.

     Two weeks prior to the enrollment deadline, courses with five or fewer registrations will be canceled, to allow those students to transfer to another course while there is still space available.

6. Faculty directors are responsible for program arrangements such as lectures, special visits, excursions, etc. All travel arrangements, as well as ticketing for theater and concert performances, will be made by the program provider. Assistance can also be given for programming elements, if needed.

7. At least one director must accompany the group from the point of origin, and both must be with the group for the duration of the course. If faculty members wish to extend their stays at the conclusion of the course, they must notify the international office of their plans no later than October 15, and pay any additional charge. If faculty do extend their stays, they must personally see that group members are safely boarded on the return aircraft that is a nonstop flight to the United States.

8. Persons under the age of 16 are not eligible to accompany or participate in these courses.

9. Faculty directors must attend the orientation session on Saturday, November 23. The schedule is as follows:
   10:00–12:30—Faculty meet.
   12:30–1:15—Students and faculty meet in large group session.
   1:30–4:30—Faculty meet with their individual groups in classrooms.
   At this time, the director should distribute a course syllabus that lists day-by-day activities and locations as well as all course requirements. The program provider will provide travel itineraries, hotel addresses, and other logistical information.

10. Grade reports are due no later than February 3, and financial reports are due no later than February 14.

_____   _____
Faculty director's signature   Date

[Source: Adapted from University of St. Thomas]

Agenda For Faculty Director's Meetings

MEETING #1: BEFORE ENROLLMENT MEETING

Welcome:
    Director
    New short-term courses
    Mentor program

Important Dates:
    Open house
    Minimum number deadline
    Orientation

Application and Selection Procedures

Open House Information

Student Orientation
- Fall meeting date
- Instructor presence at meeting
- Multiple group-specific meetings after orientation
- Info packets for international and domestic
- Working to address students' concerns

Students with Disabilities
- Identification
- Accommodations

Student Reentry
    Ice cream social

Faculty Orientation
- Fall meeting date
- Stress academic base for all programs at application/selection
- Must depart with students on departure day
- Bed bugs: student entitlement
- Transportation
- Accommodations
- Teaching style
- Expectations of faculty
- Academic expectations/grades/syllabus/no. of days
- Criteria for grading
- Evaluation of Course
- Liability: what to do in an emergency
- Group dynamics: get started on the right foot
- College policies and how they apply to:
    - travel/alcohol/vehicles
    - free time
    - religious observance time

Health/Medical Disclosure Sheet (copy)
    Student health/harassment/alcohol use/stress/security

MEETING #2: BEFORE STUDENT ORIENTATION

Who Does What: Instructor/Liaison?
- What we do to help students prepare (photos, passport, visas, health advising)
- Transportation (air, rail, bus)
- Accommodations
- Excursions/guides
- Museum visits
- Academic contacts

Budget
- Cost adjustment policy
- Refund policy
- Credit card

Health/Safety/Liability Issues
- Distribute consular information sheets, public announcements, or travel warnings from the U.S. State Department
- Student medical disclosure forms
- Motor vehicles
- Crisis management plan
- Emergency contact cards

Group Dynamics
College Policies
- How they apply to off-campus programs

Budget Issues
- Refund policy
- Financial reports

Final Reports
- Expectations
- Due dates

Presentation by College Counselor
- Eating disorders
- Anxiety disorders
- Depression
- What to do

[Source: Adapted from St. Olaf College.]

Sample 1: Director's Handbook Table of Contents

[Source: Adapted from University of Utah]

Sample 2: Handbook for Faculty Teaching Short-Term Off-Campus Programs Table of Contents

[Source: Adapted from University of St. Thomas]

Chapter 14

If You Cross Over the Sea...Program Leadership for Intercultural Development

John Sunnygard

As discussed at the beginning of this book, not all short-term programs abroad enjoy the best reputation among campus faculty or with some "seasoned" education abroad professionals. Some faculty members perceive these programs as quasi-academic Bacchanalian tourist excursions. Many education abroad professionals consider them diminutive siblings of the "junior year abroad" ideal. Poorly organized programs may encourage these stereotypes. As demonstrated, on the other hand, short-term programs can be an effective means of increasing student participation in off-campus opportunities, offering rewarding faculty development opportunities, and meeting core elements of institutional "internationalization." Properly researched, planned, and directed short-term programs can very effectively fulfill many objectives. Although it uses academic programs as the primary model, this chapter seeks to provide a development-based foundation for any "international educator" leader.

For most U.S. undergraduates, a study abroad experience will be limited to 3 to 8 weeks, usually during the summer.[1] Generally, students will be directed by a faculty member from their U.S. institution whose program was carefully scrutinized to conform to a structured set of academic guidelines. Slightly less than half of faculty directors who direct short-term programs have had some preparation for teaching off-campus programs. Faculty training is often focused on institutional policy, program recruitment, the director's responsibilities, handling university funds overseas, appropriate means of travel and accommodation, and other logistical issues.[2] A great deal of legitimate concern will be expressed for student health and safety issues, but less attention may be given to the course curriculum and the intercultural learning experience. Unfortunately in some quarters, intercultural interaction is only described as "culture shock," which, fortunately, can be overcome. Why is the program going overseas?

To design, recruit, and implement short-term programs abroad focused on cognitive and intercultural development, a three-sided model, the "Triad of Intercultural Leadership in Short-Term Programs," has been created. The triad consists of a base in intercultural development theory, with rising sides of motivation factors and program design. Experience indicates that programs that use the triad model lead to more effective long-term learning experiences.

---

[1] *Open Doors: Statistics on International Student Mobility, 2000.* Institute of International Education.

[2] Unpublished research by IES, the Institute for the International Education of Students, Chicago, Illinois. August 2001.

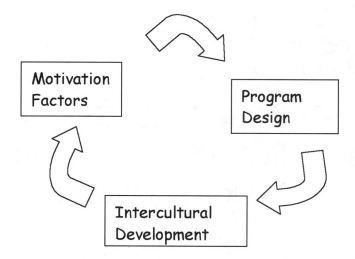

Triad of Intercultural Leadership in Short-Term Programs

Whether a faculty member has elected to teach a short-term program for pedagogical or more personal reasons, the impact on the students and the faculty director will be profound and enduring. However, sheer physical presence in another culture or country does not guarantee intercultural learning. One can, for example, teach the same Shakespeare course in Stratford, CT, or Stratford, Ontario, Canada, or Stratford-upon-Avon, England, with the same cognitive effect. Indeed, many English departments would demand that the material covered in a United Kingdom "study tour" be the Connecticut equivalent but with the addition of a few visits and a lecture or two by a local expert. Both courses will creatively teach objective "Culture"[3] in the high literary sense, and provide the education that the department expects. However, guided and critical observation of the British and U.S. cultures would not only enhance understanding of the essence of the Bard's work and the proximate opportunity of Stratford-upon-Avon; it would lead to students' more complete understanding of themselves and their British counterparts. Understanding subjective "culture"[4] is more likely to lead to intercultural competence. By incorporating the new environment, its culture, and the impact both have on student development and identity, the faculty director has become an effective international educator.

Successful short-term program directors understand how they themselves function within foreign cultures. Furthermore, they are aware of the interpersonal qualities that are affected by intercultural transitions and the dimensions of cultural difference. Faculty directors who have made the transition from *educators* to *international educators* teach not only for cognitive growth, but for affective intercultural development as well. By bringing a realistic understanding of potential participants' motivations and assumptions, they can more effectively recruit students and create the proper learning environment.

---

[3] Culture (uppercase), or *high* culture for our purposes, refers to *objective culture*, the objects and institutions of culture (i.e., art, literature, dance; social, economic, political, and linguistic systems). See Patrick Quade's Chapter 12, "It Changed My Life": Strategies for Assessing Student Learning, for additional details and references.

[4] culture (lowercase), or *low* culture for our purposes, refers to *subjective culture*, the learned and shared patterns of beliefs, behaviors, and values held by a group of people.

Intercultural Development Theories

Intercultural development theories draw from several disciplines. Three seminal theory groups have been selected that derive from research in psychology, international business, and intercultural communications. This does not represent a comprehensive survey of the growing body of intercultural theory. However, based on experience, even a cursory understanding of the key points of the ideas represented here can help explain interactions and experiences, and inform planning and curricular decisions. Furthermore, presenting students with the basic ideas of intercultural interactions and development can lead students to a more rewarding experience.

The discussion of theory will begin at a personal level, by considering four factors of how people respond in cross-cultural situations. I will then consider how a dynamic, six-dimensional model of cultural diversity informs people engaged in intercultural dealings. I will conclude by discussing Milton Bennett's "Development Model of Intercultural Sensitivity" as benchmark criteria for intercultural growth.

Each theoretical model can be viewed and applied at three levels: cognitive, interpersonal, and intrapersonal. The cognitive level, for example, the academic program, is the one most commonly approached in short-term programming. The academic program is usually the primary justification for a program, and as such warrants considerable attention. At the interpersonal level, we are concerned with relationships between people. The theories presented can help take us beyond simplistic and often misleading stereotypes of people from different cultures to informed tools for understanding and action. Students (and most faculty) returning from a successful study abroad program often declare how the experience in another culture has changed their lives and the way they view the world. Intrapersonal growth is enhanced by thoughtful planning and leadership.

When discussing a program and interpersonal interactions, examples frequently include stereotypes and generalizations with presentations of "how to." Orientation sessions may include sections on "how to get along with Moroccans," and so on. Of course, getting along with Moroccans is very important, but presenting and reinforcing cultural stereotypes does not contribute to intercultural development. Indeed, cultural stereotypes can inhibit intercultural growth.

"Know thyself." The intrapersonal dimension, or self-understanding and knowledge, is a critical part of intercultural understanding. By understanding one's own responses to uncertainty, difference, and risk, the intercultural actor can make more informed choices of behavior. The baseline, therefore, for each of these theories is self-understanding. After self-understanding, it is helpful for the faculty director to know the general and, as well as possible, the specific baselines of program participants to intercultural situations. By understanding the starting point—the baseline—the director can target areas for improvement and anticipate potential areas of difficulty. Areas for student improvement can also be creatively addressed during the planning stages.

Responses to Intercultural Interactions

Psychologists Colleen Kelley and Judith Meyers developed the "Cross-Cultural Adaptability Inventory" (CCAI) to help an individual assess her or his potential effectiveness in cross-cultural situations. "Culture shock" is a term often used to express the feelings of loneliness, frustration, alienation, and anxiety encountered after prolonged exposure to another culture. After extensive research, Kelly and Meyers identified four components of cross-cultural adaptability.

Emotional Resilience

"Emotionally resilient people like new experiences and have confidence in their ability to cope with ambiguity."[5] People often have negative emotional responses of loneliness, confusion, or frustration when they are unable to identify or understand basic cues in intercultural interactions.

Flexibility/Openness

"Open, flexible people enjoy interacting with people who think differently from themselves."[6] Open, flexible people tend to be less judgmental, more tolerant, and comfortable with those who are different from them. People who are inflexible can become distraught or disoriented by the inconsistent cues given by people different from themselves.

Perceptual Acuity

"People who are perceptually acute are attentive to verbal and nonverbal behavior, to the context of communication, and to interpersonal relations."[7] Intercultural communication involves both verbal and nonverbal communication cues that may differ significantly among cultures and lead to miscommunication or misunderstanding.

Personal Autonomy

"Personally autonomous people are not overly dependent upon cues from the environment for their sense of identity."[8] People who are highly dependent on other people and their environment for their own identity can have difficulty adjusting to new environments or people who do not issue the same comforting cues. On the other hand, people who feel alienated from their own culture's environment may feel a sense of personal exhilaration when they encounter new cues.

The CCAI offers a means of self-assessing one's response to cultural interactions based on these components. A good, honest understanding of one's own responses in the face of intercultural interactions can help one prepare for dealing with cultural situations. As students experience frustration when interacting with a new culture, these items can help the faculty director to understand and respond to the student and help provide better counseling. All involved in program development and the administrator and leadership team should be encouraged to first understand their own responses to intercultural interactions and, second, to present the components to participants. As the program progresses, one can do a status check to see how she or he is holding up.

Journal writing, or keeping an "analytical notebook" as recommended by Magistrale and Wagner,[9] is an excellent vehicle for exploring ones responses to a new culture. Writing is contemplative. Writing the days activities and one's responses and emotions to new encounters in a journal is an intellectually stimulating, emotionally soothing activity that leaves an enduring record. As discussed in Chapter 6, Designing the Academic Course: Principles and Practicalities, there is an analytical difference between an academic journal used in the evaluation process and a journal kept as a record.

---

[5] Kelley, Colleen and Meyers, Judith (1995). *CCAI Cross-Cultural Adaptability Manual.* Minneapolis, MN, National Computer Systems, Inc., 13.

[6] Ibid. p. 14.

[7] Ibid. p. 15.

[8] Ibid. pp. 16–17.

[9] Magistrale, Tony and Wagner, Kenneth (1995). *Writing Across Culture: An Introduction to Study Abroad and the Writing Process.* New York, Peter Lang Publishing.

Dimensions of Intercultural Interactions

Effective intercultural understanding, communication, and interaction are essential to the modern global corporation. Charles Hampden-Turner and Fons Trompenaars' recent work, *Building Cross-Cultural Competence: How to Create Wealth from Conflicting Values*, uses the dilemma theory to explore the tension between opposing values from a group of six "universal dilemmas." The universal dilemmas, outlined below, are represented by opposing values across a continuum. Hampden-Turner and Trompenaars believe that value (or wealth) is created when an organization successfully uses the strengths of each value system to reconcile values-in-tension. In the study abroad context, educational value is created when the international educator and students recognize and reconcile the different cultural values they encounter while abroad. Hampden-Turner and Trompenaars conducted exhaustive research that identified six value-tension pairs:

Adherents of these values believe in the primacy of…

Universalism vs Particularism		
(rules, codes, laws, and generalizations)	vs	(exceptions, special circumstances, unique relations)

Individualism vs Communitarianism		
(personal freedom, human rights, competitiveness)	vs	(social responsibility, harmonious relations, cooperation)

Specificity vs Diffusion		
(atomistic, reductive, analytic, objective)	vs	(holistic, elaborative, synthetic, relational)

Achieved Status vs Ascribed Status		
(what you've done, your track record)	vs	(who you are, your potential and connections)

Inner Direction vs Outer Direction		
(conscience and convictions are located inside)	vs	(examples and influences are located outside)

Sequential Time vs Synchronous time[10]		
(time is a race along a set course)	vs	(time is a dance of fine coordinations)

[10] Hampden-Turner, Charles and Trompenaars, Fons. (2000) *Building Cross-Cultural Competence: How to Create Wealth from Conflicting Values*. New Haven, CT and London, UK, Yale University Press, 11.

For one example, most Americans subscribe to the concept of sequential time, where time is linear and a schedule is a point on the line. It is commonly accepted (except perhaps with some college students) that one adheres to the schedule or one misses the point, forever. For members of other cultures time is circular; schedules are flexible because one cannot do everything at once and opportunities may arise again. To look at it another way, Americans are in a time joust. The "sequential" knight rides in a straight line and has one opportunity to hit the target, or the knight has to turn around and start again. The "synchronous" knight is on a merry-go-round, thrusting a sword at the dangling ring as he goes round. If the knight misses the ring, he may get another chance the next time around. For both knights, the actual moment of contact is critical, and it is hit or miss; how the knights arrive at the decisive moment is completely different.

For short-term programming, this model is instructive in at least two ways. First, the primary, universal sources of cultural differences and one's relationship to them are clarified. Second, by accepting that value arises from reconciling a dilemma, directors and students can see growth through experiencing a cross-cultural dilemma. When a student returns home from a program and demonstrates an increased sense of self-confidence, a greater understanding of the world, and increased tolerance for difference, it is an indication that he or she has reconciled some value dilemmas.

The DMIS, a Model of Intercultural Development

Milton Bennett's "Development Model of Intercultural Sensitivity" (DMIS) provides a set of developmental benchmarks of intercultural development. The DMIS has been successfully quantified by a psychometric instrument, the Intercultural Development Inventory (IDI). Both the model and instrument have been described in detail in Chapter 12, "It Changed My Life": Strategies for Assessing Student Learning. Review that chapter for further details of the model.

The DMIS has proven to be a versatile and effective means of explaining intercultural development. For the purposes of this chapter, the essential strength of the DMIS is identifying the categorical differences between ethnocentric and ethnorelative stages of intercultural development.[11] Rudyard Kipling's poem, *We and They*, is a beautiful illustration of some stages appropriate to this goal.

Father, Mother, and Me,
    Sister and Auntie say
All the people like us are We,
    And everyone else is They.
And They live over the sea
    While we live over the way,
But – would you believe it? – They look upon We
    As only a sort of They!

We eat pork and beef
    With cow-horn handled knives.
They who gobble Their rice off a leaf
    Are horrified out of Their lives;

[11] Bennett, Milton J. (1993) "Towards a Developmental Model of Intercultural Sensitivity" in R. Michael Paige, ed. *Education for the Intercultural Experience*. Yarmouth, ME, Intercultural Press, Inc.

While They who live up a tree,
    Feast on grubs and clay,
(Isn't it scandalous?) look upon We
    As a simply disgusting They!

We eat kitcheny food.
    We have doors that latch.
They drink milk and blood
    Under an open thatch. We have doctors to fee.
    They have wizards to pay.
And (impudent heathen!) They look upon We
    As a quite impossible They!

All good people agree,
    And all good people say,
All nice people, like us, are We
    And everyone else is They:
But if you cross over the sea,
    Instead of over the way,
You may end by (think of it) looking on We
    As only a sort of They!
                    —Rudyard Kipling 1926[12]

Kipling's exploration of perceptions and interpretations of different cultures almost follows the first two stages of the DMIS: denial and defense. In the first stanza, Kipling reveals the petty suspicions between family members or neighbors with his first definition of "we" and "they." Intercultural differences are denied by simply being relegated to geography and gross characterization, "everyone else is They." The next two stanzas perfectly illustrate defense, where one culture denigrates another and also declares its cultural superiority. Kipling's challenging conclusion urges us to venture over the sea, to experience cultural difference, and suggests that as a result of this experience we can move into a culturally relativistic worldview.

Awareness of cultural differences is a laudable and realistic goal of a short-term program abroad. Acceptance of cultural difference in an ethnorelativistic sense would be an ideal. With careful program structure, and by providing guided critical analysis of cultural difference, the international educator can at least help students open the door to intercultural development. If students can begin to "look [sic] on We as only a sort of They," the program could arguably be declared an intercultural success. Students will have not only mastered the cognitive elements of the program but also gained significant intrapersonal insights.

Motivation Factors

Why go "over the sea," instead of "over the way?" Some reasons are blatantly obvious. Paris is a beautiful city overflowing with art. London has a vibrant theater community. People speak Japanese in Kyoto. The Humboldt University has an immense library. Tanzania has bones. Australia has Bondi beach. Of course, there are many other reasons for going abroad as well. Understanding the motivating factors to study

---

[12] Kipling, Rudyard (1926) "We and They" in Sorti, Craig (1990) *The Art of Crossing Cultures.* Yarmouth, ME, Intercultural Press, Inc., 91.

abroad can help faculty plan a more effective program. Students and faculty often have differing assumptions, expectations, and goals of a study abroad program. Refer to "Twenty Questions for Students and Faculty" at the end of this chapter to help assess student and faculty motivation factors for study abroad.

Assumptions and Expectations

There are four players in the academic study abroad chain: the teacher, the student, the university administration, and the parent. Each has their own collection of assumptions and expectations of a study abroad program. To express basic assumptions simply: the teacher assumes that the student wants to learn; the student assumes that the program will be fun; the parent assumes that the child will be cared for; the administration assumes the teacher will be responsible (and likely that the student will not).

Similarly, each player has expectations of the study abroad program. Students expect travel, but may not expect homework. Faculty expect to teach, but may not expect to referee roommate disputes. All parties may have hidden expectations not readily expressed in planning or discussion. Bring all of the expectations and assumptions to the table to avoid misrepresentation, misunderstanding, and disappointment.

Managing Expectations

Before planning a program, take an inventory of the assumptions and expectations of all of the characters. Seek out common expectations. Carefully consider the differences. Which expectations will contribute to the program? Which expectations do you want to dispel? Students' expectations will be set by the information they receive prior to enrolling in the program. Expectations will be solidified during the predeparture orientations.

Carefully consider how the program is being presented by study abroad administrators, faculty directors, and past participants. For example, a European Union (EU) program that visits three cities will likely include frequent visits to EU institutions, lectures by local professors and governmental and nongovernmental officials, and research assignments. Students will also want to explore the cities and the nightlife, and other points in Europe. Which parts of the program will be used to describe the program? Which elements will be discussed to recruit students? Which elements will the program alumni present with the most enthusiasm?

A short-term program abroad is a holistic experience, not an isolated classroom experience. A successful program will achieve equilibrium among academic content, travel, and fun. A program should have a balance between classroom time and free time. Clearly, one cannot misrepresent or deny aspects of the program. Clubs and pubs are important venues for both students and faculty, and if dealt with maturely and proportionately, the right tone can be set. Denying the existence of nightlife, travel, and so on creates a taboo to be broken. On the other hand, placing too much emphasis on travel from a tourist's perspective or partying from an undergraduate perspective will skew student motivations in the wrong direction. Once assumptions and expectations have been established, it is extremely difficult to modify them, particularly in a short-term program abroad.

Goals

Like assumptions and expectations, each party has different goals and objectives for the program. Faculty directors and the international office should have a clear set of goals and objectives in mind for the program. The goals should be based on practical realities, academic requirements and opportunities, faculty strengths, student interest, and most importantly, the attributes of the local environment.

Goals should be made clear to students during recruiting and with promotional materials. Program and student goals and objectives should be discussed as a part of predeparture orientations. Longer-term goals should also be discussed at orientation; for example, "What do you want to bring back from this experience that you can incorporate into your academic or professional life?" or "What do you want to bring into your personal life?"

Discussing student goals begins the learning process. Often student expectations and goals are unclear and unrefined. Many students have never had this kind of learning experience before and don't know what is possible or what to expect. By learning student goals and objectives, the program and curriculum can be better informed and incorporated for immediate program relevance.

Finally, assessing assumptions, expectations, and goals can have a significant impact on the health, safety, and security of all members. Nightclubs, mountains, urban explorations, and rural wanderings all pose their own unique risks. It is always helpful to know who wants to scale the Materhorn, who wants to party, and who plans to stay in the room. When the faculty director is aware of the student's other ambitions, she or he can help the students manage their goals with the risks involved. The director can help the students determine locally appropriate means of achieving their goals.

Program Design

Program design is discussed in great detail throughout this volume, with different nuance. This chapter is focused on incorporating intercultural learning and development into the equation. The three theories discussed present frameworks and approaches to intercultural learning. Taking stock of the different assumptions, expectations, and goals of all of the players gives a clearer picture of what needs to be satisfied by the program. Careful consideration of the assumptions, expectations, and goals informs realistic objectives for planning, recruitment, program implementation, and program follow-up.

Academic and Intercultural Learning

You are planning a short-term program abroad. You are not a travel agent. The first objective must include clear learning objectives. A balance should be drawn between academic and intercultural learning objectives. Being realistic cannot be overemphasized in program planning. Most study abroad destinations offer a lifetime of learning opportunities; a 3-week program cannot possibly encounter even a fraction of the opportunities in a meaningful way.

Academic objectives should include any departmental requirements. Creativity should be used to find the right combination of classroom and nonclassroom approaches to learning. Sites provide valuable experiences for students who need to touch and feel otherwise abstract connections to the subject. However, physical sites are not the only means of connecting to a writer, scientist, or philosopher.

Invite local professors and students to lecture on the subject matter, but also to discuss the ways in which they approach the subject matter. At large, prestigious city universities that frequently receive Americans (e.g., the University of London), students are frequently too "busy" to spend time with Americans visiting for a few hours. At less renowned institutions (e.g., the University of East London), students are academically accomplished but also eager to make outside connections. Discussions with students can lead to the satisfaction of both academic and intercultural goals.

Analytical notebooks, previously mentioned, are very useful assignments. These writing assignments should be started before departure to include goals, expectations, and assumptions. Begin by asking students to look at their own cultural identities. What values do they hold? What do they enjoy doing at home? What do they expect to be different? The same? See Authoethnography Exercise in Chapter 15, Orientation and Reentry, General.

Structure and Flexibility

Clear program goals presume a structure. However, even the most structured programs in the most structured countries will require latitude and flexibility. Showing up regularly at a classroom or a lab on the home campus is very easy. Changing classrooms, locations, relying on other lecturers, and so on, increases the level of complexity and risk for delay or error. Plan to leave and arrive early at all sites. Allow open afternoons or mornings to make up for missed time or to take advantage of unforeseen opportunities.

Faculty directors and students may encounter frustrations and anxiety from being in another culture. Plan relief opportunities, breaks, and free time. Exploration of new places and people is an invaluable part of the program. However, students often do not know how to cope with new experiences and prefer to stay with what is comfortable and familiar. Let them know of possible opportunities and encourage them to explore. Again, write such opportunities down in the analytical notebook.

Short-Term Programs Abroad That Lead to Long-Term Development

A framework, not specific answers or prescriptions, has been presented for off-campus learning. Motivated, creative, dedicated international educators develop rewarding programs for their students and institutions. There is no prescription for intercultural learning, but exposure to new and different people and places combined with critical analysis and opportunity for reflection can lead to long-term rewards.

Twenty Questions for Students and Faculty

Faculty

1. Can you describe the top five goals for your study abroad program?

2. How familiar are you with your destination (e.g., have you received a map, travel book, literature, history, newspapers/magazines, values)?

3. What is your worst fear about this program?

4. Why do your students want to go on this program?

5. Why do you want to direct this program?

6. What is your plan for accessing emergency funds and evacuating your students in case of a crisis?

7. Who is responsible for helping you plan each segment of this program and carry it through?

8. What do you think will offer the greatest challenge and what are you doing to prepare yourself for that challenge?

9. What has been your previous cross-cultural experience (U.S. or abroad) and how do you think it will apply to this experience?

10. How can you keep the study abroad experience alive for students after your return?

Students

1. Can you describe the top five goals for your studying abroad?

2. How does study abroad fit in with your study plans? Your long-term career objectives? Your personal objectives?

3. What has been your previous cross-cultural experience (U.S. or abroad) and how do you think it will apply to this experience?

4. How familiar are you with your destination (e.g., have you received a map, travel book, literature, history, newspapers/magazines, values)?

5. What are five benefits that you expect to gain from this program?

6. What in your life experience do you think has helped you to prepare for this program?

7. How would you rate yourself as an international person open to diverse cultural experiences?

8. What are your fears, if any, about studying abroad?

9. What do you want to bring home from this program?

10. What will you do to make the most of this opportunity abroad?

Chapter 15

Orientation and Reentry

Joe Kinsella (<u>Academic, General</u>)

Melissa Smith-Simonet (<u>On-Site</u>)

Kathy Tuma (<u>General</u>)

<u>Academic</u>

Integrating Experiences and Ideas

For all study abroad programs, but particularly for short-term programs abroad, predeparture and reentry orientations play a critical role in making a visit to another society a valuable learning experience. Without such orientations academic travel abroad has the potential to become superficial tourism, rather than transformative learning. Therefore, as institutions develop and implement any educational programs that involve students directly experiencing people and places in the world, faculty and administrators should concentrate at least as much effort on the learning that takes place on the home campus as they do on the program abroad. Limited budgets and administrative time notwithstanding, if short-term programs abroad are to retain academic credibility, students must be able to articulate what they have learned abroad with their lives at home. Operating quality programs abroad involves operating quality programs on the home campus.

The notion that students can learn anything through travel to another place is grounded in pedagogical concepts of experiential learning (these concepts are described in Chapter 6, Designing the Academic Course). Structured around this experiential pedagogy, the concepts and activities presented here assume that successful preparation for and integration of an overseas learning experience into students' personal and academic lives involves both cognitive (i.e., "facts" and ideas, and the reasoning involved in understanding them) and affective ("common sense" and value-laden feelings that shape our behavior) aspects of learning. As a part of learning that is both cognitive and affective, framing an experience abroad with ideas and concepts that students can actively engage with local people and places is central to experiential education. Further, guiding reflection about those experiences before, during, and after returning to the home campus brings the learning process to culmination, and helps students better understand the personal changes that they feel as a result. By integrating a program abroad with predeparture and reentry seminars that highlight the interaction between cognitive and affective learning, we have found that students have more enriching learning experiences and that faculty are more satisfied with their interaction and the learning that students demonstrate as a result.

The Short-Term Challenge

Short-term programs (as has been said in earlier chapters) have often been regarded by practitioners of study abroad programs as at best an easy way out of a semester-long commitment on the part of students, and at worst a kind of superficial academic tourism that reinforces stereotypes and misunderstandings of "the Other." This is why it is critical that administrators and faculty involved carefully consider their academic and programmatic goals as they develop these types of international programs.[1,2]

Once the program has been established and the students recruited, faculty and administrators must pay careful attention to the wide range of their students' personal and intellectual needs throughout the three phases of the program: preparation, field experience, and reentry. Indeed, study abroad professionals assert that in order for any time spent abroad to be educationally valuable, it must be "embedded in an educational continuum."[3] This continuum extends from the moment a student considers the possibility of participating in a study abroad program, through the in-field learning abroad, and long after the student returns to his or her home institution and life in the United States. A well-planned and executed predeparture and reentry program ultimately makes short-term experiences abroad more meaningful personally and intellectually to the students who take part in them as well as the communities in which the students live.

A great deal of research on the effects of study abroad indicates that there is a strong correlation between the length of time actually spent abroad and the degree of impact on students' cross-cultural competence and understanding.[4] Although some recent research challenges this premise, almost any international educator will agree that there is no substitute for a semester (or longer) immersion experience for broadening students' worldviews and their perceptions of themselves as transnational actors on "global" stages.

But as students of our institutions become more diverse, and the "typical" student may be as likely to have a full-time job, a child, and family commitments as she or he is to be 18 years old and single, international educators must explore alternatives to the traditional semester or year abroad in order to facilitate an intellectually and personally transformative international experience for a more inclusive array of students. For a student who must support a family or work in order to stay in school, a short-term program abroad is often the only option available. Therefore, it is in the interest of a diverse student body and educational access to explore how we can make short-term programs meaningful educational experiences that are intellectually valued and curricularly useful.

Sikkema and Niyekawa have presented an insightful and useful model for engaging students on campus before and after traveling abroad in order to "become a cross-culturally flexible person."[5] Their approach emphasizes the development of particular skills and behaviors that are necessary in cross-cultural communication and adaptation, and is very useful in structuring the affective aspects of learning that are proposed

[1] Gochenour, Theodore (1993). *Beyond Experience: An Experiential Approach to Cross-Cultural Education*. Yarmouth, ME: Intercultural Press.

[2] Kauffmann, Norman L., Judith N. Martin, and Henry D. Weaver (1992). *Students Abroad, Strangers at Home: Education for a Global Society*. Yarmouth, ME, Intercultural Press, Inc.

[3] Hoffa, William and John Pearson (eds.) (1997) *NAFSA's Guide to Education Abroad for Advisers and Administrators, 2nd edition*. Washington, DC: NAFSA: Association of International Educators, 233.

[4] Koester, J. (1985). *A Profile of the U.S. Student Abroad*. New York: Council on International Education Exchange.

[5] Sikkema, Mildred, and Agnes Niyekawa (1987). *Design for Cross-Cultural Learning*. Yarmouth, ME, Intercultural Press, Inc.

here. But their design for cross-cultural learning assumes that while in the field students will be doing something that will engage them with local people and institutions. Although it provides an excellent conceptual outline for encouraging cross-cultural skills and understanding, Sikkema and Niyekawa's model leaves out any indication of what students would actually do on a day-to-day basis while visiting another place. In short-term programs especially this cannot be left to chance.

What, then, is to be done with short-term programs abroad? Is it possible to learn something about society, self, or "culture" during a brief visit to another place? Building these programs abroad around central ideas and issues in the host society as a course that focuses on a single topic, and provides students with the tools necessary to explore that topic lends a sense of purpose to the broader goals of nurturing cross-cultural skills of adaptation and communication. The approach we use at DePaul University is straight-forward: we start by focusing on a particular academic theme or disciplinary perspective during a predeparture seminar. These seminars introduce students to a concept, issue, or cultural phenomenon that is of interest to the faculty and pertinent in the host society. Within these conceptual lectures and discussions students are also exposed to relevant research methods or modes of critical thinking (e.g., visual sociology to explore urban geography, or theatre criticism and reader-response theory as an entrée into understanding cultural diversity) that facilitate and foster ideas about the overall program theme. This can be done through a series of meetings, and/or assigned readings with a single reflection paper or, minimally, guided discussions. If time is tight, utilizing Web technologies such as Blackboard or other online instructional tools can help routinize these discussions while you encourage students to explore ideas on their own. At DePaul, in addition to these discussions and readings students are required to maintain a daily journal that focuses on questions and observations encountered as they prepare and develop a focus to their program abroad. This journal provides a space for students to reflect on their individual goals (personal and academic) while giving them practice in reflective writing on a regular basis that will assist them in recording their thoughts and experiences while abroad.

Students are then taken abroad, and encouraged to continue their exploration of these ideas and concepts while meeting and interacting with local people. Throughout their time in the field students are required to maintain their journals, in which they are to reflect on their daily activities and their reflections on the conceptual program theme. On several DePaul programs a series of journal prompts are used to evoke action and reflection. Ideally, students are given lectures by both local guests and the accompanying faculty, and are provided with group discussion time to process their feelings, thoughts, and experiences in the field.

Finally, a structured series of reentry group discussions and presentations give students the chance to process and digest what they have seen and done abroad, and serves as a kind of capstone for students' international learning experiences. After a short-term program abroad, a reentry seminar is particularly useful for faculty to help students integrate their new knowledge and cross-cultural awareness with their lives back home and to assess the students' learning through sustained contact after returning.

These predeparture and reentry seminars should be part of the academic credit granted for a short-term program abroad, and students' grades should be contingent on successful participation and completion of assignments before, during, and after the time spent abroad.

Creating the Frame

The remainder of this chapter will detail a best practices approach for designing predeparture and reentry classroom seminars to frame in-field experiences during short-term programs abroad. These recommendations are based on 15 years of experience working in the study abroad profession, running programs at DePaul University in Chicago in which the in-field component lasts between 3 weeks and 3 months (a single quarter). In addition, my anthropological work around ethnographic methodology and phenomenology, and putting together my own ethnographic research projects in Zimbabwe and Uganda have reinforced my conviction that field-based methodological training is a powerful tool in preparing students to be astute observers while engaging people in another society. Examples will be drawn from a number of short-term programs operated at DePaul, in particular: "Amsterdam, Rotterdam, Brussels and Prague: Comparative Perspectives in Urban Development" and "Modern British Theatre: Text, Performance, Gender, and Criticism." These two programs typify the best of short-term programs at DePaul. With an institutional commitment to economic access to education and serving nontraditional student populations, DePaul has been an excellent environment in which to develop these types of programs.

What follows is neither a comprehensive nor exclusive list, but highlights what I believe to be the potential strengths of short-term programs abroad. Predeparture and reentry seminars are an important mechanism to assuage the inadequacies of the short-term program format vis-à-vis semester- and year-long programs. At the root of this argument is the supposition that short-term study abroad cannot and *should not* have the same learning goals and objectives as longer programs, with broad objectives to build cross-cultural awareness and skills. Rather, short-term programs must be conceived of as focused learning experiences that are facilitated and orchestrated by faculty dealing with limited topics within the target society. This is not to suggest that general cross-cultural skills of adaptation, and/or culture-specific skills (e.g., language learning, personal flexibility, appreciation for differences, etc.) are not learnable in a short-term program abroad format. To be academically honest with our students, however, educators involved with short-term programs must acknowledge that the same *depth* and *kind* of learning possible in a semester- or year-long program is *less* possible through a short visit to another society. The strength of any short-term program, therefore, lies in the ability of educators to effectively link "doing" and "reflecting," "experiencing" and "comprehending" within a short timeframe. This is the foundation of experiential learning.

The learning that takes place in any study abroad program should be considered a process that extends from predeparture preparations to readjustment processes back home. The time actually spent abroad is only a part of the whole learning experience. In *NAFSA's Guide to Education Abroad for Advisers and Administrators, Second Edition*, Hoffa, Pearson, et. al. speak of a "three-phase, inclusive learning process" that prepares students personally and practically for a semester or longer immersion experience abroad while motivating them to "learn more about the host culture…and become familiar with the process of cross-cultural adaptation."[6] Their "culture-general" approach is an excellent way to help students understand cross-cultural perspectives, and develop skills of cross-cultural adaptation and flexibility.

By definition, however, short-term programs abroad do not enjoy the luxury of time for students to really experience cross-cultural adaptation in a profoundly personal way. While a student living abroad for a year, for example, can eventually learn about interpersonal relationships and particular cultural practices through sustained and repeated interaction, these skills of cross-cultural communication and understanding take

---

[6] Hoffa, William, and John Pearson (eds.) (1997) *NAFSA's Guide to Education Abroad for Advisers and Administrators, 2nd Edition*. Washington, DC: NAFSA: Association of International Educators, 233-234.

time to develop. In a short-term format, therefore, it is necessary for faculty to actively focus the attention of their students on a particular set of ideas that are pertinent to the host society and to give them a set of tools by which they can systematically explore those ideas in the field. Ideally, this may take place during predeparture seminars, run as regular on-campus class meetings for an abbreviated period of time prior to departure (at DePaul we recommend that predeparture and reentry contact total between 5 and 8 hours for each course unit offered for credit). If seminars are required, the key is to communicate to students the same expectations regarding attendance and participation in these on-campus meetings as would be demanded in a "regular" on-campus course.

A Word on Experiential Learning and Anthropology

The concept of experiential learning is often employed to describe and legitimate study abroad programs. Working from another perspective, however, it is useful to examine the components of what is considered to be the process of learning from experience in order to structure an entire study abroad program, from predeparture through reentry. David Kolb's circular process of experiential learning that involves a dialectical relationship between concrete experiences and abstract concepts, reflection and experimentation, is an excellent conceptual model around which to structure program activities and goals (see figure, "Structural Dimensions Underlying the Dialectical Processes of Experiential Learning"). According to Kolb, "experiential learning can be described as a four-stage cycle involving four adaptive learning modes—concrete experience, reflective observation, abstract conceptualization, and active experimentation."[7]

STRUCTURAL DIMENSIONS UNDERLYING THE DIALECTICAL PROCESSES OF EXPERIENTIAL LEARNING[8]

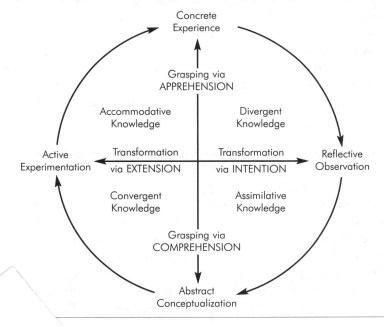

---

7 Kolb, [...] *[...]l Learning: Experiencing as the Source of Learning and Development.* Englewood Cliffs, NJ: Prenti[...]

8 [...] *[...]rning: Experiencing as the Source of Learning and Development.* Englewood Cliffs, NJ: [...] [...]n of Pearson Education, Inc., Upper Saddle River, NJ.

In short-term programs abroad, students must be taken through this cycle repeatedly in a guided manner so that they will be able to apprehend the differences they encounter, and understand the impact of the study abroad experience on their own identities and values.

From an anthropological perspective, this cyclical process is illustrative of the ethnographic methodology known as "participant-observation," in which the researcher establishes routine interactions with local people around some task or project (concrete experiences) in order to participate in the daily lives of a group under study. Engaged in these ongoing activities while continually reflecting on experiences and interactions with people in the form of field notes, participant-observation is a holistic approach to understanding abstract concepts about a particular group, which then shapes further interaction and inquiry. This grounded approach to research has been found to provide researchers with both intuitive and intellectual grasps of the cultural practices of groups of people, and is the cornerstone of ethnographic knowledge. As an anthropologist, therefore, it is tempting to suggest that we should create apprentice ethnographers of all study abroad students as a way to prepare them for living abroad (see Autoethnography Exercise at the end of this chapter). In the case of short-term programs abroad, close faculty participation in the theoretical and methodological preparation of students will assist them in managing the cognitive aspects of learning in such a condensed format while apprehending the new (and emerging) world around them.

Kolb's model of experiential learning is made up of a "four-stage cycle involving four adaptive learning modes...learning is the result of the interaction, conflict, and resolution of these different learning modes."[9] In Kolb's model, which is grounded in the work of Jean Piaget, learning necessitates the apprehension and comprehension of particular experiences to be transformed through some sort of action, either mental or physical, on the part of the learner. The key to understanding Kolb's model of experiential learning, therefore, is in the relationship and tensions between what he identifies as the "prehension" and "transformation" dimensions of these learning modes, represented by the cross axes in the figure. These two dimensions of learning, which each have dialectically opposed adaptive tendencies toward the world, are best understood as the ways in which we "grasp" at understanding (prehension consisting of experiences and ideas) and what we do once we have grasped (transformation consisting of reflection and experimentation). This model is particularly helpful when organizing predeparture and reentry seminars as a way to structure the relationships between the experiences students have and the ideas those experiences evoke, and how those experiences and ideas are transformed into knowledge through reflection and experimentation.

As role models of cross-cultural adaptation, faculty directors must also understand how their own skills and appreciation for diversity are a significant part of affective aspects of an international learning experience. While focusing students' attention on the opportunities for intense cross-cultural learning encounters during a sojourn abroad, faculty directors should be aware of how their own behavior is perceived and modeled by their students. In this way the faculty directors of short-term programs must be prepared to serve not only as sources of factual information and theoretical orientation for students, but must also be able to model the skills necessary to function in a foreign milieu—they must be good examples of cross-cultural adaptability and sensitivity. It is the job of the study abroad professional, therefore, to ensure that faculty understand their expanded educational role in undertaking programs of this sort and to help them explore pedagogical means through which to integrate the cognitive and affective aspects of learning.

---

[9] Kolb, David A. (1984). *Experiential Learning: Experiencing as the Source of Learning and Development.* Englewood Cliffs, NJ: Prentice Hall, 40-41.

Seminar Format

The ideal format for a short-term program abroad involves a series of weekly seminars that run 3 to 5 weeks during the semester immediately before, and 3 to 5 weeks immediately after travel. Whether the travel portion of the program is developed and administered by home-institution faculty or the international office, or is a predesigned course working with a program provider with local faculty abroad serving as instructors, the bottom line is that students participating in a short-term program must be given time to clarify academic and personal goals prior to departure by focusing their attention on a narrow set of concepts related to the site. If you are a lone administrator sending students on programs without faculty from your institution, you should consider having students sign up for independent study courses with appropriate faculty who can help them focus their attention prior to departure. The absolute minimum recommended is to give students an ongoing journal assignment that requires them to set intellectual and personal goals and engage in an ongoing process of reflecting on those goals while abroad (see Study Abroad Program In-Field Journal Assignment at the end of this chapter).

Ideally, predeparture and reentry meetings are structured as seminars. The content of these meetings should be a blend of lecture and discussion about assigned readings, and delivery of factual "practical" information. Reading assignments should introduce students to an aspect of the place to be visited, as well as a methodological approach that is to be employed while abroad.

As part of their methodological preparation students should also be required to maintain a journal throughout the entire period. Reflection on discussions and personal insights should be recorded in this journal, which students use to generate journal summaries for class each week. These summaries are based on guiding questions or prompts offered by the instructor, designed to get students into communities and places abroad while thinking about the course focus (see Study Abroad Program In-Field Journal Assignment at the end of this chapter).

In designing predeparture and reentry seminars, you should also consider utilizing experiential techniques to acquaint students with the affective aspects of cross-cultural learning. Information-based techniques should be balanced with an experiential approach in order to reinforce for students the holistic nature of the education abroad experience, and to acquaint them with the ongoing process of reflection about their experiences. Excellent ideas for in-class experiential techniques can be found in publications from Intercultural Press.

Seminar Design: Focus, Prepare, Integrate

Because the time spent abroad on a short-term program is brief, and therefore contact with local people and social institutions can be fairly cursory, the integration of a particular disciplinary exploration of the places and people to be visited (e.g., urban growth, poverty or artistic expression), along with "practical" information about travel, safety, and program logistics before departure is absolutely necessary. This section will give you some guidelines for developing predeparture and reentry seminars and materials.

Clearly there can be as many models for these activities as there are educators who design them, but there are important issues that should be addressed during some sort of on-campus programming that is to complement a brief experience abroad. First and foremost of these issues is the need for faculty involved to focus student attention on the concepts and ideas to be explored before they depart. As topical explorations of specific issues in specific locations, predeparture and reentry seminars provide conceptual orientation for students throughout the three phases of a study abroad program. Teaching students about appropriate methodological approaches gives them tools needed to systematically explore these concepts. By integrating theoretical and methodological concepts, the predeparture and reentry seminars are designed to give students focused trajectories on which to briefly explore the cultural practices and social issues of people from another place while simultaneously giving them some activity or routine through which to apprehend themselves as socially and culturally positioned actors in the emerging "global" society.

As a frame for their experience abroad, pre- and post-travel meetings should do the following:

• *Focus* students' attention on a particular set or ideas of concepts related to the places to be visited, and academic and personal expectations on obtainable goals in light of the particular program. This preparation should in some way *build students' awareness of themselves* as part of particular cultural traditions and be used as a springboard toward deeper cross-cultural understanding or global comprehension, and toward cultural relativism.

• *Prepare* students logistically for their program abroad by providing "practical" information (e.g., packing, money, safety, etc.).

• Help students to *integrate* their international experience into their personal and academic lives back on campus after their return. In terms of personal internalization, the reentry seminar should provide a forum in which students are encouraged to reflect on observations, interactions, and personal changes since returning home. Academic integration suggests a conceptual value of study abroad toward institutional learning goals and curricula. Students should also be afforded the opportunity to demonstrate knowledge they have gained and helped to articulate how they see this knowledge as beneficial to their academic, professional, and personal lives.

If institutional structures and resources permit, encouraging faculty to develop short-term programs abroad in pairs allows for the possibility of a theoretical/methodological approach in which one faculty member focuses on a theoretical topic (e.g., urban growth in Europe or identity in British theatre) and the other offers a disciplinary approach to field methodologies (e.g., visual sociology or literary critique). For revenue-conscious deans, it is important to emphasize that this model generates two courses worth of tuition revenue, and that having two faculty members participating in a single program goes a long way in limiting liability and ensuring safety in the event of a crisis.

Predeparture Seminar: Theoretical Focus, Methodological Practice, and Cultural Awareness

Most short-term programs abroad cannot give students the same kind of immersion experience that semester- or year-long programs can. Students need to be told this up front. From this frank discussion should come an outline of the academic and cross-cultural goals of the program, and students should be required to articulate reasonable personal and academic expectations that are in tune with their interests and skills and match the broad goals of the courses.

Theoretical Focus

Academic goals must be rather precise examinations of particular topics related to the area of travel. "Exploring culture" is not an appropriate academic goal, since it provides little to no focus on academic content (what, after all *is* culture, and how does one go about exploring it?). Faculty developing short-term programs should be encouraged to utilize the field site as a "text" through which they will explore a particular research problem or sociocultural, physical, or historical phenomenon (whatever their discipline). This is the aspect of the seminar that most resembles a "typical" course. This theoretical or topical exploration should be broad enough to help students develop their specific interests within the same conceptual paradigm.

Methodological Practice

Predeparture meetings should also focus on developing field research projects that deal with the topic or topics at hand while encouraging students to meet people and explore the places they will visit. Again, it is important to be clear with students that their short-term experience abroad necessitates a very focused and intensive sojourn that pretty much has them following the lead of their faculty director or directors. Helping students understand methodology will further this.

In a number of short-term programs operated at DePaul, paired teams of faculty offer theoretical and methodological focuses around which students are encouraged to build their specific research/program project. In the program "Amsterdam, Rotterdam, Brussels and Prague: Comparative Perspectives in Urban Development," for example, students are asked to explore "the particular urban forms exemplified by the cities of Amsterdam, Rotterdam, Brussels, and Prague, and the social and economic forces that have shaped these European cities over time…." Through the lens of a camera students are guided through an exploration of the history and urban development of these cities while they continually reflect on their own position within social urban geographies and class structures. Two professors whose areas of interest are in human geography and urban planning and renewal oversee the in-field portion of the program. As a method for exploring various aspects of the urban spaces to be visited they have their students focus on "visual/visible signs and symbols of contemporary issues of urban development" in order to explore "comparative central city redevelopment, gentrification, changing social and cultural urban geography…through photography and other methods and forms of fieldwork…." As an easily-understood method for "capturing experiences" (or collecting data), photography provides an outstanding memory stimulus through which students can continually reflect on their experiences at different points in time.

Journals are also maintained as a mechanism to hone students' skills at reflective observation and abstract conceptualization about their thoughts and feelings in relation to the conceptual work being explored. In addition, the journal can facilitate reflection about students' personal and academic goals, cultural values, and the emerging global society as they prepare to engage in a cross-cultural immersion experience abroad. The journal is a way to help students "discover" their own emerging cultural identities in relation to, and as part of, crisscrossing networks of global media, social organizations, and human movement. This discovery of self-knowledge will come about through guided and continuous reflective observation and journaling within the context of students' preparation for, participation in, and return from a study abroad experience. During the London theater program, in which students spend 3 weeks in London viewing plays and reflecting on how cultural identity is enacted both on stage and in the audience, students are required to maintain a particularly interesting group journal online.

Cultural Awareness: Toward Cultural Relativism

In order to maintain focus on the place to be visited, a "culture-specific" approach should be employed in order to expose students to some of the cross-cultural issues and challenges they might face in a particular place. Broader cross-cultural goals of a study abroad program are certainly appropriate goals of short-term programs, but because of the brevity of the visit, educators must pay careful attention to

(1) the deconstruction (and/or inadvertent perpetuation) of sociocultural and nationalistic stereotypes within the context of the course and travel, and (2) the modeling of skills necessary to successfully operate in diverse cultural and social environments. An understanding of the anthropological concept of "cultural relativism" will assist in breaking down these stereotypes. Faculty directors can serve as models for students, sharing their expertise and experiences of functioning in the target society, and helping students understand through real-life situations what it means to work in an international milieu. This is an aspect of the short-term program abroad that must be attended to with thought and careful consideration. Faculty must be able and willing to model skills in cross-cultural adaptation and should speak openly with students about how they can nurture these skills within themselves.

Opposed to "culture" conceived of as a normative set of rules, cultural relativism is a conceptual stance employed by anthropologists in the field that demands them, when observing any sort of behavior or cultural practice, to try to understand those practices from the point of view of the people doing them. When observing new or unusual practices of people outside our own societies, cultural relativism requires us to suspend any kind of judgment about those practices until we can better understand the motivations and cultural assumptions of the actors. The concept of cultural relativism is rooted in Franz Boas' heavily empirical research into the production of language in Baffinland and British Columbia. Boas, who worked at the turn of the 20th century with Native North Americans, argued that cultural phenomena are "historically conditioned and transmitted by the learning process," and that they are themselves, "determinants of our very perceptions of the external world."[10] In other words, as they began to grapple with ethnographic examples of a developing concept of "culture," anthropologists in the late 19th and early 20th centuries came face-to-face with the facts of human variability. This variability, as had previously been postulated, was due to varied levels of evolution that specific groups of people had or had not achieved; European culture, from this perspective, was imagined to be the highest form of culture. Employing a "comparative perspective," Boas and his students encountered cultural practices that challenged this ethnocentric view, that disrupted the "grand scheme" of cultural evolution, and eventually replaced anthropological theories based on "cultural stages of savagery, barbarism, and civilization" with an understanding of the "multiplicity of cultures" as based on, and legitimated through often very different histories, beliefs and cultural practices.

Reentry Seminar: Internalization, Integration, and Demonstration of Knowledge

The post-field program enables the students to re-interpret, integrate, and formulate their learning into a whole experience. It enables them to stand back and see the structure or connectedness of things. It also helps them avoid closure at a time when they are still uncertain about the new concepts and consciousness they have been exploring within themselves. It is important for the students to keep the learning alive and moving; they cannot, as happens too frequently with a course, finish and say, "Well, that was an interesting experience." Learning has just begun and should not be filed away and regarded as complete.[11]

---

[10] Stocking, George W., Jr. (1968). *Race, Culture, and Evolution: Essays in the History of Anthropology.* New York: The Free Press, 156-160.

[11] Sikkema, Mildred, and Agnes Niyekawa (1987). *Design for Cross-Cultural Learning.* Yarmouth, ME, Intercultural Press, Inc., 50.

Whereas this is probably the most important phase in a study abroad program if sustained learning is to be established, it is also the phase that is most often neglected. This may have to do with a persistent concept of learning in the United States that envisions learning as a one-way process, in which data is simply transmitted to an individual for storage. Paulo Freire refers to this one-way notion of education as the "banking account concept" in which information is simply deposited into the head of the learner by a putatively knowledgeable teacher. According to an experiential pedagogy, however, learning is an ongoing process of exchange between learner and teacher in which the experimentation with new-found knowledge is just as important for the learner as is the "factual" information. The reentry seminar, therefore, is an excellent time for faculty and students to collaboratively explore the experiences they have shared abroad, and to come up with new insights about themselves and societies in which they operate.

The reentry seminar should also help students recognize the personal growth that they have undergone as a result of the program abroad, while getting them to understand specific concepts and ideas related to the program site. While still in the field, students should be encouraged to begin reflecting on the changes that have taken place within their own concepts of themselves and prepare for the potential of "reverse culture shock" in which they could feel alienated from family and friends. Whereas reverse culture shock is not as major an issue with short-term programs abroad, very often students indicate that they have formed new friendships with students on their program and feel a sense of loss when they realize that they have experienced an important, life-changing event without their friends and family. The phenomenon of being asked "how it was," only to be faced with glossy stares as they begin to tell a story from abroad is a common one, and one that puts strains on relationships at home.

For the success of a learning experience to be fully realized, from an experiential perspective, there must be a structured means through which students bring the experience "home" and apply what they have learned to their everyday lives. Like a collection of photos, placed in a picture book and left on the shelf to collect dust, the collection of experiences from abroad must not be allowed to collect dust in the minds of learners. On the contrary, for learning to occur, the emotional and cognitive growth must be internalized personally and integrated intellectually. To do this, some sort of outlet for creative intellectual development and expression must be provided.

At DePaul there are two models emerging for this reentry seminar. One involves several follow-up meetings of the group during the semester immediately after their return. Like the predeparture seminars, these are regular course meetings in which students are guided through some form of analysis of their experiences and the "data" they collected while in the field.

Personal Internalization

Both of these aspects of reentry are significantly more acute after a long-term stay abroad, but they should not be neglected for students whose visit to another society has been shorter. Students should be encouraged to reflect on the changes they have gone through, and the "new" person they now imagine themselves to be. Very often the learning on a short-term program, if everything goes well, can be as disruptive of established identities as on semester- or year-long programs.

This continued process of internalization "enables the students to reinterpret, integrate and formulate their learning into a whole experience" within the context of their home culture.[12] During the reentry phase, the faculty directors are encouraged to engage themselves in a similar process of reflection along with their

---

[12] Steinaker, Norman W., and Robert M. Bell (1979). *The Experiential Taxonomy: A New Approach to Teaching and Learning.* New York: Academic Press.

students. "Behavior that is not sustained by peers, by society, or by a respected authority seldom becomes permanent in a human life." This leadership role of the faculty member will both strengthen the bonds established abroad, and will be an active demonstration—another experience, if you will—of the learning that has been expected of the students. In this sense, the role of the faculty director truly does become that of a role model.

All students participating in programs at DePaul are required to complete a journal summary (see Study Abroad Program Final Journal Assignment at the end of this chapter) in which cross-cultural learning goals are evaluated against Kelly and Meyers' Cross-Cultural Adaptability Inventory (CCAI).[13] (See John Sunnygard's Chapter 14, If You Cross Over the Sea...Program Leadership for Intercultural Development, for further discussion on the CCAI.) I have found this inventory to be a useful tool that helps measure critical skills of adaptation and observation. Students are not given a grade for this journal summary, but they are invited to discuss (either in person or as part of regular returnee group meetings) their reflections and continued goals in the area of cross-cultural communication.

Academic Integration and the Demonstration of Knowledge

Academic integration is another area of reentry that is often given short attention by teachers and administrators of study abroad programs. Students returning from any experience abroad seek out ways to make their newly found international identity meaningful within the context of their academic degree. It is important for educators involved to help students develop an integrated understanding of their international experiences as a part of their academic career. Part of this simply involves students discussing their experiences in other classes and venues on campus.

The desire to demonstrate what one has learned abroad is a natural, but very often frustrating part of returning from a study abroad experience. This is the point at which students are compelled to engage in a level of conversation that they had not previously been accustomed to participating in. Students returning from an experience abroad are constantly asked to summarize their experiences in one or two sentences by friends, family, and academics alike. The unprepared students are always taken by surprise when, on reflection, they are unable to perform this sort of summary. If they attempt to enter into a more substantive explanation of their experiences, they are often met with blank stares or simply cut off by an impatient audience. What quickly becomes apparent to the returned study abroad student is that their experience is to a great extent somewhat incomprehensible to people who have not shared similar experiences.

As has been suggested, in order for overseas learning to be an experience of growth, the learner must be able to use the experience abroad to enhance future experiences in his or her life. First, however, students must develop skill at articulating their experience. A final research project or other creative expression of what they have learned serves as a means through which students can focus their life-altering experience toward a specific area of interest. The research project also serves as a means through which students can potentially develop their experience into further research, or simply gain a more in-depth understanding of a particular aspect of the people and places visited.

In addition to writing, students should be given the opportunity to talk to other students about their experience. Hiring students as assistants and/or inviting them to speak at recruitment and predeparture seminars are excellent means through which the student can feel a tangible sense of accomplishment, as well as

---

[13] Kelley, Colleen, and Judith Meyers (1995). *Cross-Cultural Adaptability Inventory Manual.* Minneapolis, MN: National Computer Systems, Inc.

assist the study abroad office in the task of encouraging other students to apply. This reentry seminar, therefore, is a powerful tool in perpetuating the learning that began long before the plane left the runway. As educators committed to promoting and developing quality programs abroad, we must be extraordinarily conscious of the ways in which students are able to build their international learning into their lives as emerging actors on global stages. Hopefully the suggestions found here will promote an ongoing conversation as to how best to do this.

General

Short-term programs abroad do not afford students the luxury of time to understand the lay of the land in their host countries. To enable students to make the most of the time they do have on site, they need to have as much advance preparation as possible.

Of course, much of what students learn in the orientation meetings and handbooks will not mean much to them until they are on site. But if you have provided the sufficient academic, logistical, and cultural information, it will make sense to them once they have landed.

In addition to the expected benefit of increased student preparedness, a solid orientation program can also help to reduce institutional liability. If it can be documented that Student A was advised against Behavior B, your institution will be in a better position in any legal situations.

Orientation Meetings

Make every effort to have at least one orientation meeting with the students. If you are administering a number of programs, it makes the best use of time to have one single general information meeting for participants in all programs, facilitated by the international office. Individual group meetings led by the faculty director can follow this general meeting. In fact, having the small group meetings immediately following the general session can help to ensure that students will attend. Students may not be missed in a meeting of 300 participants, but it will certainly be obvious if they do not attend the meeting of their group of 15.

Sample Agenda for a General Student Orientation Meeting

7:00	Welcome by director of international office
7:05	Comments from former student participant: what to expect
7:15	General safety presentation by campus security director
7:30	Group dynamics presentation by experienced faculty director
7:45	Psychological issues presentation by counseling center staff
8:00	College policies abroad presentation by dean of students
8:15	Cross-cultural issues presentation by experienced faculty leader
8:30	Health issues presentation by college physician
8:45	International studies office staff: reminders and Q&A
9:00	Small group meetings: faculty director and students

Orientation Handbooks

Written information needs to be given to students, too, usually in the form of a predeparture handbook. Students may receive their handbooks before or after the general meeting—there are advantages to each. What is most important is that the relevant details need to be given to students in writing, because they will only recall brief bits of what they hear at the orientation meeting. When a question comes up, students should refer to the printed materials for answers.

Required Information

In all cases, be careful not to assume advance knowledge on the part of the students. They may not have any idea how to go about obtaining a passport; the only visa they know is a credit card; and they may not know that it is not safe to drink the water in some areas (and yes, that includes ice.)

Information that should be given both at orientations and in writing includes the following.

Logistical

✓ The need for a passport, visas, and other essential documents should be explained. Explain the process for getting a passport. If students already have passports, ask them to check the expiration date. If a visa is needed, give students the necessary forms and instructions to obtain one.

✓ International travel arrangements should be spelled out clearly in writing by the travel agent or other service provider, and shared with the students in writing, with extra copies for family and friends. Tell students what time to arrive at the airport and where to meet the group. Talk to them about security measures they are likely to experience in airports.

✓ What is and is not included in the program fee (e.g., housing, home stays, and meals) should be clearly spelled out in the course description. If there is to be a home stay, students should be given as much information as possible about the host family, including family members' names and ages, and if available, the address and phone number. Students should be encouraged to bring hospitality gifts.

✓ Students should be advised about how much additional cash will be required to cover meals not included, recommended amounts for personal spending, additional travel, and so on. They should be given advice on how to carry the funds (e.g., will a credit card work or do they need travelers' checks, cash, or local currency?).

✓ Packing recommendations and airline luggage restrictions: include a list of suggestions about appropriate clothing to bring, how many formal outfits should be taken, and so on. Encourage the students to pack what they think they need and then walk at least four blocks with their fully loaded suitcase. If they cannot do it, they need to lighten the load.

✓ Phone and e-mail services abroad: tell students that access to these services may be more limited than in the United States. If students buy phone cards, make sure that they know how to use the cards correctly. Students have been surprised to receive large phone bills from hotels despite the fact that they were using a prepaid card. It is fine to visit an Internet café occasionally to touch base with home. But encourage students to spend their precious time exploring the culture—better to take in one more museum than to spend an afternoon sending e-mails to friends.

Academic Policies

✓ Faculty directors should provide syllabi and class expectations, a schedule of class meetings (before, during, and after travel), and in-field activities.

✓ Grading and assessment policy: like any course, expectations must be spelled out clearly. See Chapter 6, Designing the Academic Course.

✓ Policy to add/drop courses after program has begun (e.g., if a student wishes to withdraw from a course after the program has begun, what are the academic and financial penalties?).

✓ Academic policies about plagiarism and disciplinary procedures should be clearly articulated.

Health, Safety, and Legal Issues

(Chapter 16, Safeguards for Short-Term Programs, provides extensive information on the items listed here.)

✓ Inoculations (if necessary) and requirements for medical examinations before departure.

✓ Precautions and recommended procedures for transporting prescription and over-the-counter medicines.

✓ Explanation of how medical emergencies will be handled, and the general availability of medical facilities in the host country.

✓ Advice on how to keep oneself healthy before, during, and after travel; include information about "jet lag" and "traveler's flu."

✓ Caution about depression and eating disorders; ask students to be frank in sharing medical information with you about such issues.

✓ Risks of being sexually active with other group members or local people during program.

✓ The policy on alcohol and drug use abroad should also be distributed separately in writing.

✓ Health insurance coverage: explain the institutional policy. If health insurance is the responsibility of the student, make that clear.

✓ The list of emergency contacts and telephone numbers can be printed on wallet-size cards to ensure that students always know how to call for help.

✓ Encourage students to access the U.S. State Department Web site (http://travel.state.gov). The U.S. State Department publishes a number of pamphlets that include both country-specific recommendations, as well as general travel advice for Americans traveling abroad.

Group Building

Short-term programs abroad are intense experiences that require group cohesion and cooperation. During orientation, discuss issues around "group travel" and the attendant stress this may put on students and their intergroup relationships. Make sure students understand that there are times when the wishes of the individual must be sacrificed for the good of the group.

In predeparture discussions about academic/theoretical aspects of class, get group members to talk openly about their personal reactions, ideas, and ideologies, and discuss differences of opinion among group members fairly and openly. This not only builds trust among students, but also provides for great discussions about relative perspectives and respect for different opinions.

Build learning communities. Each person in the group should be familiar with the academic and personal goals of other members, and the faculty director should foster an environment of trust and mutual support.

Country/Culture Awareness Exercises

There are a number of exercises that the faculty director can do with the students to get them thinking about where they are going and how it might differ from their own environment. The Autoethnography Exercise at the end of this chapter is a good tool for promoting cultural awareness.

General Reentry

The "togetherness" of the short-term program abroad will create a strong bond among the students. Once the program has ended, they will feel somewhat bereft without their traveling companions. The international office, the faculty director, or both should create times to bring the groups back together to talk about their shared experiences.

Program specific debriefings. If possible, international office staff should schedule a 1- to 2-hour meeting with each group to discuss all aspects of the program—academic, logistical, and social. Give students the opportunity to let you know what worked well and to give suggestions for improvement. This can also be a time for students to discuss any readjustment problems they may have and to find out that their group-mates share those issues.

Welcome back events. Schedule an event (e.g., dinner or an ice cream party) and invite all students returning from short-term programs. This gives students a chance to talk with participants in other programs and to share experiences.

Written evaluations. Because of the nature of these programs, students may be loathe to discuss any negatives at the group meetings. Using a written evaluation allows the students to criticize and make suggestions in an anonymous way. (See Chapter 12, "It Changed My Life": Strategies for Assessing Student Learning.

On-Site

The on-site student orientation is one of the most important moments of your study abroad program. Your orientation meeting will set the tone for the overseas experience the students are about to commence.

A good orientation should address the practical issues as well as the cultural challenges the students are about to face. Your meeting makes everything real because the students are now (at last) in the host country and your task at hand is to facilitate their transition to the new environment.

While preparing your meeting agenda, remember that certain practical issues should be addressed regardless of the home institution, the field of study, or the length of the program. However, each orientation should be tailored to the specific type of student, the length of the program, and the nature of the material being studied.

Important goals to keep in mind throughout the orientation preparation and process are to give the program a solid beginning, to provide a strong foundation for the program, and to establish trust and respect among the students and yourself. Finally, and most importantly, your on-site orientation is meant to prepare and inform the students for the weeks ahead.

Ideally, on-site orientation should be broken down into layers: the arrival-and-survival orientation, the general orientation, the academic orientation, and the accommodation orientation. By breaking down your orientation, the students have time to focus on the subject at hand and are less overwhelmed than when they hear and try to process everything at once. Remember, students need time to get settled, as well as time to sleep and to get over jet lag, for them to absorb information in an appropriate and timely fashion.

Arrival and Survival

It is extremely useful to have a welcome letter ready and waiting for each student upon the group's arrival in the host country. Students receive the letter when they check in. It should be brief, yet it must contain pertinent and important information including:
- program obligations such as times and places of important first program meetings;
- a map of the area where they will be living (with pharmacy, ATM, police station, subway stop, and food shops clearly marked);
- directions to and from the housing location to the site of your general orientation meeting; and
- information on how to call home.

It is a good idea to check in the group all together. A group check-in facilitates tasks such as handing out items such as keys and linens, and explaining rules, regulations, curfews, and security. It makes pointing out important facilities, such as kitchens, cafeterias, bathrooms and showers, laundry, and Internet access much easier, too.

A walking tour of the neighborhood is always useful and appreciated by the students. Be sure to point out:
- public transportation stops
- ATM machines
- the supermarket
- the post office
- the pharmacy
- the police station
- historical sites
- parks

A walking tour is also a good time to give students a few important safety tips for the host city or country. Stick to basic and simple things to remember such as not walking home alone late at night. Keep in mind that your students are generally extremely tired and that your more in-depth safety talk will be at your general orientation meeting the following day.

General Orientation

General orientation should be held as close to the arrival of the students as possible, though it is better not to have it on the actual day of arrival in the host country. Experience has shown that covering important topics on arrival day is ineffective because students are too tired to absorb or learn anything of importance.

Tips on running a successful orientation meeting include the following:
* Have a specific agenda of subjects to cover.
* Try to be brief yet complete in your explanation of the subjects discussed.
* Have more than one person present the information, to keep student attention.
* If available, use visual aids such as slides, posters, transparencies, handouts and copies, and Microsoft® PowerPoint presentations.
* Allow some time for questions and answers after each topic is covered, but keep the meeting moving.

Each participant should receive a packet of information and a program calendar. Your orientation packet should include written material about the topics covered at the meeting for later reference. Your packets should also include maps, timely periodicals or articles about the host city or country, any in-house publications you may have, as well as information on local happenings, concerts, exhibits, and events occurring during the program's duration.

Topics to be covered at your general orientation meeting should include the following:
* the program calendar and introduction
* money and banking
* telephone and post office
* transportation
* health and safety

Program Calendar

When reviewing the program calendar with your group, make sure the students understand the dates when classes begin; when exams will be held (to be discussed further and in greater detail during your academic orientation); departure points and times for any museum visits, trips, or excursions; and the end date of the program, which is obviously important for planning the group's departure from the program accommodations and host city.

Money and Banking

During the money and banking segment of your orientation, it is useful to have some of the local currency on hand for students to refer to while you explain the notes and coins used in the host country. Be sure to explain how and where to change currency in the host city, as well as local banking hours. Assume that most of your students have never traveled abroad before and supply them with reliable and convenient addresses for banks and exchange bureaus. Finally, it is always a good idea to explain how students can have money wired to them in case of an emergency or wallet theft; provide information on local Western Union offices.

When discussing money and banking, explain sales tax in the host country as well as local tipping practices. Because student budgets are personal and can vary enormously, it is generally not useful to discuss budgeting at length, though reiterating that planning ahead will help students' budgets is always worth mentioning. Also, it is a good idea to point out items or services that are particularly expensive in the host city.

Communications

Communication is an important part of any orientation and is best presented by discussing it in terms of telephoning, post office services, and e-mail access.

Telephones. Explain to students how telephones work in the host country: are pay phones coin operated or do they take cards? If phone cards are needed, tell students how and where to purchase the cards. Be sure to have up-to-date prices.

Inform students of the calling rates within the host country and internationally. Cover all possibilities, including direct dial, collect calling, and U.S. phone credit card calling; provide students with the necessary dialing codes. Explain how students can call home and how people from home can call students. Many parents will be dialing overseas for the first time and will not know how to place the call; if you inform the students, they can tell their folks. Suggest to students the least expensive way to call and remind them of the time differences!

Cell phones have taken off in Europe and more and more students are purchasing cell phones during the first days after they arrive in the host country. You may want to try to find the best deal available to students or work out a deal with a local company especially for your students. Although it is impossible to know everything about cell phones because the choices are vast and beyond what most of us ever imagined available, try to at least inform yourself of the general way cellular calling works in the host country so that you can point students in the right direction.

Things to note regarding cell phones: Will the phone have international calling access? Will it have voicemail? Do students pay to receive calls? Are the phones available with a prepaid card system, to avoid unpaid bills? Will students need a bank account to establish a contract with a local phone company?

Have a reliable address or two ready for phone stores should your students decide to buy or rent cell phones.

Cell phones are a great help in that they allow parents and friends to contact students directly without waiting to be passed through a receptionist in a dormitory or having to learn the local language to leave a message. Cell phones have also lightened the stress and tension related to telephone use in home-stay situations.

Post Office. Local post office information should be made available to the students. Inform them of the post office's hours and the rates for sending post cards and letters via airmail. Give students an idea of how long they can expect to wait for a letter or a package. You should warn students of possible customs taxes on large packages, and of things that will not clear customs easily. Be sure to mention any other relevant services available to them at the post office. For example, in France, La Poste is also a bank and a money exchange, and it has Western Union facilities.

E-mail. Regarding e-mail, most students have no intention of living without it, no matter where in the world they are! If your program facilities do not have a computer, be sure to identify Internet cafés with flexible hours and good rates, or tell students how to find one themselves.

Transportation

An important section of your orientation will cover transportation in the host city or country. Many students will have never taken public transportation in their lives. Try to plan an activity in the first day or so where students can take public transportation with you the first time. That way their transportation orientation is "live and in person."

Give a clear, basic explanation of the subway and/or bus system in the host city. Include the hours the system operates and anything pertinent or special to the system that students will need to know. Make sure each student has a map, and during your meeting run through a couple of sample trips to places in town they might visit. Mention areas that are better off avoided in the evenings or parts of town that are undesirable. Be sure to give students the correct vocabulary for purchasing tickets or passes and have current prices available.

A short discussion of using taxis is also helpful. Provide students with approximate costs and hailing procedures, again always keeping in mind that your students may have never taken a taxi before. Wherever possible, supply students with a phone number to call a taxi should they need to get home late at night. Make sure the company you suggest is legitimate and reliable.

Health and Safety

Certainly one of the most crucial parts of your general orientation meeting is the discussion of health and safety. It is useful to provide the students with a list of doctors they can contact should they become ill. Ideally, these doctors would speak English so that the students could communicate more comfortably. Information on local hospitals and pharmacies is useful as well. Be sure to explain to students how health care is paid for in the host country: are students expected to pay first and be reimbursed by insurance later? Inform them of how much a typical visit to the doctor will cost as well as what mode of payment is accepted. If the program provides insurance for the students, make sure you have a copy of the policy and that you have read it over and understand it as you will no doubt at some point during your program be asked to give a sick student an explanation of it.

Students should be given the phone number to call for ambulance, fire, and police—the host-culture equivalent of 911 in the United States.

Because student safety is always a top priority, the topic should be addressed formally at general orientation. However, staying safe is an ongoing process for your group, so you should be available to discuss safety issues at any time during the program. Sometimes some of the best safety discussions with students happen in more casual settings and situations, for instance at a group meal or on a long train ride.

Students need to think about their safety at all times and should be instructed, reminded, and encouraged to make good decisions for themselves throughout their time abroad.

The safety section of your orientation is a good time to review the rules and regulations of student conduct. This includes discussion of use of alcohol and drugs. Know your program's policy on alcohol use as well as the legal drinking age in the host country. When discussing alcohol, be clear about what may be tolerated (e.g., a glass of wine at dinner with their host family) versus what will be considered grounds for expulsion from the program. Remind students that one of the keys in staying safe in a foreign environment is keeping their wits about them to recognize anything that doesn't feel right and to make good decisions. If student thinking is clouded by alcohol or drug use, their chances of making the best choices and decisions are not as good, hence putting them at a higher security and safety risk.

U.S. student safety abroad since the events of September 11 is a crucial part of any on-site general orientation. Now, more than ever, we need to provide open communication and plans should the unthinkable happen.

Prepare an emergency card to give to each student showing simple steps to take in case of emergency. Keep it simple and to the point. The card should have emergency contact numbers, including the U.S. consulate in the host city.

Encourage communication within your group. For example, ask students to provide you with information about their destinations on travel weekends and breaks. Should you ever need to account for everyone at short notice you at least have an idea of where the students are and when they are expected back. Students understand the need for the information they are providing and are typically very cooperative.

It is important to get the tone of this section of orientation just right. You need students to understand the seriousness of what you are discussing, as well as the importance of having a "what if" plan of action, but you do not want to cause confusion or panic or have students dwelling on the topic unreasonably. Think about your presentation carefully beforehand to ensure projection of the right feeling.

Accommodations Orientation

Accommodations may be the most challenging part of getting your group settled in the host country. Experience shows that students who are comfortable and happy with their program housing acclimate to their new environment more easily than those who are unhappy with their lodgings. Therefore, preprogram preparation and selection of student housing is vital to the overall success of your program.

During your housing meeting with the students be clear about general rules and regulations. Be extra clear on program rules about excessive noise, parties, curfews, and overnight guests. Students should receive clear instructions on telephoning from their place of residence, as well as information and instructions about kitchen, cafeteria, and laundry facilities.

The type of housing your program offers may influence how you present the accommodations section of orientation. Below are some tried and true ways to orient students to various standard housing options.

Residence Halls

Present rules and regulations of the residence hall to the students clearly. It is always better to tell students exactly what they are responsible for before the program begins than to try to backtrack later should anything go wrong.

Presenting house rules in the form of a contract that the students read and sign is an effective way to get them to heed regulations. In this contract you should be clear on the following issues:
- Obligations and procedures regarding students' keys and lockouts of their rooms.
- Responsibility for damage to the residence and the need to replace anything broken or damaged.
- Obligations and procedures regarding guests and visitors.
- Rules and regulations regarding noise, parties, making curfew, etc.

◆ Obligations and procedures regarding housekeeping. Will custodial staff clean students' rooms, or are the students responsible for cleaning their rooms themselves? What about trash? What are students responsible for regarding cleaning linens and towels?

◆ How does the telephone system in the residence work? Are phones automatically connected and able to call anywhere? Are the phones prepaid or will students have phone bills to pay?

Home Stays

Students in home stays tend to be much more nervous than other students about their housing. And why not? After all, for the most part they have moved out of their parents' house and been on their own for a couple of years and now they are moving into somebody else's parents' house with a new set of rules and procedures. Students in home stays are always worried about language barriers, whether they will like their host family, whether the host family will like them, and whether or not it will all work out between them. They need to feel confident in your choice of their home stay situation and of your understanding of what they are looking for in their home stay selection.

Students will want to know how the program selects their host families. Briefly explain the procedure: is there a person on the staff who is in charge of family stays or does the program work through an agency? In the latter case, be sure that the agency is reputable and that it understands the type of student on your program. Be clear regarding meals, kitchen privileges, and academic schedules that may interfere with family meal times. Clarity on prices and rents is obviously important, as well as whether or not laundry facilities and telephone access will be available to your students.

On the day of arrival, meet with the students as a group to talk about their home stay situations; go over the general rules and regulations that apply to every family. Field general questions and remain positive! Reassure students that in most cases, the extra anxiety they may be feeling and the extra effort they will be making is well worth it. Experience has shown time and again that students in home stays improve their language abilities far beyond those living in a student residence or student apartment and that the experience of living with the local people is one they will carry with them throughout their lives.

Review with the students some guidelines on having a successful family stay. Reiterate what they are responsible for regarding rent, phone bills, and meals. Of course students will have already heard all of this back in their predeparture orientation in the United States, but generally students listen a lot more closely once they are on site.

After you have met with the students as a group, each student should have a short individual meeting with whoever has organized their housing for them. At the individual meeting details about the family can be discussed. Have an information card prepared for each student with the name, address, and phone number of their host family as well as directions to and from the home to the site of your general orientation meeting. Prepare a list of family-specific living guidelines for students to have and to read before they move in.

If it is not possible for the host family to pick up the student from your office or arrival site, try to send students via taxi to their new homes. Finally, arrange for students to have a welcome lunch or dinner with their hosts on the day of arrival.

Apartments

Students staying in apartments will need much of the same information as students in home stays. On the day of arrival have the apartment address and phone numbers ready for each student, as well as information about the students' floors, codes, and keys. Try to send students to their apartments via taxi, and as with the home stays, provide directions from each individual apartment back to the site of the general orientation. As with students living in a residence hall, provide a map of the neighborhood with the post office, subway station, ATM, police station, pharmacy, and grocery store clearly marked.

To help the students feel at home and to make sure the apartment is being treated properly, it is important to have someone who knows the apartment do a short orientation once the students have moved in. This person could be the apartment owner, a staff housing coordinator, or a person from the real estate agency. Make time to explain and show the students how different appliances work, how to get the heat and water on, or simply how to jiggle a tricky lock. Doing so will save everyone time, money, and headaches down the road.

Orientation is a good time to review apartment contracts. Be as specific as possible on rules and regulations as well as any utilities the students are responsible for paying. Go over security deposits, including what could possibly be deducted from the students' deposits at the end of the program. Be clear on the "do's and don'ts" of apartment living in the host country. Do not assume students know; often, student apartments in the United States are located together, and the only neighbors are other students. In the experience abroad, this will most likely not be the case and students should be told what they can expect as well as what is expected of them as neighbors.

Food in the Host Culture

At some point during your on-site orientation, the subject of food in the host culture should be addressed. Topics include the importance of food in the host culture and the rituals of meals in the host culture.
It is useful to explain to students the different options they have for eating out, such as restaurants, cafés, bistros, and so on. Briefly discuss what kinds of foods students can expect to find in the host culture, what things cost, and general cultural differences regarding food.

If food shopping is greatly different in the host country than it is in the United States, it is worthwhile to chat with students about appropriate procedures at the local market and review with them communication and interaction with small shopkeepers. Depending on how fluent students are in the local language, you may want to provide them with an easy reference list of food terms. Often, U.S. students are surprised to learn of the culinary delights the rest of the world enjoys that are not readily available at home.

Finally, a talk about vegetarianism outside the United States may be useful. More and more U.S. students describe themselves as vegetarians, yet they may not be prepared for the reception of vegetarianism in their host families or local restaurants. This part of your food talk may or may not be necessary for your students depending on the host culture.

Academic Orientation

One of the most important aspects of your on-site orientation is the segment pertaining to student academics because, after all, that is the very reason students are abroad in the first place.

Students will have been given information about classes offered and credits earned before they leave the United States. It is important to review this information with them once they are on site. Again, as with every other aspect of your orientation, students tend to listen better once they are on site.

Begin with a review of classes offered by the program. Give information and background on any local institutions your group may be enrolled in. The best way for students to be familiarized with their new school is to organize another, separate orientation meeting for your students with someone from the school. Ideally, this meeting should take place before classes begin.

Have a general talk with your group about procedures for registration, dropping and adding classes, and general academic administration. Students need to know who will be acting as their academic coordinator while they are abroad. If there is no one on site to fulfill this role for them, then students need to know whom they should contact at the sponsoring U.S. institution.

Go over the students' class schedules. Be clear about where they need to be and when. Students abroad often need more support from their faculty director since local educational institutions outside the United States operate very differently than the ones at home. Furthermore, students abroad are generally expected to be much more independent and self-starting than they needed to be back home since U.S. academic institutions tend to do much more hand holding than do overseas institutions.

Review the attendance policies in effect on your program because attendance may not be a factor/requirement at the students' home schools. Make sure students know what they are responsible for should they be absent, what constitutes an excused absence, and what is required in terms of make-up work.

Provide information on where to purchase textbooks. If any books are to be purchased before leaving the United States, students obviously would bring these texts with them. However, often there are books and workbooks to be purchased on site. It is useful for participants to know when and where to get the books and to have an idea about their cost.

Set up individual academic registration and confirmation meetings with each student during the first week abroad. That way, there is no confusion about exactly which courses students are signed up for, the number of credits they will be receiving, and what their academic obligations and requirements are.

Prepare the necessary paperwork to be completed and signed to facilitate the meeting. This will help keep meetings moving along and will provide you with an accurate academic record for each participant on your program.

Conclusion

Remember, orientation is an ongoing process throughout the entire program. After all your meetings, presentations, walking tours, and cultural lectures are done, the process continues. For the cultural learning and understanding of the host culture to continue, you and your team need to be available throughout the time abroad to act as a sounding board, to give guidance, to help, or sometimes just to lend a sympathetic ear. The more prepared the students are for their study abroad experience, the better, deeper, and more enriching the experience will be for all concerned.

Study Abroad Program
Journal Assignment

Congratulations on being accepted to the Liberal Arts and Sciences Study Abroad Program! As you prepare for this experience (one that many returning students claim has changed their lives) you have been asked to maintain a personal journal in which you will record your thoughts, feelings, and observations about yourself and the place to which you are planning to travel. During this process of preparation you should use your journal to reflect on three areas of learning, which are explained in more detail in the three "Learning Threads" below. Briefly, your journal should help you to accomplish the following

Learn about your own cultural practices, values, and "common sense." In so doing, you are also encouraged to think about how your society and cultural background have prepared you to communicate and live in another cultural environment (i.e., how do you deal with stress and ambiguity).

Learn about your program and your expectations for the program. What do you hope to accomplish during your study abroad experience? What role(s) do you expect to take on as a participant in this program? What precisely do you plan to do in order to achieve those goals and objectives? Do you think your role(s) will inhibit or further those goals?

Where are you going? You should be reading as much as you can about the place you're going. Talk to others who have been there; check the Web for interesting details about the city; read, read, read!!!

This journal will be the primary tool through you will learn about your study abroad experience as a whole, and in turn share with me your reflections on this learning. You should reflect on your personal experiences in your journal on a regular, ongoing basis, writing in it no less than three times per week.

I will also ask you to bring your journals to orientation meetings so that you can include spontaneous thoughts and observations evoked through these meetings in your ongoing reflections. I will <u>never</u> ask you to surrender your journal to me, nor will I ever ask you to share specific pages with me. I <u>will</u> ask you to summarize your observations at periodic moments during the next 6 months, and I <u>may</u> also ask you to share those observations with your fellow students. Please be prepared with examples of what you've written for our first orientation meeting.

In the end, this journal is for you. You should consider your journal as essential to the success of your program as finding a place to live or getting the airplane ticket. Your journal, along with your photos, will constitute your memory of your experience abroad. You owe it to yourself to make a sincere effort at maintaining this dialogue with yourself. **At the end of your program I will collect a 4 to 5 page summary from each of you as a condition of my submitting your grades to the registrar's office.** In other words, you will not be graded for your journal or summary, but you will receive your grades in exchange for the summary. I wish you luck in your preparation, and success as you explore and engage the emerging world of the transnational!

Three Learning Threads

I. Who are you?

Throughout your preparation you should be learning about yourself and your cultural values, "worldviews," and how those values inform your identity. Who are you and what makes you you? To get you going on this task, I have included a "value statements exercise" that you should read and reflect on in your journal. Please complete and bring this exercise with you to your first orientation meeting.

During the cross-cultural workshops you will also be asked to reflect on common stereotypes of Americans that are often held by foreigners. How do you think encountering these potentially conflicting attitudes and stereotypes will affect your experience abroad? What strategies can you come up with that will help you deal with the stress of encountering these attitudes? This stress is often associated with a phenomenon known as "culture shock." Have you ever experienced culture shock? If so, write about some of your feelings about those experiences. If not, what do you imagine culture shock to be like? Please note that I did NOT ask you if you think you will encounter culture shock—you will. My intention here is to get you to come up with strategies for dealing with culture shock in a healthy, productive way.

II. What are your goals and objectives for participating in this program?

Your decision to participate in this challenging cross-cultural experience is a significant commitment. What do you hope to "get out of" the program? You should come up with at least one objective each month of preparation, and in your journal think about how you plan to accomplish these objectives through specific goals. Do you anticipate any difficulties in accomplishing your goals? What specifically do you think you will need from those of us administering the program in order to succeed? For example, one objective you might set is to become more fluent in the target language. A goal that will help you meet this objective would be regular attendance at your language classes. Can you think of any other goals that would help you achieve your objective of fluency?

What does it mean to "immerse" oneself in a culture? What is culture? What do you know about the program that you feel will help you gain greater insight into the lives and practices of the people you will be meeting?

III. Where are you going?

During your interviews I asked each of you to try to imagine (or remember) what your destination city smells and tastes like. Hopefully you have been indulging yourself in dreaming about your destination.

In asking you to maintain this ongoing dialogue with yourself, I hope that you will begin to create the program in your head (and your journal). Include in your journal your excitement, anticipations, hopes, dreams, fears, and anxieties about going abroad. In other words, I am asking you, in a focused manner, to seriously think about what you are getting yourself into. In the end this is your program, and the degree of success you achieve is ultimately your own. Good luck with your task.

[Source: Adapted from DePaul University]

Study Abroad Program
In-Field Journal Assignment

Guided Reflections

As you begin your new adventure, learning and living abroad, please use the following weekly questions and "prompts" to guide your journal reflections. These are not meant to dictate what you write in your journal, but should be used as a way to focus your thoughts and reflections about your experience abroad as it is happening. Remember, this is your journal; these questions are a way to keep your journal focused on what you are learning and experiencing, but should not dictate what you do abroad.

Your journal reflections will be critical as you begin to put together your final Journal Summary at the end of your program. If you have any questions regarding this on-going assignment, please feel free to e-mail me at XXX@XXX. **As a reminder, a journal summary must be turned in at the completion of your program in order to receive credit for your courses.**

Have a *safe* and *wonderful* time abroad!
Explore, experience, and learn!

In-Field Journal Reflection #1

Now that you have arrived, you should begin to observe your reactions to and feelings about your living situation, your classes, the school you are attending, and your classmates (both other DePaul students and other students and host family members). In this first in-field journal summary assignment, write about one thing that surprised you and one thing that you expected about your:

1. Living situation
2. Classes
3. Host city
4. Classmates

What other things about your new environment have been particularly confusing, frustrating, or otherwise uncomfortable? Explain in detail and using as many examples as possible.

In-Field Journal Reflection #2

By the second week you should have some sort of daily routine established. What are you doing every day? Have you noticed any times that you feel the need to be alone? What do you do during these times? Are you spending time with other North American students on a regular basis? If so, explain the context. Have you made any local friends?

What nonprogram trips have you gone on? Have you visited (or made plans to visit) any places of interest to you? If so, describe your experiences there. What other activities are you doing to achieve your personal learning goals? Do you feel that you are adapting to your new environment well? What makes you feel this?

In-Field Journal Reflection #3

Describe the three closest contacts you have made to date with people from the host society. These might include members of your home-stay family, teachers, other students, or members of your own family who live abroad. Describe one or two situations in which you spent significant time with these people, how you felt about the interaction, and (if appropriate) what you discussed.

In-Field Journal Reflection #4
Go to a typical "tourist" attraction or event in your host city. Describe where you went, what you saw, and how you felt during your visit. How was the event or the site presented to you as a tourist? Take pictures and incorporate them into your journal.

Try to imagine what the people who designed the site think this event will communicate about this place. Who do they think you—as a tourist/member of an audience—are?

In-Field Journal Reflection #5
At this point in your time abroad you should have made significant contact with local people. Describe three interactions that you have had in which "American culture" was discussed. What did your contacts say about Americans? What did you say/how did you react? How did these conversations make you feel?

In-Field Journal Reflection #6
Describe something totally new or unexpected that you have learned about your host society. How did you learn about this? Is there anything that you could have done prior to departure that might have prepared you for this?

In-Field Journal Reflection #7
Reflect on the learning goals you set prior to your departure (remember those learning goals?). Are these goals appropriate for your experience to date? What have you been doing to achieve these goals? Are there any goals that you wish to modify, add, or remove?

In-Field Journal Reflection #8
Describe the first time you left your host city for more than two nights. Where did you go? What did you do? How did you feel when you returned? What did these feelings teach you about your sense of security and feelings of "home"?

In-Field Journal Reflection #9
What has changed most significantly about your perception and attitudes toward the host society since your arrival? Look back at your journal entries you wrote prior to your departure. What has surprised you? What did you anticipate? Explain. Do you feel that you are being accepted by your hosts (at school, at home, and on the street)? What makes you feel this way?

In-Field Journal Reflection #10
As you prepare to return to the United States, what kinds of feelings are you experiencing? Is there anything that you did not do that you wish you could have done earlier (place to visit, people to see)? What is your proudest accomplishment? What do you wish you had done better?

[Source: Adapted from DePaul University]

Study Abroad Program
Final Journal Summary Assignment
Winter 2002

Due: 10 April 2002

Spend a day or two rereading your journal from the beginning. Remember the day you interviewed with me, and first heard of this journal assignment. Do you recall the way you felt, the excitement of starting your journey abroad? Were you anxious about anything? What goals did you set for yourself? Who were you then?

As you read your journal, consider how you have changed over the last term. Have you been able to achieve the personal and academic goals that you set for yourself in the months prior to departing? What do you wish you had done differently? About which accomplishments are you particularly proud?

After reading your journal and reflecting on your experience abroad, write a page or two on each of the four broad questions below. Please be specific and precise when you recall experiences or events. I am not looking for large amounts of prose here, and would appreciate concise and clear answers to these questions. Try to avoid overly vague references, and focus on the experiences you had abroad, and how they made you feel (e.g., "I remember when I finally felt comfortable speaking Spanish with my host family. It was during supper the second week in Madrid..."). Please include stories and short narratives about your time abroad that will help me better understand you, your goals, and your accomplishments.

If you have specific complaints with the program, the administration of DePaul or your host institution, your field director, or some "logistical" aspect of the program, please do not focus on them here. While these negative feelings certainly would play a part in formulating your answers, and certainly may be presented here, this is not a program evaluation, per se. I am trying to better understand what you learned about yourself and your hosts while you negotiated the program—and your life—abroad. You should have been given a chance to complete program and course evaluation forms while at your study abroad site. If you did not, please let me know immediately.

If you have any questions, please feel free to contact me before your paper is due.

Good Luck!

Please write in clear, concise language using correct grammar. All summaries must be typewritten, and will be accepted as MSWord e-mail attachments (but not as e-mail text).

Question #1
Tell me about the most surprising, confusing, or strange difference about a person from your host society (e.g., a habit, a phrase, a way of doing something, etc.) that you observed while abroad. Be specific. Do not talk about "Parisians" or "most people." Give me concrete

examples about particular people. Describe the emotions you felt when you encountered this difference (e.g., did you laugh, were you frustrated, etc.), and then describe if your reaction changed during the time you were abroad. Did you ever grow accustomed to this difference? (FO)

Question #2
Think of three people from the host society with whom you felt particularly close. Explain your relationship to them, and if you plan to maintain contact in the future. For each of these people, write how you imagine they would describe you, as an American and as a student. Do you feel that these people understood you as a North American student? Describe the place where you most frequently encountered each of these people (e.g., in class, at home, in a park, in a pub, etc.). (PAC)

Question #3
Write the key values, beliefs, or identities that you used to describe yourself in the journal entries you made before you left. Again, please be specific and use direct quotes from your journal to tell me who you were before you left. Then compare that person with the person you are now. Are you the same? Did you change? (PA)

Question #4
Reflecting on the events you recorded in your journal, write about specific situations in which you felt:
1. Confused or embarrassed
2. Angry
3. Exhilarated
4. Alone and/or sad
5. At peace

Focus on briefly describing the events(s) and the people involved in each situation, and then tell me how you felt and what you did. (ER)

[Source: Adapted from DePaul University]

Sample Table of Contents for a Predeparture Orientation Handbook

[Source: Adapted from University of Kansas]

Autoethnography Exercise

Autoethnography is your view of your own cultural background and the values and interests that come from it. It is important to what we will call "positioning" in terms of the country-specific culture we experience in a short-term course abroad. Positioning refers to the perspective, or lens, that each of us brings to our observations and interpretation of another culture. From knowing our position vis-à-vis another culture, we can better be aware of how our views and backgrounds might affect what we see and the way we interpret what we see.

Please write on the front and back of this page about your own cultural background, using the following areas as a guide:

- Your religious background; how important it is to you; values from that background.
- Your cultural/ethnic background; how important it is to you; values from that background.
- Rituals or traditions that you celebrate as part of your culture or your family. Describe what is important to you about this tradition or custom, and why?
- Do you belong to some cultural or social group that you strongly identify with?
- Political leanings: do you have strong feelings about certain political issues?
- What values do you have that you think are part of U.S. history and culture? How strongly do you feel about these values? What do you do when these values are attacked?
- Your lifestyle: in what ways do you think your lifestyle is "typically American?"
- Interests and hobbies: course-specific ideas, such as have you ever studied art, dance, theater or film, or performed in a play or dance or attended performances?
- Brainstorm words and phrases that would describe your likes and dislikes, your identity, or your values.
- Have you ever experienced prejudice against who you are, or against a group to which you belong?
- What are your favorite American stories?

Course- and Country-Specific Example: Egypt

- Without thinking too much, write down all the words and phrases you have associated with the Middle East, Egypt, Arabs, and/or Muslims. These may be from media, movies, books, or your own personal experience.
- What background do you have in Middle Eastern history or culture?

[Source: Pamela Nice, University of St. Thomas]

What Do You Need to Know and Do Before You Go?

This exercise is intended to spur you to think about all of the things that you need to do to prepare yourself for your study abroad program. It is not a comprehensive checklist or to-do list, but it might give you some ideas for making your own list. Have fun!

Check yes if a statement is true, no if it is not...yet. Count up your yes responses.

How many yes responses did you get?

20 or more	You are a regular Marco Polo! Have a great adventure studying abroad!
15–19	Almost ready! You just need to polish a few globes before you go.
10–14	You have more than just packing to do before departure...
less than 10	Are you sure you know where you are going? Use the time before you go wisely!

Is this true of you?	YES, of course!	Uh...NO, not yet
I have a passport and have made copies to leave at home and take with me.		
I know how to say "thank-you" in my host country language.		
I know the entry requirements to my host country for persons of my nationality.		
I have spoken with a native of my host country.		
I know what electrical current is standard in my host country.		
I have read a magazine, newspaper, or book from my host country in the last 3 to 6 months.		
I can locate my host country and study site on the map.		
I have had physical, dental, and eye checkups in preparation for going abroad.		
I have gotten written prescriptions to take with me for glasses and any medications I take regularly, and plan to take a supply for my entire stay.		
I have searched the Web, viewed television, or listened to a radio broadcast from my host country in the last 3 months.		
I am familiar with any predeparture health recommendations for the region I will visit.		
I know the type of government in my host country.		
I have checked the exchange rate for my host country in the past month and have practiced converting amounts in my head.		
I know how I'm going to take money overseas, and know how I will get emergency funds if necessary.		
I can sing the national anthem of my host country.		
I have copied all credit cards and other important documents to leave at home in case of loss or theft.		
I know the predominant religion of my host country.		
I can draw freehand a reasonable map of my host country and surrounding countries.		
I know the time difference between my home town and my study site.		
I know the country telephone codes for the United States that I will need to call home from overseas.		
I know the name of the head of government of my host country.		
I know how much a meal will cost in my host country.		
I am receiving financial aid and I have seen an office of study abroad financial adviser to make sure arrangements are in place.		
All my payments and forms for study abroad are in and up to date.		

[Source: Adapted from University of Kansas]

Study Abroad Orientation Quiz

Complete this open book quiz and turn it in at orientation by **9:45am** to get a complimentary gift. Page numbers refer to the yellow student handbook. Several questions have more than one correct answer.

1. What is a safe way to carry valuables such as money and documents? (pp. 26-27)

2. What are three things that you should leave behind when going abroad? (p. 24)

   a)_____
   b)_____
   c)_____

3. Does the U.S. Constitution protect you when you are outside the United States? (p. 28)

4. What information will you find on the U.S. State Department Consular Information sheet for the country you will visit? (pp. 24-25)

   a) Unusual health conditions
   b) Where you can find other Americans
   c) Crime and security situation
   d) The phone numbers of area hospitals
   e) Drug penalties
   f) Political disturbances and areas of instability

5. The overseas U.S. embassy can: (p. 28)

   a) Get you out of jail.
   b) Provide a list of English-speaking lawyers.
   c) Provide temporary payment of medical bills.
   d) Provide a loan if you run out of money.
   e) Help your family track you down, if you have registered your presence.
   f) Replace your passport, if lost or stolen.

6. Why should all international travelers be concerned about AIDS? (p. 13-14)

   a) Standards for screening blood transfusions and sterilizing needles are not the same worldwide.
   b) Travelers are exposed to more public toilets, so will be at greater risk of contracting the virus.
   c) Availability, quality, and social acceptability of condoms is not the same worldwide.

7. List the precautions you will take for packing (12, 23-24):

   Eye glasses _____
   Prescription drugs_____
   Luggage ID _____
   Personal ID _____

8. Describe three strategies you, personally, will employ to ensure that your health remains good while you are abroad. (pp. 11-12)
   a)_____
   b)_____
   c)_____

9. Describe three common pick-pocket techniques (p. 26)
   a)_____
   b)_____
   c)_____

10. If you lose or are robbed of your passport, credit cards, plane ticket, and money, what will you do? What precautions can you take to make replacement easier? (pp. 24, 27)

11. You have a long weekend coming up and you would like to go traveling. What do you do? (pp. 38-39)

    a) Ask natives or your on-site director for suggestions
    b) Leave your itinerary with a friend or the director
    c) Travel with a friend for safety and companionship

12. Name three coping strategies you can use when faced with feelings of culture "shock" or cultural fatigue (pp. 20-21).
    a)_____
    b)_____
    c)_____

True or False?

____ ATMs are now universal. It is no longer advisable to take some money in travelers' checks. (p. 31-32)
____ Federal Express will not ship prescription medications overseas. I should take all I need with me. (p. 12, 34)
____ In most cases, the best defense against unwanted male attention is a severe glare and an angry retort.
____ Foreign hospitals will, in most cases, not take a U.S. health insurance card for payment; the individual must pay the bill and be reimbursed by her/his health insurance company. (p. 9)
____ It is best to exchange MOST of the money you will take abroad BEFORE you depart. (p. 31)

[Source: Adapted from University of Kansas]

Self-Test: Safety Scenarios

Answers to most questions will be found in the student handbook for short-term and summer programs. If you are in doubt about safe solutions to any of the scenarios, however, do not hesitate to consult the office of study abroad.

1. **This is your first experience** in the country you are visiting and initial adjustment is a bit tougher than you thought. You haven't slept in 5 days, you're not hungry, you're beginning to get a cold. All you want to do is curl up in your bed and ignore everything. Classes are the last thing on your mind.

   - What are some coping strategies that might help you out?
   - Should you seek help? If so, from whom?

2. **You and three friends** take an overnight train back to your host city after a weekend excursion on your own. You four are the only people in the train compartment, so you've piled your luggage in the middle toward the window. It's not a restful journey and you don't think you really got to sleep at all. However, when you arrive at your destination, your bag/purse is missing!

   - What happened?
   - What valuables could be missing?
   - What is your next step?
   - What can you do to prevent this?

3. **You are traveling on a break.** On arrival in your destination, you find that the well-known, inexpensive hostel where you had planned to stay is full. In fact, you were so sure you'd be able to stay at this place, you gave the address and phone number to your (seemingly) overprotective mother and told her you'd call her when you arrived.

   - What do you do?
   - What are your resources?
   - What would you do differently next time?

4. **Two men on a train befriend you**, an older fellow and one closer to your age. They are friendly and seem harmless. After about 45 minutes of conversation, they offer you some of the beverage they are drinking.

   - Should you accept?
   - Why or why not?
   - What are the risks?

5. **You were warned**, but you thought, "what's the harm in bringing *one* little joint?" The following week, however, you get caught smoking it in your dorm room.

   - What are the consequences?
   - Who can help you out?

6. **You are 20—not of age to drink** in the United States, but legal in the country in which you are studying. You take advantage of this with gusto. You find that you can purchase alcohol at any time of the day, and begin to do so, sometimes before class. Things seem to be getting a little out of control, but you don't seem to be able to stop.

   - What are some of the negative consequences of continuing like this?
   - Consider health, safety, academics.
   - Are the consequences just personal or are they more far-reaching?
   - What can you do?

7. **You are in the kitchen** preparing dinner and you are alone. You cut yourself with a knife and you know you'll need stitches. Before you pass out from loss of blood

   - What precautions have you taken for this sort of emergency?
   - What emergency contact numbers should you have?
   - What questions should you ask at the on-site orientation about obtaining medical care?

8. **You're on a bus alone at night.** You start talking to the people next to you. You get up to get out of the bus, and you notice the people next to you are also going to exit. You are uncomfortable with the situation.

   - What do you do?
   - How would you avoid this situation?

9. **You notice a political demonstration.** It looks interesting! What do you do? (choose one)

   - Be a passive observer rather than an active participant.
   - Join in and "do as the Romans do!"
   - Assess the situation. What are clues that you should leave the area immediately?

10. **You arrived 2 weeks ago**, and you've noticed that you attract more sexually-oriented attention than you are comfortable with. You feel a bit threatened.

    - What can you do to reduce the likelihood of attracting attention?
    - Should you consult someone? If so, who? What questions will you ask?

[Source: Adapted from University of Kansas]

Chapter 16

Safeguards for Short-Term Programs

Mickey Slind and Sarah E. Spencer

Designing, directing, and administering study abroad programs, especially if they are short-term, presents a special challenge for faculty and administrators. It is assumed that students and faculty directors should be encouraged to take responsibility for their own health and wellness. However, administrators have the additional responsibility of informing students and directors of unusual hazards, such as specific health, safety, and liability concerns, that may await them overseas, and of coordinating an appropriate and effective support system.

Liability issues are becoming increasingly complex on campuses. Every effort should be made to implement institutional policies, sound operating procedures, and responsible programming. However, convincing students and faculty to concentrate on good preventive care and to be in tune with wellness practices is the key to success.

In summary, everyone must be proactive. This section will highlight what areas to focus on in health, safety, insurance, liability, and crisis management.

Short-Term Considerations

Whereas semester- or year-long programs allow the luxury of time to solve many problems that may occur overseas, the critical short-term issue is *lack of time*. Whereas questions of health and safety, risk, and liability are the same in all programs, the impact on the program, its director or directors, and its students can be profound when encapsulated into the limited time period of a short-term program. The questions are not only related to health and safety, but to academics as well. If a student becomes ill at the beginning of a 3- or 4-week program, and is unable to attend class for a week or two, how will credit be earned when so much time has been lost?

If a student has an accident while on a program that travels extensively, as many short-term programs do, who stays behind to attend to the student's medical needs while the group moves on to the next site? What kind of local health care is available and how can your faculty director access it should the occasion arise? Have you warned your students of any aspect of your program that may carry a higher risk of injury or danger? These are just some of the important issues that face administrators of all programs, but particularly those that are considered short-term.

Predeparture Preparation

As covered in Chapter 15, Orientation and Reentry, preparing students to study abroad, especially for short-term programs, is essential. As you develop orientation programming and written materials, health and safety issues such as immunizations and on-site risks, insurance, and basic host country medical systems must be included. The following topics should be considered:

- basic hygiene
- medical insurance
- medical kit
- immunizations
- disease prevention
- eye care
- mental health issues
- emotional problems
- anxiety and stress
- nutrition
- eating disorders
- environmental health issues
- preexisting conditions
- health care delivery overseas

- sexuality and relationships
- principles of safe sex
- information on sexually transmitted disease, including HIV/AIDS
- contraceptive needs
- alcohol (responsible use of) and drugs (prescription and controlled substance)
- personal security
- road safety and car rental concerns
- accident and injury prevention
- altitude sickness
- jet lag
- emergency situations

It is important that all students and their faculty directors receive the same predeparture and on-site information and that the appropriate person reinforces the importance of these concerns during the program. Students, faculty directors, and administrators should understand how to respond to health emergencies.

The Basics

Contingency plans, such as the Example of a Crisis Management Plan: Off-Campus Programs at the end of this chapter, will help you to respond to emergencies. When preparing students for their overseas experience, remind them to get sufficient rest prior to their departure, to eat properly and carefully while abroad, and to follow a pattern of healthy living, at home and abroad. Students who travel independently prior to the beginning of the program frequently arrive exhausted and ill. Students should be advised to carefully consider their travel plans and to take a proactive role in their own self-care.

Predeparture written materials, such as a student handbook, will help reinforce this general message and other site-specific information.

Health Issues

Students, and some faculty directors, may assume that since they are participating in a short-term program, health issues do not need to be addressed. As you prepare students to study abroad, take into account the following specific considerations.

The Medical Report

As demonstrated in Chapter 11, Student Selection and Enrollment, clear procedures and policies must be defined as programs develop, especially with regard to refund policies if a student withdraws or a program is canceled.

Although the administrator or faculty director cannot ask for medical information before a student is selected to participate, many programs do request that students complete a medical report or health information form after acceptance (see Short-Term Study Abroad Medical Report" at the end of this chapter).

There is some debate over requesting health information at all or whether a physician's signature should be required. However, by having students self-disclose any illness such as asthma or diabetes, or required medication, assistance can be anticipated and provided. The collected information is strictly confidential, and faculty directors should have copies to review and take abroad.

Before moving forward, always check with your organization and legal counsel for appropriate language and whether a form such as the "Medical Report" can be used.

Immunizations

If your program visits a country where immunizations are recommended or required, you may wish to work with a local health clinic (either institutionally or community-based, depending on your circumstances) to provide information, support, and the immunizations. Many clinics have a health education component and often are very supportive of efforts toward ensuring students' good health overseas. Health educators, on campus and in the community, can form a partnership with administrators to deliver appropriate predeparture information to students and faculty directors. They will also advise on immunizations that are recommended or required, based on information from the Centers for Disease Control and the World Health Organization.

Students must be informed of recommended immunizations or medicines well before departure to follow the appropriate steps. A country- or program-specific information sheet, such as the Costa Rica Programs: Immunization Recommendations at the end of this chapter, is highly recommended. If student access to travel clinics is difficult, you may wish to set up travel clinics at a time when participants can receive appropriate inoculations as a group.

Region-Specific Health Issues

Extra precautions are necessary when short-term programs travel to areas with particular health risks, and there are many excellent resources to use, such as the Centers for Disease Control and Prevention and the International Association for Medical Assistance to Travelers (IAMAT). Areas of concern and advice to participants include the following:

How To Treat Diarrhea

Symptoms of diarrhea can range from mild to very severe and can occur with little warning. Here are some recommendations to participants for treating diarrhea:

- Replace fluids. Dehydration is one of the problems associated with diarrhea. The goal of treatment is not to suppress the symptoms of diarrhea, but to correct the body's fluid imbalances.
- Add salt to diet.
- Avoid dairy products (they inhibit the body's absorption of salt).
- After 1 to 2 days, use medications such as Imodium, Lomotile, Pepto-Bismol, or Paregoric to relieve abdominal cramps. These medications should be used only for 2 to 3 days to give symptomatic relief.
- If symptoms persist longer than a few days, consult a physician.
- If diarrhea is accompanied by a high fever, shaking chills, and/or blood in the stool, consult a physician immediately.

Diarrhea

✓ Do not drink the local water or ice unless it is 100 percent safe (and still, question the source of information).

✓ Travelers should avoid salads, thin-skinned fruits (such as grapes), milk and milk products, and seafood that is far from where it was originally caught.

✓ Cooked foods should be thoroughly cooked.

Malaria

✓ Found mainly in rural areas and areas with night-biting mosquitoes.

✓ If going to an area where malaria is prevalent, a physician should be consulted for the best type of preventative medicine.

✓ Travelers may not donate blood for 3 years after leaving a country where malaria is found.

Diphtheria/Tetanus

✓ Tetanus is particularly prevalent in rural areas.

✓ Diphtheria and tetanus are easily prevented with a DPT or DT inoculation; this inoculation is recommended every 5 years.

Tuberculosis (TB)

✓ Greater number of incidences in many region-specific areas.

✓ Student may have a TB test upon return.

HIV/AIDS

✓ 80 percent of HIV-infected people acquire the infection through sexual contact.

✓ May also be contracted through blood transfusions or injections with contaminated needles that have not been properly sterilized.

✓ Sexual contact should be avoided or a latex condom used correctly for every sexual contact.

✓ If regular injections are needed, bring your own supply of needles and syringes.

✓ If regular blood treatment is needed, bring your own supply of blood products if possible.

Cholera

✓ Transmitted through contaminated food and water.

✓ Immunization needed if traveler will have close contact with local population in areas with a high incidence of cholera.

Hepatitis A

✓ Common in countries where sanitation is poor.

✓ Infection comes from person-to-person contact or through contaminated food and water.

✓ Since the incidence of hepatitis A is growing worldwide, it is recommended that all travelers be immunized.

Hepatitis B

✓ Widespread in many developing countries. Spread in the same way as AIDS.

✓ Travelers spending more than 6 months in an infected area or engaging in at-risk behavior should receive vaccination.

Polio
✓ Disease that occurs in the developing world outside North and South America.
✓ Most U.S. citizens have had their primary immunization series.
✓ Booster required every 10 years if traveling to areas where disease is prevalent.

Rabies
✓ Infection from a bite, scratch, or, less commonly, lick from an infected animal.
✓ Travelers who will have frequent animal contact would benefit from a rabies preexposure vaccine series before departure.
✓ Anyone potentially exposed to rabies must seek prompt medical attention.

Typhoid
✓ Transmitted from person-to-person contact or through contaminated food and water.
✓ Vaccination recommended for travelers to risk areas.

Yellow Fever
✓ Viral disease carried by mosquitoes in some areas of Central and South America and tropical regions of Africa.
✓ Travelers to disease areas, or those transiting through a disease area and entering another country, may be required to show a certificate of vaccination against yellow fever for legal entry.

Special Precautions

If the program involves research in the field or physically rigorous activities, local conditions need to be confirmed and students need to be advised of any necessary precautions that should be taken before the program departs. If there are unusual activities or high risks involved, you should inform participants. Examples include sports or physical activities, political instability, environmental concerns, and health issues. Environmental concerns include anything from poisonous snakes and insects, to air or water pollution, to extreme traffic hazards.

Prescription Drugs

Most of us at some point take two different kinds of medications—prescription and over-the-counter drugs. Before leaving, students and faculty directors must plan for what medications they will need while abroad.

Suggestions for Prescription Medications
♦ Take a minimum supply of a one and a half, if not a full double supply.
♦ Be very careful to keep medications in a place where they cannot be lost or stolen. Keep all medications in carry-on luggage.
♦ Keep medications in their original containers to avoid problems in customs.
♦ Upon arrival at the destination, keep medications in two separate places.
♦ Prescription medicines are not always the same abroad as in the United States. Do not plan on having U.S. prescriptions filled while abroad. If carrying a prescription, have the physician write the drug's generic name, instructions, dosage, and reason for prescribing the drug.
♦ Check with the physician before departure for advice on how to adjust when to take medication, reduce the risk of over- or underdosing from the time difference between home and destination.

Suggestions for Over-the-Counter Medications

♦ Over-the-counter drugs may not be the same as in the United States.
♦ Travelers should consider bringing their preferred over-the-counter brands of:
   ✓ headache and fever medicine
   ✓ vitamins
   ✓ diarrhea and constipation medicine
   ✓ antacid
   ✓ antihistamine
   ✓ motion-sickness tablets
   ✓ decongestant
   ✓ hydrocortisone cream

Glasses and Contact Lens Wearers

Suggest that participants take along an extra pair of glasses or contact lens, as well as a lens prescription.

Medic Alert

If a participant has any serious condition not easily recognized, such as allergies, diabetes, or epilepsy, he or she may want to acquire a Medic Alert emblem. For more information, contact:

Medic Alert Foundation International
P.O. Box 1009
Turlock, CA 95380
800.633.4260

Adjusting to the Heat

If students will be traveling to a country with a year-round warm climate, they need to think about how they will adjust to the weather, especially if their home environment has the opposite climate. Extreme changes in climate and temperature variations will affect both the comfort and health of those who are not prepared. For the most enjoyable time in the heat, suggest that students:

♦ minimize the amount of time they are in direct sunlight;
♦ drink plenty of fluids, especially water;
♦ wear loose-fitting clothing that is made of cotton or another material capable of absorbing perspiration;
♦ wear light colors, especially white, which will reflect sunlight;
♦ wear a wide-brimmed hat of a light material; and
♦ use sun block.

Sexually Transmitted Diseases, Including HIV/AIDS

Sexually transmitted diseases, such as gonorrhea, syphilis, and herpes continue to pose health risks in almost every country. The HIV virus, which causes AIDS, is not only transmitted sexually, but also through contaminated needles and blood supplies, and thus presents a general health risk abroad. If a student should require surgery, medical evacuation should be carefully considered. Invasive medical procedures such as transfusions and injections may be high risk because the instruments and blood may not be safe or screened. Needles and syringes should be single-use, disposable, and prepackaged in a sealed container. Travelers to high-risk areas of the world may consider carrying these items along in their travel medical kit for use in case of emergency.

Overseas Medical Care

Should a student or faculty director require medical care while overseas, they should recognize that there are cultural and medical differences in health care. In some countries, physicians are far less likely to prescribe drugs than doctors in the United States, and in others, patients' families provide food and feed the patient. Prepare students for the unexpected, both in occurrence and in practice. There may be a severe shortage of medicine or an unavailability of technology. On the other hand, students may be surprised at the efficient care they will receive in many countries as compared to the United States, and at a much lower cost.

To prepare, check with the health officer or nurse at the U.S. embassy or consulate in the host country, who can identify local health care resources should they become necessary. Names and addresses of several embassy-recommended physicians can be obtained before participants become ill or need medical attention, saving precious time in an emergency.

International Association for Medical Assistance to Travelers

Consider becoming a member of the International Association for Medical Assistance to Travelers (IAMAT), a nonprofit organization that provides medical information for countries around the world. For more information, visit www.iamat.org.

Overseas Decisions

Most travelers' complaints are colds, intestinal upsets, and minor aches and pains—conditions that require no professional medical assistance. Food- and waterborne diseases are the number one cause of illness to travelers. It is only when these complaints escalate or when other emergency situations arise that require further treatment that decisions for local care or evacuation should be made. Confirm that all participants have insurance for medical evacuation.

If a member of the group requires emergency assistance overseas, ask the program provider, on-site coordinator, or the hotel for assistance. Taking a taxi to a hospital or emergency room is another easy, quick solution. If language is a problem, try to obtain the services of someone who can translate for you. Even an experienced faculty director with good command of the language may have difficulty obtaining information without a vocabulary that covers basic medical terms.

Safety Issues

Like health concerns, most safety problems can be drastically reduced with good predeparture information, planning, and action.

What to Bring

- Safety begins while packing. Travelers should dress conservatively to avoid being a target, and as much as possible, avoid the appearance of affluence.
- Travel light.
- The minimum number of important documents necessary should be carried, and plan a place or places to conceal them. Passport, cash, and credit cards are most secure when locked in a hotel safe. When carried on the person, conceal them in several places rather than putting them all in one wallet or pouch. Avoid handbags, fanny packs, and outside pockets, which are easy targets for thieves.

- An extra set of passport photos.
- A copy of birth certificate.
- Travelers should label their luggage and put name, address, and telephone number inside and outside of each piece of luggage. They should use covered luggage tags to avoid casual observation of identity or nationality and if possible, lock that luggage.
- Note credit limits on each credit card brought. Make certain not to charge over that amount while overseas. The credit card company should be asked how to report the loss of the card. Remember that 800 numbers do not work from abroad, but the company should have a number that can be called while overseas.
- Two photocopies of the passport identification page, airline tickets, and driver's license. One photocopy should be left with family or friends at home, the other packed in a place separate from where valuables are carried.
- A copy of the serial numbers of the traveler's checks should be left with a friend or relative at home. Travelers should carry their copy in a separate place and cross their numbers off the list as checks are cashed.

What to Leave at Home

- Valuable or expensive-looking jewelry.
- Irreplaceable family objects.
- All unnecessary credit cards.
- A copy of the itinerary with family or friends.
- Copies of passport, credit card numbers, itineraries.

Security

The U.S. State Department's Consular Information Sheets are available for every country of the world. They describe entry requirements, currency regulations, unusual health conditions, the crime and security situation, political disturbances, areas of instability, special information about driving and road conditions, and drug penalties. The information sheets also provide addresses and emergency telephone numbers for U.S. embassies and consulates. In general, the sheets do not give advice. Instead, they describe conditions so that travelers can make informed decisions about travel.

In some situations, however, the U.S. State Department recommends that U.S. citizens defer travel to a country. In such a case, a Travel Warning is issued for the country and posted on that country's Consular Information Sheet.

Public Announcements are another means by which the U.S. State Department disseminates information about terrorist threats and other relatively short-term and/or transnational conditions posing significant risks to the security of U.S. travelers. Announcements are issued when there is a perceived threat usually involving Americans as a particular target group. In the past, Public Announcements have been issued to deal with short-term coups, preelection disturbances, violence by terrorists, and anniversary dates of specific terrorist events.

The Bureau of Consular Affairs' World Wide Web home page address is http://travel.state.gov. It includes Consular Information Sheets, Travel Warnings, and Public Announcements; passport and visa information; travel publications; background on international adoption and international child abduction services; and international legal assistance. It also links to the U.S. State Department's main Internet site at http://www.state.gov which contains current foreign affairs information.

Consular Information Sheets, Travel Warnings, and Public Announcements are available on the World Wide Web (see insert on previous page); at the 13 regional passport agencies; at U.S. embassies and consulates abroad; or by sending a self-addressed, stamped envelope to: Overseas Citizens Services, Room 4811, Department of State, Washington, DC 20520-4818. They are also available through airline computer reservation systems when you or your travel agent make your international air reservations. You can also access them via telephone (202.647.5225, from a touch-tone phone), by fax (202.647.3000, using the handset as you would a regular telephone (the system prompts you on how to proceed)), or by bulletin board (view or download the documents using a computer and modem by dialing the CABB on 301.946.4400—the login is "travel," the password is "info"). There is no charge to use these systems other than normal long distance charges.

Wardens

Consider registering the group with the U.S. embassy in the country or countries to be visited, and identify a warden if possible. Wardens are designated contacts that the U.S. embassy or consulate will reach in case of an emergency. Embassy information can be found at www.embassyworld.com.

Precautions to Take While Traveling

Safety on the Street

All participants should use the same common sense traveling overseas that they would at home, and they should be especially cautious in or avoid areas where they are likely to be victimized. These include crowded subways, train stations, elevators, tourist sites, market places, festivals, and marginal areas of cities. [Source: Department of State Publication 10399, Bureau of Consular Affairs, revised 1996.]

Specifically, travelers should be warned:

- Do not travel alone, especially at night.
- Do not use shortcuts, narrow alleys, or poorly lit streets.
- Avoid public demonstrations and other civil disturbances.
- Keep a low profile and avoid loud conversations or arguments. Do not discuss travel plans or other personal matters with strangers.
- Avoid scam artists. Beware of strangers who approach offering bargains or to be a guide.
- Beware of pickpockets. They often have an accomplice who will jostle, ask for directions or the time, point to something spilled on clothing, or create a disturbance to distract the traveler. A child or even a woman carrying a baby can be a pickpocket. Beware of groups of vagrant children who create a distraction while picking pockets.
- Wear the shoulder strap of a bag across the chest and walk with the bag away from the curb to avoid drive-by purse snatchers.
- Try to seem purposeful when moving about. Even if lost, the traveler should act as if they know where they are going. When possible, ask directions only from individuals in authority.
- Know how to use a pay telephone and have the proper change or token on hand.
- Learn a few phrases in the local language to signal a need for help, the police, or a doctor. Make note of emergency telephone numbers that may be needed: police, fire, your hotel, and the nearest U.S. embassy or consulate.

- If confronted, do not fight back. Travelers should give up their valuables since their money and passport, unlike themselves, are replaceable.
- Carry the hotel name, address, and telephone number in the local language and in English.

Safety in Hotels

- Keep hotel doors locked at all times. Meet visitors only in the lobby.
- Do not leave money and other valuables in the hotel room while out. Use the hotel safe.
- Let someone know when to expect your return.
- If out late at night alone, do not get on an elevator if there is a suspicious-looking person inside.
- Read the fire safety instructions in the hotel room. Know how to report a fire. Know where the nearest fire exit and alternate exits are located. Count the doors between the room and the nearest exit. This could be a lifesaver if required to crawl through a smoke-filled corridor.

Safety on Public Transportation

If a country has a pattern of tourists being targeted by criminals on public transport, such information is mentioned in the Consular Information Sheet under the "Crime Information" section.

- Only take taxis clearly identified with official markings. Beware of unmarked cabs. Ask for, and where appropriate, negotiate the fare before entering cab.
- If the way is being blocked by a stranger and another person is very close behind, move away. This can happen in the corridor of a train or on the platform or station.
- Do not accept food or drink from strangers. Criminals have been known to drug food or drink offered to passengers. Criminals may also spray sleeping gas in train compartments.
- Do not be afraid to alert authorities if feeling threatened in any way. Extra police are often assigned to ride trains on routes where crime is a serious problem.

How to Handle Money Safely

- Change travelers' checks only as currency is needed to avoid carrying large amounts of cash. Countersign travelers' checks only in front of the person who will cash them.
- Do not flash large amounts of money when paying a bill.
- Make sure credit cards are returned after each transaction.
- Deal only with authorized agents when exchanging money. Do not change money on the black market.
- Be careful when using an ATM machine. Keep the 4-digit code secure.
- If possessions are lost or stolen, report the loss immediately to the local police. Keep a copy of the police report for insurance claims and as an explanation of the situation. After reporting missing items to the police, report the loss or theft of:
  ✓ travelers' checks to the nearest agent of the issuing company;
  ✓ credit cards to the issuing company;
  ✓ airline tickets to the airline or travel agent; and
  ✓ passport to the nearest U.S. embassy or consulate.

How to Avoid Legal Difficulties

Travelers can be arrested overseas for actions that may be either legal or considered minor infractions in the United States. They should be aware of what is considered criminal in the country visited. Consular Information Sheets include information on unusual patterns of arrests in various countries when appropriate.

Remember!

When students and faculty are in a foreign country, they are subject to its laws and are under its jurisdiction, not the protection of the U.S. Constitution.

Some of the offenses for which U.S. citizens have been arrested abroad are as follows:

Drug violations. More than one third of U.S. citizens incarcerated abroad are held on drug charges. Some countries do not distinguish between possession and trafficking. Many countries have mandatory sentences—even for possession of a small amount of marijuana or cocaine. A number of Americans have been arrested for possessing prescription drugs, particularly tranquilizers and amphetamines, that they purchased legally in certain Asian countries and then brought to some countries in the Middle East where they are illegal. Other U.S. citizens have been arrested for purchasing prescription drugs abroad in quantities that local authorities suspected were for commercial use. If in doubt about foreign drug laws, ask local authorities or the nearest U.S. embassy or consulate.

Photography. In many countries travelers can be harassed or detained for photographing such things as police and military installations, government buildings, border areas, and transportation facilities. If in doubt, ask permission before taking photographs.

Protection Against Terrorism

Terrorist acts occur at random and are unpredictable, making it impossible to protect participants absolutely. The first and best protection is to avoid travel to areas with a persistent record of terrorist attacks or kidnapping. The vast majority of foreign states have good records of maintaining public order and protecting residents and visitors within their borders from terrorism.

Most terrorist attacks are the result of long and careful planning. Just as a car thief will first be attracted to an unlocked car with the key in the ignition, terrorists are looking for defenseless, easily accessible targets who follow predictable patterns. The chance that a tourist traveling with an unpublished program or itinerary would be the victim of terrorism is extremely slight. In addition, many terrorist groups seeking publicity for political causes within their own country or region may not be looking for U.S. targets.

Nevertheless, the following pointers may help participants to avoid becoming a target of opportunity. They should be considered as adjuncts to the tips listed in the previous sections on how to protect travelers against the far greater likelihood of being a victim of crime. These precautions may provide some degree of protection and can serve as practical and psychological deterrents to would-be terrorists.

♦   Be aware of what is discussed with strangers and watch out for anyone who may be eavesdropping.

♦   Try to minimize the time spent in the public area of an airport, which is less protected. Move quickly from the check-in counter to the secured areas.

♦   As much as possible, avoid dress and behavior (e.g., baseball hats, college sweatshirts, fanny packs, loud voices) that may identify you as an American.

- Keep an eye out for suspicious abandoned packages or briefcases. Report them to airport security or other authorities and leave the area promptly.
- Avoid places where Americans and Westerners are known to congregate, such as McDonalds and other fast food restaurants, and U.S.-owned companies, such as The Gap.

High-Risk Activities

Certain activities carry a high risk. Institutions that sponsor programs that include activities such as horse-back riding, surfing, scuba diving, skiing, mountain climbing, or swimming as a part of the program-related excursions or activities should consider carrying a rider on their insurance policy to cover the increased risk and exposure. Weigh the risks to the group of the proposed activity, and pay special attention to safety issues when providing predeparture orientation. Inform students of any dangerous situations that may occur. Obviously, risks in a backcountry archaeology program or a jungle trek may be quite different from those in Paris or Hong Kong.

Alcohol and Drug Use or Abuse

Rule number one: use of illegal substances is absolutely prohibited. It should be made clear to students that anyone caught using illegal substances will be immediately removed from the program. It should also be made clear that penalties for use of illegal substances in other countries can be much stronger than in the United States and there is nothing the faculty director or the U.S. embassy can do to assist someone caught breaking the laws of the host country.

Use of alcohol in off-campus programs can be a problem, especially for those students who have suddenly achieved legal drinking age. First, check to see whether your institution has a policy prohibiting the use of alcohol at college-sponsored functions. If so, you need an interpretation from your risk manager or legal counsel about how that policy should be applied on an off-campus program.

In any case, the issue of alcohol use should be addressed with students. You may wish to consider a policy such as the one that follows:

Responsible use of alcohol is when:

1. A student abides by the laws of the country or state in which he or she is living.
2. A student does not miss any scheduled event because of the effects of alcohol consumption.
3. A student does not become ill due to the effects of alcohol consumption.
4. A student does not engage in inappropriate behavior toward other individuals as a result of alcohol consumption.
5. A student does not engage in destructive behavior toward property as a result of alcohol consumption.
6. A student does not engage in behavior that causes embarrassment to the other members of the group, the faculty member(s) or the in-country host(s) as a result of alcohol consumption.
7. Students in a group do not facilitate/encourage or ignore a fellow student who is abusing alcohol. Providing alcohol to persons under the legal drinking age is illegal and against policy. Transporting quantities of alcohol to program sites with the intent of sharing the alcohol with members of the group is considered to be irresponsible use of alcohol.

[Source: Adapted from St. Olaf College]

Students are encouraged to use good judgment if consuming alcohol at private homes or other accommodations during nonprogram hours. Student groups are encouraged to discuss issues related to alcohol abuse by other members of their group with the program supervisor/instructor.

If a student becomes incapacitated due to alcohol overuse, or if he or she is in need of medical attention, others are strongly encouraged to contact the faculty member or program site supervisor immediately, to protect the health and well being of the affected student.

Traffic and Vehicles

Advise students to be aware of traffic patterns. It is easy to become confused in countries where drivers use the opposite side of the road. Consequences for drinking and driving are very severe in most countries.

Warn students to be sure that any equipment they rent or use (bicycles, mopeds, motorcycles, cars) is operationally safe. If the faculty director or any member of the group plans to rent a car anywhere, inquire about driving regulations, learn traffic signals, and make sure they can legally drive in the country. Some programs may prohibit students from renting vehicles.

Swimming

Swimming carries a high level of risk unless you are in a well-chlorinated pool. However, even pools can be a health hazard. Of special concern is the risk of disease from contaminated lakes and rivers that can cause a variety of skin, eye, ear, and intestinal infections. Ocean swimming is usually the cleanest, but it is always good practice to check with the local authorities before venturing into unknown bodies of water. Tides and undertows can be deadly to the uninformed swimmer. Beaches and coastlines that are marked with the international code for "no swimming allowed" are to be avoided.

Insurance Matters

Any student participating in a short-term program abroad should be required to produce evidence, prior to departure, of adequate health and accident insurance. Your organization should set the terms of what is determined to be adequate for specific circumstances and programs. You may wish to require mandatory insurance, which can be built into the program fee or purchased separately. A point in favor of mandatory insurance is that the organization has prescribed the basic coverage, and you can be assured that each participant has satisfied the requirements.

Contracting for Study Abroad Insurance Coverage

Before requiring a certain type of insurance for participants in your program, check with your institution's legal counsel or risk management office to clarify the liability situation for university- or college-sponsored programs. If your organization has its own comprehensive policies, does the coverage extend overseas? Who is included? Is there an age limit? Does the student have to be enrolled full time to qualify? Are faculty directors covered as well? These are some of the questions that should be discussed before selecting an insurance provider.

The policy should cover the participant for the entire period of the program, and should include medical expenses related to sickness or injury, medical evacuation at a limit for the program's site, and repatriation in case of death. Does it include medical evacuation back to a student's home or to a health care delivery site overseas? What exclusions are there for medical evacuation? Who will make this decision and under what conditions? When establishing an insurance plan for a program, other things to consider are supplementary lost baggage, stolen property, or trip cancellation/interruption insurance.

Preexisting Conditions

Preexisting conditions have been a very complex area of insurance coverage. How is a preexisting condition determined and by whom? What is excluded? Is the student fully informed of the exclusion? There is nothing worse than telling a parent, partner, or guardian that the student's health insurance does not cover significant medical costs overseas.

Claims Process

Carefully review the insurance policy for its claims process. Are payments made directly to the hospital and/or physician overseas, or do they require the student to pay and then file for reimbursement? If the latter is true, students must be informed of the importance of retaining receipts for payment for medical treatment. Without a receipt for services rendered, the student may never be able to collect on the claim. In addition, has the claims process been made clear to students and faculty directors? If the student is required to pay in full at time of treatment, he or she will need to produce a credit card with an adequate credit line to allow for payment. If credit cards cannot be used and faculty directors have to pay out of group funds, students should agree to repayment by signing a document written by the faculty director.

Student Options for Insurance

International Student Identification Card

Many organizations require the International Student Identification Card for all study abroad participants. The card covers basic health and accident insurance coverage, as well as medical evacuation and repatriation of remains, but it only covers a small portion of expenses for major accidents or illness. It should be viewed as supplemental and not primary insurance coverage.

Insurance Through Parents, Spouse, School, or Other Insurance

Participants should talk with their family and insurance agent to find out exactly what coverage includes. They may want to consider the following:

- Does the plan include hospitalization coverage for accidents and illnesses while abroad?
- What is the maximum amount of coverage provided?
- Are there deductibles? If so, what are they?
- Will the plan include emergency room expenses?
- What is the coverage for medical evacuation (i.e., returning to the United States to be given the appropriate medical treatment for injury or illness; sometimes includes returning on an airplane with a medical unit)?
- In the event of death, what is the coverage for repatriation (i.e., return of bodily remains after death to country of origin)?

- What should the student do under the plan if he or she has to pay cash up front and has no money?
- Does the plan cover visits to the doctor or medication prescribed while abroad?
- What are the procedures for filing a claim, and how long does it take to get reimbursed after filing?
- If it is a trip cancellation plan, what are the guidelines regarding preexisting conditions?
- When does the plan begin and end?
- Does the plan enable the student to have continuous coverage before, during, and after he or she goes abroad?
- Is the plan the primary or secondary carrier? If secondary, when does the coverage begin?
- Is there a booklet explaining coverage in detail?

Trip Cancellation Insurance

Trip cancellation insurance protects students financially if they have to cancel or interrupt their study abroad program for *medical reasons*. If cancellation from the study abroad program occurs after the final deadline for any reason, students usually forfeit not only the deposit but also the entire program fee. For more information on trip cancellation insurance, see the Web Resources section at the end of this book.

Disclosure of Insurance Information

More organizations are requesting proof of insurance from the companies that provide services for study abroad programs. Ask your risk manager or legal counsel if this is necessary. See the "Proof of Insurance" example at the end of this chapter.

Liability Issues

Liability issues will never go away, and no organization can eliminate all liable situations, on campus or overseas. The key with any education abroad program is to reduce your liability whenever and wherever possible. For short-term programs abroad, take the following steps to reduce your liability:

- Make sure that all administrators and faculty directors understand what defines "appropriate and inappropriate personal and professional behavior" on campus and overseas.
- Review your program with an eye to eliminate potential threats.
- Conduct a legal audit—by your legal counsel or attorney hired to coordinate with the international office—to review the program's policies and procedures.
- Be sure your legal counsel has reviewed all of your program documents that are contractual in nature for validity, duration, enforceability, exceptions, and/or conflicts. Promotional materials should be reviewed annually to ensure that the program is accurately represented.
- Add a disclaimer to publicity and promotional materials to protect the administrator against unforeseen changes in program arrangement, including such things as currency fluctuations or increased airfares.
- If your program involves unusual or high risks, inform the participants of the potential risks, and be sure your publicity and promotional materials state the risks clearly. In addition, never promise what you cannot deliver.

For detailed information on legal issues and education abroad, see *NAFSA's Guide to Education Abroad for Administrators and Advisers*, p. 363–366.

Liability Waivers

The most important thing you can do to reduce your liability is to require students to read and sign a release, disclaimer, agreement, or liability waiver. When students who are legal minors are allowed to participate, require their parents or guardians to also sign and receive copies of relevant forms and materials.

Included at the end of this chapter are examples of liability waivers and study abroad agreements from a variety of schools:

The University of Kansas (public university)
✓ Student/Parent Liability Release
✓ Provider's Proof of Insurance
✓ Medical Report Form
✓ Conditions of Participation

St. Olaf College (small, private, liberal arts college)
✓ Parent Waiver and Release
✓ Student or Participant Waiver and Release
✓ Off-Campus Interim Agreement Form

University of St. Thomas (large, private university)
✓ Short-Term Study Abroad Agreement

Crisis Management

While it has always been important for an institution to have a well-developed crisis management plan, recent events have made such a plan even more important. Your credibility with students, parents, and even your own administration is enhanced by an effective crisis management plan.

Disaster can hit a program with sweeping effects: a debilitating health problem might require a student to withdraw; the faculty director might suffer a stroke or heart attack; one of the group may be lost or abducted; a group member abusing alcohol can manifest behavior that is destructive to himself or herself and the program. As an administrator or faculty director, you must be aware of the many types of problems that may endanger your students and the program. They may never happen, but to be aware is to be prepared.

Considerations

1. Does your organization have an existing crisis management plan to deal with a domestic crisis, such as the death of a student on campus?
2. Is there a 24-hour number in place for faculty or students to call?
3. If a program provider is retained, is he or she available 24 hours a day?
4. Has your crisis management plan been approved by senior administration and leadership?

At the end of this chapter you will find examples of plans for crisis management, suspension or cancellation and evacuation of study abroad programs, and preventative actions for faculty directors overseas.

Sending Students Home

There are many reasons why a student may need to return home during a short-term program abroad. Some returns will be voluntary, such as for medical reasons or a death in the family. Other returns will be disciplinary, prompted by the action (or inaction) of the student. A policy should be developed for when and how to send students home. This policy should be well understood by your office as well as your faculty director or on-site director.

In any situation, facts and details must be thoroughly documented by those involved on-site as well as by staff at the home institution. Some campuses and programs develop forms to guide this documentation, such as the Incident Report example at the end of this chapter.

Medical or Psychological Reasons

When a student needs to return home for a medical or emotional/psychological reason, you should have a plan to determine whether the student needs to be accompanied. This can be very problematic, especially if you are managing shorter programs. Students are adults, and cannot be forced to return against their will. Professional advice must be sought on the student's condition, and the best procedure should be determined. Since emotional problems and mental illness are usually excluded by medical insurance policies, your program should be prepared to assist the student and the student's family. A ticket may have to be arranged for whoever would accompany the student home under these circumstances.

Disciplinary Cases

Unfortunately, there may be circumstances that necessitate sending a student home, especially if the student breaks published rules of the organization or the code of conduct. Again, it is vital to have published expectations of behavior in all written materials, such as a student policy handbook. See Sample Disciplinary Rights and Procedures for Study Abroad Programs, Academic and Nonacademic at the end of this chapter.

Each faculty director will have different thresholds for student behavior and it is important to articulate these expectations to students at the predeparture orientation, in the syllabus, and again after arrival on-site.

Behavior Contracts

If a student break a rule for the first time, the faculty director may write a "behavior contract," a document that lists the infraction and asks for the student's signature. See the sample Behavior Contract at the end of this chapter.

Expelling a Student from the Program

If a student violates the rules of conduct a second time, or the student's first violation (such as drug use) warrants expulsion from the program, you may be required to expel the student. See the Sample Expulsion Form at the end of this chapter.

If a student does need to be sent home, consider the following helpful hints from others who have been faced with the difficult decision to expel a student:

+ Faculty directors do not need to make these decisions on their own. A network should be in place to support the faculty director, the group, and the situation.

+ An extreme case may call for a student to be expelled from the home institution as well as from the study abroad program. In such cases, working with your dean of students and legal counsel is imperative.

+ The logistical issues, such as the group's location far away from the departure city, may be the most challenging. Work with your program provider or travel agent to limit the cost of the expulsion to the other students on the program.

+ Check to see whether a student is a minor or legal audit (21 years or younger) and make sure that all study abroad students waive their FERPA rights as discussed in Chapter 11, Student Selection and Enrollment.

Conclusion

With all of the precautions and warnings, and the listing of health issues and hazards, administrators, faculty directors, or short-term providers should not give in to the temptation of seeing a problem or lawsuit lurking behind every administrative decision or indecision. U.S. institutions send thousands of students overseas every year, with very little incidence of health emergency or catastrophe.

Costa Rica Programs: Immunization Recommendations

Following are immunization recommendations by the Centers for Disease Control to protect you while traveling abroad. Talk with your parents to see if these immunizations/medications are covered by your hospitalization insurance. If so, make arrangements with your local clinic or a travel clinic. If they are not covered by your hospitalization insurance, it will likely be less expensive to obtain the immunizations/medications from the campus health services office.

** *If you plan to take the immunizations from the campus health services office, let them know as soon as possible so that sufficient supplies can be ordered.*

- -

Polio: Initial primary series plus one injection to persons traveling to developing countries. ($25)

Tetanus-Diphtheria: Need booster every 5 years when traveling. NOTE: Because of a shortage of Tetanus-Diphtheria vaccine, the campus health services office cannot give this vaccination. Check with your personal health care provider if you need a booster.

MMR: Must have had first dose after 1 year of age. A second immunization is recommended. ($35)

Hepatitis A: First dose prior to departure, second dose 6 months to 1 year later. ($55 per injection)

Hepatitis B: Series of three injections. First dose when possible, second dose 1 month later, third dose 6 months to 1 year after first injection. ($18 per injection if 19 years old; $36 per injection if 20 and over)

OR:

Twin Rix: If you haven't been immunized against either Hepatitis A or Hepatitis B, you can get this immunization which protects against both. Three injections total. ($80 per injection)

Typhoid: One injection at least 2 weeks, or more, before departure. ($45)

Malaria: Chloroquine. Begin taking 1 week before entering infected area; take one tablet weekly while in infected area; continue until you've taken four doses after leaving infected area. Your physician can write a prescription that you can fill at your local pharmacy.

NOTE: It is recommended that you have a Tuberculosis screening before you leave and 3 months after you return. ($3)

NOTE: Because some of the above recommendations require sequential dosing, and because there may be issues of interaction, you should contact the campus health services office or your health care provider early to plan a course of action.

- -

ALL OF YOUR IMMUNIZATION RECORDS ARE AVAILABLE AT THE ON-CAMPUS HEALTH SERVICES OFFICE. CHECK WITH THEM TO SEE WHICH OF THE ABOVE IMMUNIZATIONS YOU NEED.

** FOLLOW THE ADVICE OF YOUR PERSONAL PHYSICIAN OR HEALTH CLINIC PROFESSIONAL IF IT DIFFERS FROM THE ABOVE.

[Source: Adapted from St. Olaf College]

Short-term Study Abroad Medical Report

The purpose of this form is to determine your health history and any special medical needs you may have when you study abroad. Information provided will be treated confidentially. Any information considered important and essential will be forwarded to your faculty director for the purpose of serving you as promptly and correctly as possible, should you require medical or counseling services during your term abroad.

To Be Completed By Applicant

Name (please print)			Height	Weight	Sex
					☐ F ☐ M

Course Name

Are you generally in good physical condition? ☐ Yes ☐ No	If no, please explain.
Are you currently being treated for any physical condition? ☐ Yes ☐ No	If so, please explain.

Are you a diabetiic? ☐ Yes ☐ No	Have you ever had epilepsy or other seizure disorders? ☐ Yes ☐ No	Do you have asthma? ☐ Yes ☐ No

Do you have a heart condition? ☐ Yes ☐ No	Do you have or have you had any eating disorders? ☐ Yes ☐ No

What diseases have you had in the past five years (if any)?

Have you ever been treated for an emotional disorder? ☐ Yes ☐ No	If so, please describe.* * Please explain to the extent that this information should be known by the staff concerned with your well-being
Do you have any allergies to foods, medications, enviornmental factors, insects, etc? ☐ Yes ☐ No	If so, what happens when you come into contact with the allergen?
Are you taking any medication? ☐ Yes ☐ No	If so, please describe.
Are you on a restricted diet (vegetarian)? ☐ Yes ☐ No	If so, please describe.
Do you anticipate needing any health care or counseling while abroad? ☐ Yes ☐ No	If so, please describe.

If there is any additional health information that would be helpful for the faculty director to be aware of during the study abroad experience, please describe below.

Medical Insurance

All students are required to be covered by a medical insurance policy while they are abroad. Please check your insurance company to see if your benefits extend to your stay abroad.

I am insured for any medical expenses which may incur while I participate in the Program. This policy is with:

Insurance Company	Policy Number

I certify that all responses made on this Medical Report form are true and accurate, and I will notify the administrator) hereafter of any relevant changes in my health that occur prior to the start of the program. I understand that this form is for information purposes only and in no way implies that the administrator takes responsibility for my health.

Student Signature	Date

[Source: Adapted from University of St. Thomas]

Provider's Proof of Insurance

**DISCLOSURE OF INSURANCE INFORMATION
(Name of Home Institution here [hereinafter "Home"])**

Name of your institution _____

A. Please provide Home with information about insurance for transportation services (e.g., buses, automobiles, vans, etc.) that your institution provides to Home students. Please include a copy of the proof of insurance.

Name of insurance company: _____

Insurance policy number: _____

B. Please provide Home with information about property (e.g., fire, theft, etc.) insurance for the buildings and property at your institution where Home students live and study. Please include a copy of the proof of insurance.

Name of insurance company: _____

Insurance policy number: _____

C. Please provide Home with information about liability insurance against accidental death or injury of Home students at your institution. Please include a copy of the proof of insurance.

Name of insurance company: _____

Insurance policy number: _____

Note: If you contract with other agencies to provide transportation, accommodations, or other services to Home students, please provide us with their insurance information as well.

Please return this completed form, with attachments to Host in the envelope provided.
Thank you.

[Source: Adapted from St. Olaf College]

Student/Parent Liability Release, Health Insurance Certification, Medical Release, and Conditions of Participation

INSTRUCTIONS TO STUDENT (and parent, guardian, or spouse):

• Please read the following *and sign the statements that follow in the presence of a notary. Make a copy for your personal records and return the original of this form* to the Office of Study Abroad by the date stated in your acceptance letter.

• **One completed copy** of this form must be on file at the Office of Study Abroad **before** a student can participate in a KU Study Abroad program.

I. Liability

In conducting study abroad programs, the University of Kansas (KU) makes every effort to provide for the welfare and safety of the participants. On many programs, the official representative of KU at the study abroad site will make such rules and regulations for the conduct of the participants as will reasonably safeguard the health, well-being, and safety of all such participants, taking into consideration KU policies on student Rights and Responsibilities in addition to the laws of the host country. Recognizing, however, that participation in the program is voluntary and that there are certain inherent risks that the participant must assume, the participant understands that neither the university, nor any cooperating institution, assumes any responsibility for damage to or loss of property, personal illness or injury, or death while a participant is in the program.

While the university will assist in providing information on health care and insurance, it is the individual student's responsibility to ascertain that he or she has adequate health and accident coverage, valid during his or her stay abroad, **and has informed himself or herself of the proper health precautions for the world region to be visited.** As proof of adequate insurance, health insurance information and a policy number must be provided on page 2 of this form, and the completed, notarized form must be on file at the KU Office of Study Abroad before a student may participate.

Should a participant be placed in a position where, because of his or her incapacity to act, the question arises as to whom may act on the participant's behalf or as his or her parent's, guardian's, or spouse's agent. Thus, the KU representative abroad shall be the duly

Keep one copy for your records

Student Name _____

KUID or SSN _____

Program/Term_____

appointed attorney-in-fact for such student and for such parent, guardian, or spouse.

The University of Kansas strongly discourages students owning or operating vehicles while participating in study abroad programs. Traffic congestion and different traffic laws and regulations, civil and criminal, can make driving motor vehicles in foreign countries extremely hazardous. Insurance requirements, or other financial responsibility laws, vary from country to country. If, however, a participant is determined to operate a motor vehicle while abroad, he or she recognizes that KU assumes no financial responsibility for legal aid, or for the care of the participant should he or she be involved in an accident while operating a motor vehicle.

Opportunities for individual travel are plentiful and the university does not wish to discourage participants from taking advantage of them. The university, however, undertakes no responsibility for the participant when he or she is traveling independently during the course of the study abroad period.

II. Overseas Health Insurance Coverage

It is important to realize that most U.S. health insurance coverage is not recognized overseas. The student will normally have to pay for medical service, and fill out a claim form to be returned to the home company for reimbursement. It is imperative for students to know the limits of their coverage, and to carry at least one claim form to be signed by appropriate medical persons abroad to facilitate reimbursement.

Study abroad programs can be physically and medically rigorous and the possibility of illness or an accident is always a concern. Therefore, it is strongly advised that participants have a physical examination to receive assurance from a physician that they are able to participate. Additionally, it is advised that the student meet with the director or study abroad adviser prior to departure and provide confidential information of special conditions and/or needs such as, but not limited to, allergies, medication, treatment programs, or other medical concerns, so that if problems arise they are not a surprise.

III. Medical Emergencies

An American student abroad is expected to be able to cope with day-to-day occurrences, but occasionally events arise that are of an emergency or medical nature and which require medical care, hospitalization, or surgery for a student participant. So that such treatment can be administered without delay, we ask that each participant sign the statement on the following page authorizing the University of Kansas representative abroad to secure, at the expense of the participant, any treatment deemed necessary.

Participants on University of Kansas study abroad programs are covered for the duration of their program by MEDEX Assistance Corporation for emergency medical evacuation and assistance services which include repatriation of remains in the event of death. Detailed information about MEDEX services and a MEDEX card are enclosed. Participants should read these materials carefully and carry their cards at all times while participating on the KU study abroad program.

IV. Release/Certification Statements

As a condition of participation, each participant is required to sign the following statements and provide health insurance policy information as an indication that the above conditions and limitations are understood and accepted. A parent, guardian, or spouse must also sign to indicate that these conditions have been acknowledged.

A. Liability Release Statement

I hereby release the University of Kansas and any cooperating institution and their officers and agents from any and all claims and causes of action for damage to or loss of property, medical or hospital care, personal illness or injury, or death arising out of any travel or activity conducted by or under the control of the University of Kansas or cooperating institution.

B. Insurance Certification Statement

I hereby certify that I am covered with health insurance which I have determined to be adequate and satisfactory for any injury or illness that might befall me while I am participating in a University of Kansas study abroad program. I acknowledge that the University of Kansas and its representatives have not made any representations to me concerning the adequacy of my health insurance and I further acknowledge that it is my sole responsibility to ensure that my health insurance coverage is adequate for my needs.

_____

Insurance company

_____

Policy number:

C. Medical Release Statement

In the event of injury or illness to the undersigned, I hereby authorize the representative of the University of Kansas, at my expense, to secure necessary treatment, including the administration of an anesthetic and surgery, and such medication as may be prescribed. It is further agreed that, if my condition so required, I may be returned to the United States at my expense. I agree that if the University of Kansas makes any payments on my behalf, I will reimburse the university for such payments.

_____
Student's name (please print)

_____
Student's signature

_____
Parent/guardian/spouse name (please print)

_____
Parent/guardian/spouse signature

State of:_____ County of _____. Subscribed and sworn to before me, a Notary Public

within and for the County and State above set out this _____ day of _____.

_____
Notary

_____
My appointment expires

[Source: Adapted from the University of Kansas]

Conditions of Participation on Study Abroad Programs

In consideration of being allowed to participate in a Study Abroad Program,

I, _____, hereby understand and agree to the following conditions of

participation:

•**Orientation:** I am responsible for the content of all predeparture and orientation materials. KU students are required to attend a predeparture orientation on campus.

•**Program Rules:** The program director and staff have the authority to establish rules and guidelines necessary for the operation of the KU study abroad program for the health and safety of the entire group, and if I violate the established rules, I will be subject to disciplinary action, which may include dismissal from the program.

•**Rules:** As a participant in a study abroad program, I am subject to the Code of Student Rights and Responsibilities. The Code is printed in the Office of Study Abroad (OSA) Student Handbook.

•**Host Country Laws:** As a visitor to a foreign country, I will be subject to the laws of that country. Violations of the local law of the host community or country are referred to and handled by the appropriate local law enforcement authorities.

•**Academic Policy:** Because this is an academic program, I am responsible for attendance at classes and on scheduled trips, and for completing assigned work. Failure to participate fully in the program may constitute academic misconduct and result in dismissal from the program.

•**Behavior in Host Country:** As a foreign study participant, I am a guest in a host country. It is essential that all participants respect norms of conduct and patterns of behavior that may be different from standards at home. Such norms will be discussed at orientation meetings with the program director and/or on-site staff.

•**Use of illegal drugs** during the entire period of the program is strictly prohibited. Students in the program found using or possessing illegal drugs in any form are subject to immediate expulsion.

•**Violent behavior, or sexual harassment**, or other conduct disruptive to the program or offensive to the host culture may result in dismissal of program participants.

•**Financial Responsibility:** My participation in the program is contingent upon making all payments or financial aid arrangements by the stated due dates and completing and submitting all required forms before the start of the program. I further understand that failure to submit forms or payments may result in late enrollment penalties or my being dismissed from the program.

•**Voluntary or involuntary departure from the program** before its completion does not automatically result in academic withdrawal. While the Office of Study Abroad may assist, I am responsible for resolving my enrollment status if I leave the program early. I further understand that I am solely responsible for any and all costs arising out of my own voluntary or involuntary withdrawal from the program prior to its completion, including withdrawal caused by illness or disciplinary action by representative.

Student Signature   Date

[Source: Adapted from the University of Kansas]

PARENT WAIVER AND RELEASE
OFF-CAMPUS PROGRAMS

I am the parent/guardian of _____ (name of student or participant). I consent to my son/daughter/ward's participation in the _____ (name of program), which I understand will necessitate travel. In consideration for my son/daughter/ward's participation in the program, I agree as follows:

I. My son/daughter/ward has sufficient health, accident, disability, hospitalization, and personal property insurance to cover him or her during his or her participation in the program. None of the fees paid for the program are used to pay for such insurance. The College has no obligation to provide such insurance.

2. I authorize any representative of the College to secure dental and medical treatment for my son/daughter/ward if he or she is injured or becomes ill while participating in the program, including without limitation anesthetic and surgical treatment, and to sign authorization forms necessary to obtain the treatment. I assume full responsibility for all costs relating to or arising out of the treatment.

3. I give permission for my son/daughter/ward to travel independently on weekends and academic holidays at his or her expense during the period covered by the program and after the conclusion of the program. The College is not responsible for my son/daughter/ward while he or she is traveling independently.

4. I hereby release and discharge The College, and its regents, officers, employees, agents, successors, and assigns, on behalf of myself and my legal representatives, heirs, successors, and assigns, from any and all claims, liabilities, and costs which I or any of my legal representatives, heirs, successors, and assigns may have or claim to have relating to or arising out of my son/daughter/ward's participation in the program, including without limitation my son/daughter/ward's injury, illness, and death, and from all acts of negligence on the part of the college, its regents, officers, employees, or agents.

5. I agree to indemnify, defend, and hold harmless The College, and its regents, officers, employees, agents, successors, and assigns, from any and all claims, liabilities and costs asserted by or on behalf of my son/daughter/ward or any of my son/daughter/ward's legal representatives, heirs, successors, and assigns, or by or on behalf of me or any of my legal representatives, heirs, successors, and assigns, within the scope of the release in Paragraph 4 above.

This waiver and release will be governed by the laws of the State of Minnesota.

I have read carefully this waiver and release and the Student or Participant Waiver and Release that my son/daughter/ward, with my permission, has signed. I understand and voluntarily agree to be bound by the provisions of this waiver and release and the provisions of the Student or Participant Waiver and Release.

Date: _____   _____
                                 Signature of parent/guardian

Print name _____

Home address _____

_____ Phone #_____

Health insurance provider_____ Policy #_____

[Source: Adapted from St. Olaf College]

STUDENT OR PARTICIPANT WAIVER AND RELEASE
OFF-CAMPUS PROGRAMS

NAME_____ PROGRAM _____

SEM I_____SEM II_____YEAR_____INTERIM_____

I am applying for participation in the above program and, if I am a student, have the opportunity to gain academic credit through enrollment in the program. In consideration for my participation in the program, I agree as follows:

l. The College has the authority to establish rules for the operation of the program, and I will comply with those rules. The program supervisor may terminate my participation in the program for violating the rules or for behavior which is disruptive or which could affect adversely the reputation of the program. If I am a student and my participation in the program is terminated, I will receive no academic credit.

2. I authorize any representative of The College to secure dental and medical treatment for me if I am injured or become ill while participating in the program, including without limitation anesthetic and surgical treatment, and to sign authorization forms necessary to obtain the treatment.

3. Any independent traveling I do on weekends and academic holidays during the period covered by the program and after the conclusion of the program will be at my expense. The College is not responsible for me while I am traveling independently.

4. I hereby release and discharge The College, and its regents, officers, employees, agents, successors, and assigns, on behalf of myself and my legal representatives, heirs, successors, and assigns, from any and all claims, liabilities, and costs which I or any of my legal representatives, heirs, successors, and assigns may have or claim to have relating to or arising out of my participation in the program, including without limitation my injury, illness, and death, and from all acts of negligence on the part of the college, its regents, officers, employees, or agents.

5. I agree to indemnify, defend, and hold harmless The College, and its regents, officers, employees, agents, successors, and assigns, from any and all claims, liabilities and costs asserted by or on behalf of me or any of my legal representatives, heirs, successors, and assigns within the scope of the release in Paragraph 4 above.

This waiver and release will be governed by the laws of the State of Minnesota.

I have read this waiver and release carefully and understand and voluntarily agree to be bound by its provisions.

Date: _____   _____
                                     Signature of parent/guardian

NOTE: Your application is not complete until this form has been signed (both sides)and returned to International & Off-Campus Studies.

RETURN 2 COMPLETED COPIES, KEEP ONE COPY FOR YOUR FILES

[Source: Adapted from St. Olaf College]

OFF-CAMPUS INTERIM AGREEMENT FORM
International and Off-Campus Study

Name of program_____

My signature below indicates that I,_____:
(PLEASE PRINT NAME)

1.   agree to adhere to the payment schedule as outlined in the Off-Campus Interims Brochure;

2.   agree to inform the International and Off-Campus Study Office in writing should I need to cancel participation in the program to which I have been accepted;

3.   understand that cancellation fees for my program are payable as outlined in the Off-Campus Interims Brochure;

4.   have read and understand all of the general information in the Off-Campus Study Interims Brochure and on the Off-Campus Interims Application;

5.   understand that every effort will be made to protect the health and safety of students on the program. International and Off-Campus Study cannot guarantee a risk-free environment nor accept responsibility for accidents or illnesses on an off-campus study program.

6.   recognize the need for the following rules, agree to abide by them, and realize that I could be sent home for violating them and know that a decision to terminate my participation in the program is final, non-appealable, and at my own expense:
   a.   I will not buy, sell, or use drugs at any time.
   b.   I will not engage in abusive use of alcohol.
   c.   I will not engage in disruptive behavior.
   d.   I will participate in all classes and scheduled activities unless I am ill.
   e.   I will abide by dress and cultural codes suitable in the cultures visited.
   f.   I will avoid demonstrations, especially in politically volatile countries.

7.   have read, understand, and will abide by the "Philosophy, Policies, and Procedures" material;

8.   agree to participate in any orientation meetings, and/or retreats for my program;

9.   agree to complete and return to the International & Off-Campus Study Office all documents required by them to make arrangements for my program.

_____   _____   _____
Student's Signature   Student Number   Date

I understand that my son or daughter has read and agreed to the above.

_____   _____ _____
Parent's Signature   Date

Please return one copy of this form to the IOS Office with your application or as soon thereafter as possible.

[Source: Adapted from St. Olaf College]

Short-Term Study Abroad Agreement
University of St. Thomas

This is a Release of Legal Rights -- Read and understand before signing.

Name of student:_____

Program: _____

I,_____(student's name) will be participating in a cross-cultural study abroad program ("Program") in _____ for _____term, _____, offered through the University of St. Thomas International Education Department. I hereby agree as follows:

1. Risks of Study Abroad

I understand that participation in the Program involves risks not found in study at the university. These risks include: traveling to and within, and returning from, one or more foreign countries, foreign political, legal, social, and economic conditions; different standards of design, safety, and maintenance of buildings, public places, and conveyances; and other matters which may be described in brochures and other written information concerning this Program which I have received and reviewed. I have made my own investigation and am willing to accept these risks.

2. Independent Activity

Although the University of St. Thomas ("University") is sponsoring this course, I understand that neither the University nor any of the faculty directors or travel arrangers will be supervising me at all times. I will have the opportunity and the right to independently leave the group periodically, subject to the faculty director's requirements for participation in and attendance at classes and other activities that are a required part of the Program. Therefore, I will be responsible for my own safety and cannot hold the University liable for any injuries to my person or property or any other losses as a result of my participation in the Program.

3. Institutional Arrangements

I understand that the University does not represent or act as an agent for, and cannot control the acts or omissions of, any host institution, host family, transportation carrier, hotel, tour organizer or other provider of goods or services involved in the Program. I understand that the University is not responsible for matters that are beyond its control. I hereby release the University from any injury, loss, damage, accident, delay, or expense arising out of any such matters

4. Early Departure

If I decide to leave the Program before completing my course of study, I will provide the University with advance written notice of my intention to leave the Program. If I leave the Program prior to its completion, the University has no liability to provide or arrange for transportation, housing, dining or other services to me in connection with my early departure.

5. Standards of Conduct

A. I understand that each foreign country has its own laws and standards of acceptable conduct, including dress, manners, morals, politics, drug use, and behavior. I recognize that behavior violating those laws or standards could harm the University's relations with those countries and the institutions therein, as well as my own health and safety. I will become informed of, and will abide by, all such laws and standards for each country to or through which I will travel during the Program.

B. I will comply with all rules and regulations issued by the University, faculty directors, or any coordinating institution. It is within the faculty director's discretion to determine that my violation of such rules and regulations warrants my termination from the Program. **In that event, I may be sent home at my own expense**. I agree that the University has the right to enforce its rules and regulations, in its sole judgment, and that it will impose sanctions, up to and including expulsion from the Program, for violating these rules and regulations or for any behavior detrimental to or incompatible with the interests, harmony, and welfare of the University, the Program, or other participants. I recognize that due to the circumstances of foreign study programs, procedures for notice, hearing and appeal applicable to student disciplinary proceedings at the University do not apply. If I am expelled, I consent to being sent home at my own expense with no refund of fees. **I also agree that I will (a) not buy, sell, or use drugs at any time, (b) not engage in abusive use of alcohol, (c) participate in all classes and scheduled activities unless ill, and (d) abide by dress and cultural codes suitable in the countries visited.**

6. Program Changes

The University may, in its sole discretion, determine that circumstances within a foreign country may require the cancellation of the Program within that country. The University will provide me with as much advance notice as possible of its intention to cancel the Program in which I will participate. I also understand that the University, the on-site coordinators, or the foreign government may prematurely terminate the Program. I understand that the University's fees and Program charges are based on current airfares, lodging rates, and travel costs, which are subject to change. If I leave or am expelled from the Program for any reason, there will be no refund of fees already paid. I accept all responsibility for loss or additional expenses due to delays or other changes in the means of transportation, other services, or sickness, weather, strikes, computer problems, or other unforeseen causes. If I become sick or injured, I will, at my own expense, seek out, contact, and reach the Program group at its next available destination. The University bears no liability for any losses or claims incurred by me in connection with my own early termination from the Program or the University's termination of its participation in the Program. If I decide to remain in the foreign country after receiving notice of the University's intent to terminate the Program, I bear complete responsibility and liability for my own care and safety.

7. Health and Safety

A. I have consulted with a medical doctor with regard to my personal medical needs. There are no health-related reasons or problems that preclude or restrict my participation in this Program.

B. I am aware of all applicable personal medical needs. I have arranged, through insurance or otherwise, to meet any and all needs for payment of medical costs while I participate in the Program. I recognize that the University is not obligated to attend to any of my medical or medication needs, and I assume all risk and responsibility therefore. If I require medical treatment or hospital care in a foreign country or in the United States during the Program, the University is not responsible for the cost or quality of such treatment or care.

C. The University may (but is not obligated to) take any action it considers to be warranted under the circumstances regarding my health and safety. I hereby authorize the University and/or faculty directors to procure all necessary medical assistance while I participate in this Program and to authorize any competent medical person to do all things reasonably necessary to treat any injury or illness that occurs during my participation in the Program. I agree to pay all expenses relating thereto and release the University from any liability or any actions.

8. Assumption of Risk and Release of Claims

Knowing the risks described above, and in consideration of being permitted to participate in the Program, I agree on behalf of my family, heirs, and personal representatives to assume all the risks and responsibilities surrounding my participation in the Program. I and my heirs and successors and assigns agree to release, indemnify, and hold harmless the University of St. Thomas, its past and present trustees, officers, employees, agents and the heirs, successors, and assigns of each from any and all loss, cost, damage, liability, or expense (including reasonable attorney's fees) resulting in or arising from my participation in the Program (including periods in transit to or from any country where the Program is being conducted).

9. Program Charges

I am responsible for any and all required payments and charges applicable to the Program. I understand the Program's cancellation policies and fees and agree to abide by them. I have read, understand and will abide by the terms of the *Short-Term Study Abroad & Away Policies and Procedures* book included with the application.

10. Health Insurance

I am insured for any medical expenses, which I may incur while I participate in the Program. This policy is with _____ and my policy number is

_____ .

I have carefully read this Assumption of Risk and Release Form before signing it. No representations, statements, or inducements, oral or written, apart from the foregoing written statement have been made.

This Agreement shall be effective only upon receipt of my application by the University of St. Thomas, and shall be governed by the laws of the state of Minnesota, which shall be the forum for any lawsuits filed under or incident to this Agreement or to the Program.

Student Signature:	Date:

I, (a) am the parent or legal guardian of the above student; (b) have read the foregoing Assumption of Risk and Release Form (including such parts as may subject me to personal financial responsibility), (c) am and will be legally responsible for the obligations and acts of the student as described in this Assumption of Risk and Release Form, and (d) agree for myself and for the student to be bound by its terms.

Parent/Guardian Signature:	Date:

This signature is only necessary if the student is considered a dependent for federal income tax or financial aid purposes.

[Source: Adapted from the University of St. Thomas]

Example of Crisis Management Plan: Off-Campus Programs

Orientation information, both printed and oral, contains information for faculty and students about health and safety issues related to international and off-campus travel. Adherence to this information, along with appropriate behavior, caution, and common sense, can prevent many of the crisis situations discussed below.

Conditions Requiring Crisis Management

The administrator must be contacted under the following circumstances:

- Serious illness, injury, or death;
- Emotional or psychological stress that requires intervention;
- A participant is the victim of a crime (e.g., theft, assault, rape, harassment) or is accused of committing a crime;
- An in-country situation arises that causes concern (e.g., a political uprising or a natural disaster);
- Conduct issues at the discretion of the faculty director; or
- Any other international situation that could warrant concern, either U.S. domestic or foreign.

Course of Action

Some off-campus programs have substantial on-site support. It is expected that there will be collaboration between the on-site organization and the administrator. Most organizations should also have a crisis response team, either as part of the institution's administrative structure or international programs. Listed below are some possible actions to take in various crisis situations you might encounter while abroad.

Ill or Injured Student or Faculty Director

- On-site personnel (e.g., faculty director, student, program provider) contact the appropriate local authorities (e.g., police, U.S. embassy, medical personnel) to begin the local action necessary to handle the situation.
- On-site personnel contact the home campus 24-hour number (usually the security office). If possible, identify the person you wish to speak to and give an accurate description of the situation.
- A representative from the 24-hour number will notify the appropriate person, who will call you back; in all cases, the program administrator will be notified.
- May contact other personnel for assistance, such as the American International Assistance Service in Houston, TX, (International Student ID Card) to involve them in evaluating the situation. Telephone: 800.626.2427.
- Administrator will phone the emergency contacts of the person or persons involved in the crisis to apprise them of the situation, if not notified by the faculty director or the on-site coordinator. (FERPA rights should be waived to contact student's emergency contact.)
- Necessary action will be taken: provision for medical care in-country, emergency evacuation, etc.

Death of Student or Faculty Director

(Follow your organization's protocol.)

- On-site personnel contact the appropriate local authorities (e.g., police, U.S. embassy, medical personnel) to begin the local action necessary to handle the situation.
- On-site personnel contact the home campus 24-hour number.
- Administrator will contact director of the crisis response team.
- Organization's protocol will be followed.
- Working rule: All persons involved should always have another person in the room when discussion of these situations is taking place (e.g. phone conversations).

Student or Faculty Director With Emotional or Psychological Problems

- On-site personnel contact the appropriate local authorities (e.g., police, U.S. embassy, medical personnel) to begin the local action necessary to handle the situation.
- On-site personnel contact the home campus 24-hour number.
- Administrator will contact on-campus counseling personnel. Counselors will be in touch with student, faculty director, and on-site coordinator to evaluate the situation and make necessary recommendations.
- Administrator will contact the emergency contact of the student or faculty director, if appropriate.
- If appropriate, administrator should work with contact legal counsel.

Student or Faculty Director Is the Victim of a Crime (e.g., theft, assault, rape, harassment)

- On-site personnel contact the appropriate local authorities (e.g., police, U.S. embassy, medical personnel) to begin the local action necessary to handle the situation.
- On-site personnel contact the home campus 24-hour number.
- Administrator may contact the director of the crisis response team, if appropriate.
- If the incident is between two students of the group, the dean of student life has primary responsibility and university policy will apply.
- If the incident is between a student member of the group and the faculty director, the appropriate dean/V.P. (vice president) has primary responsibility and policy will apply.
- If the incident is between a member of the group and an outside party, action taken will depend on legal requirements of the host country and wishes of the victim. Legal counsel will be contacted by the administrator or the dean of student life, if necessary, for appropriate advice.

Student or Faculty Director Is Accused of Committing a Crime

- On-site personnel contact the appropriate local authorities (e.g., police, U.S. embassy, medical personnel) to begin the local action necessary to handle the situation.
- On-site personnel contact the home campus 24-hour number.
- Administrator may contact the director of the crisis response team, if appropriate.
- If the incident is between a member of the group and an outside party, action taken will depend on legal requirements of the host country and wishes of the victim.
- Legal counsel will be contacted by the administrator, if necessary, for appropriate advice on the role of the organization in the situation.
- In consultation with the on-site coordinators, administrator will contact the emergency contact of the student or faculty director employee if desired.

List Contact Numbers and Web Sites

[Source: Adapted from St. Olaf College]

Suspension/Cancellation/Evacuation of Study Abroad Programs

Criteria for Suspension/Cancellation of Program and Evacuation of the Students

The decision to suspend or cancel a study abroad program will be based on conversations with any of the following:

- Cosponsored program staff in-country;
- University officials at a partner university;
- U.S. embassy officials in-country;
- Other officials from U.S. agencies and/or nongovernmental organizations; or
- Appropriate U.S. State Department country desk officer(s).

The decision will also be based on the administrator's own assessment of the following events (not in rank order):

- Declaration of war by the United States against the host country or an adjacent neighbor;
- Declaration of war by a third country against the host country;
- Significant terrorist activity in the program city/country;
- Inability of the faculty director or on-site coordinator to organize and carry out an academic program.
- Disruption of public utilities and/or services;
- Widespread civil unrest, violence, and/or rioting;
- A declaration of martial law in the program city/country;
- Recommendation of suspension/cancellation by the on-site coordinator;
- Travel warning and/or specific directive by the U.S. State Department and/or U.S. embassy; or
- Faculty directors who do not feel comfortable taking students to that country, or on-site recommendations.

Procedures

The organization's crisis response team procedures will be in effect.

Specific Procedures for Any Program

- If the students are on an organized excursion outside of the program city and there is a civil emergency, the on-site coordinator and faculty director in charge of the excursion shall take the group to a secure location and contact the U.S. embassy/consulate and administrator for instructions.
- If the students are traveling independently, an effort will be made to contact them according to the contact information and itineraries they have left behind. The students will be advised as to the proper course of action.
- If the students are in the program city, the on-site coordinator will identify a meeting space. The U.S. embassy will give instructions on the evacuation, dependent on airlines operations. The administrator will do his or her best to coordinate return transportation to home destinations in the United States.

Communication Procedures

The Administrator will:

- keep students and on-site coordinators in-country in the loop;
- communicate with the participants' emergency contacts, especially in the event that the organization decides to move the students and/or cancel or suspend the program;
- keep staff of international office well informed; and
- communicate directly with the college president, crisis response team, deans, and directors and keep the organization's community informed with the appropriate information.

Withdrawal Policy

The appropriate committee will be called to determine the program's financial situation and the process for reimbursing participants after withdrawal from the host country.

- If administrator cancels a study abroad program due to an U.S. Department of State Travel Warning, a full refund will be made.
- If administrator cancels a study abroad program for any other reason, every attempt will be made to return payments. Refunds will be aggressively negotiated on the behalf of students.
- If a student and/or parent voluntarily request withdrawal from a study abroad program, recoverable costs will be returned.
- If student and/or parent voluntarily request withdrawal and administrator subsequently cancels or suspends the program, every effort will be made to return recoverable costs.

[Source: Adapted from Kalamazoo College]

Preventative Actions for Faculty Directors Overseas

Before Departure

- Leave a copy of your passport (first two pages) with the international office or department in case of replacement.
- Confirm that your emergency contact is updated with human resources.
- Confirm that the international office and department has received the latest itinerary, with all phone, fax, and e-mail numbers.

On-Site

- Make sure that all students and faculty have been listed with the U.S. embassy.
- Keep emergency contact numbers for each student. Establish a procedure for reaching the contacts in case of an emergency.
- Make sure students know how to reach you 24 hours a day in case of an emergency.
- Caution students about speculative communication and advise them to wait until clear information is available before contacting home.
- If students plan to travel independently, they should notify faculty directors of:
  - ✓ their planned itinerary, giving as much information as possible about location (city/country), hotel/hostel, or other addresses and phone numbers and any other contact information;
  - ✓ their mode of transportation, that is, all scheduled plane and train information, including from-to, departure, and arrival dates and times and plane or train numbers;
  - ✓ their cell phone number if they have one (list the full number, including access and country codes).

[Source: Adapted from University of St. Thomas]

Sample Disciplinary Rights and Procedures for Study Abroad Programs, Academic and Nonacademic

In all off-campus programs, students are subject to the rules of conduct as stated in this student policy handbook or as set down by the faculty director.

In these cases the faculty or staff person who is in charge of supervising the off-campus/study abroad program will have the full authority of the dean of students (for nonacademic violations) and the dean of the college (for academic violations) to adjudicate disciplinary violations of the rules of conduct.

When feasible, the faculty or staff person in charge should make every effort to informally resolve problems that arise. However, if a formal process is required, the following procedures for adjudicating violations of the rules of conduct should be followed:

1. The staff or faculty member who administers the program on-site will notify students of alleged violations in writing.

2. A meeting will be held between the accused student and the faculty or staff member after the student receives the violation letter to determine if the student violated the rules of conduct.

3. After the meeting, the faculty or staff member will determine whether or not the rules of conduct have been violated and, in consultation with the director of international programs and the dean of students or dean of the college, determine sanctions, if applicable.

4. The student will receive a decision letter stating whether it has been determined that the student violated the rules of conduct and the appropriate sanction, if any. A copy of the decision letter will be forwarded to the dean of students or dean of the college for inclusion in the student's disciplinary file.

5. There is no appeal of discipline occurring in connection with the off-campus/study abroad program. Faculty or staff in charge of the administration of the program have full authority for imposing sanctions, including sending the student home prior to the completion of the class or program.

6. In extreme cases, the faculty or staff member who oversees the class or program may, in consultation with the director of international programs and the dean of students or dean of the College, immediately suspend a student from the program and send the student home at the student's expense. The decision of the faculty or staff member is final.

[Source: Adapted from the University of St. Thomas]

Behavior Contract

I, [student name], failed to [list infraction]. I understand that this requirement is meant to benefit the group, and that my behavior is a disruption to the successful functioning of this academic experience.

I understand that my actions impact the group, and that I must keep the group interests in mind when making decisions about my behavior.

I understand that if a similar infraction of course requirements occurs, I will be sent home at my expense, in accordance with policy.

Student signature _____

[Source: Adapted from the University of St. Thomas]

Sample Expulsion Form

[Student name], you have repeatedly violated the behavioral expectations set up in the study abroad agreement that you signed before departing for this course. In that agreement, you stated that you would comply with all rules and regulations issued by the organization, the faculty director, or any coordinating organization, and that you would:

a) not buy, sell, or use drugs at any time;

b) not engage in abusive use of alcohol;

c) not engage in disruptive behavior;

d) participate in all classes and scheduled activities unless ill; and

e) abide by dress and cultural codes suitable in the countries visited.

You were clearly reminded of [list infraction] during the predeparture meeting with the faculty director on [list orientation date], and in the contract you signed on the day after your first infraction [list date of behavior contract].

Minimally, you have violated the conditions of the study abroad agreement by:

[List specific incidents.] _____

As stated on page X of the student policy book, "In all study abroad programs, students are subject to the rules of conduct..." and, "There is no appeal of discipline occurring in connection with a study abroad program." At the faculty director's discretion, you will not face further disciplinary action when you return.

Your behavior has not only been a clear violation of your contractual obligations, but also has been disruptive and disrespectful to your classmates and to your faculty director. At the orientation, and repeatedly thereafter, your faculty director has emphasized that this is first and foremost an academic experience. Through your behavior you have demonstrated a lack of commitment to that priority.

Arrangements have been made for your early departure. [List travel specifics.] Your parents or guardians will be notified by [administrator] to expect your early return.

Statement authored by faculty director.

I have read and understand this statement.

_____

Student signature
(not required)

[Source: Adapted from the University of St. Thomas]

Incident Report

Please fill out this form as completely as possible. In the event of any legal action this form will serve as the basic official college record of what transpired and what actions were taken by responsible college officials at the scene of the incident. Attach extra sheets as necessary and any documentary evidence. Fax a copy of your report to _____ as soon as possible. Submit the complete original report and all supporting materials to _____ upon your return to the United States.

Date of incident_____   Location of incident _____

Time of incident_____   Were you present?_____

Name of student involved (*please use a separate form for each student*):

_____

Names of other students involved: _____

_____

Brief description of what happened: _____

_____

_____

Who provided this description if you were not a witness (*please list all names*):_____

_____

If you were not present, when were you informed? _____

What actions did you take? _____

_____

If the student was transported to a hospital or clinic, please provide complete name of the facility, its phone and fax numbers, and address _____

_____

Names and phone numbers of all physicians who examined or treated the student

Dr._____   Phone:_____

Dr._____   Phone:_____

(turn over)

Exact names of any medications prescribed to the student (*please keep _all_ packaging/inserts*):

Rx: _____

Rx: _____

Rx: _____

Rx: _____

Was the student conscious and capable of making informed judgments about his or her medical treatment?_____

If the student was not capable of making medical decisions, who made any decisions?

_____

What if any follow-up care was recommended?_____

_____

_____

Were the police or legal authorities notified of the incident or present at the scene?_____

Names and phone numbers of responsible legal authorities in charge of the case:

_____ Case#: _____

Was the U.S. or relevant embassy notified:_____Name and number of responsible

consular officials involved in this incident:_____

_____

Dates/times of contact with international student office and/or parents:

_____

_____

_____

_____   _____   _____
Signature   Date   Time

[Source: Adapted from St. Olaf College]

PART V
Reflections from the Field

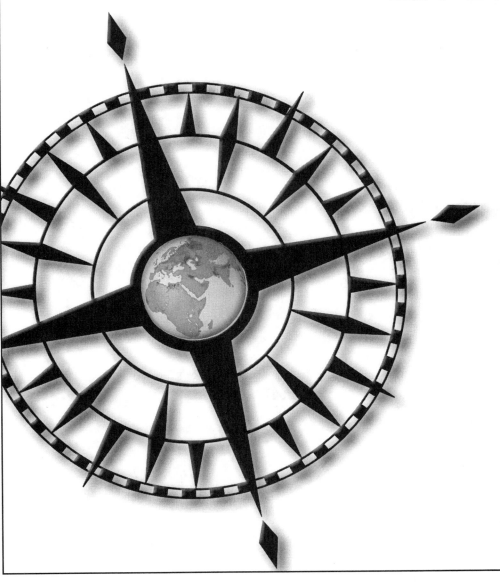

Chapter 17

Reflections on Field Experience

Ron Lee

Friends ask me, why did I do this for so long? Why put up with the risk, the anxiety, the frustration, and the strain of organizing and leading a study program abroad for a bunch of college kids who might really have in mind a month-long party?

My response is in part an honest admission of a kind of masochism; an admission that you can get hooked on savoring how good it feels when the program is over and you get back home. But my more serious response represents the first of several "don't underestimate..." bits of advice. In the midst of that anxiety, frustration, and strain, never underestimate how huge an impact your program can have on the students. Over a period of 25 years I led eight 1-month programs in London, a 5-month program in Southeast Asia, and two 5-month programs in the Middle East. With every one of those programs I discovered, almost as a startling revelation, that students who I thought were drifting through the program in a haze of indifference were in fact being profoundly impacted or changed.

It is not uncommon for this discovery to come a few years after the program, in an unexpected Christmas card or an invitation to a wedding or just a note out of the blue, in which this student, who most of the time appeared bored or half asleep, tells you that your program changed his or her life and that the memories will last forever. Study abroad works; it is indeed challenging, but for me it has been the most rewarding teaching I have been privileged to undertake. And short-term programs abroad work. It's just that everything happens faster.

Because it all happens faster, you must be willing to do careful advance planning. There won't be time to work out major changes in the program once you are on site. I have done some work as a theater director, and I suppose that I approach the planning for a program abroad a bit like approaching a production. I spend a lot of time trying to envision the whole experience. I think about setting and change of scenes, about timing and rhythm, about the plot, about characters and their interaction and development, and about my role as the "director" and as a kind of coach.

Casting the production, of course, is critical. But one of the biggest challenges (and perhaps problems) in working with short-term programs is that faculty directors may not have much of a voice in the selection of the students. Practice varies a great deal among institutions, but it is not unusual for students to be in a program simply because they were the first ones to sign up. I would strongly urge faculty directors to work out with their study abroad offices some role for themselves in selecting the students. The success of the program and of the group experience is influenced considerably by the make-up of the group itself. It is very helpful if the faculty director has the power to refuse to enroll a student who has, for example, a record of disciplinary problems, or alcohol or substance abuse.

It is now true that families have the means not only to send their student on a program but also for one or both of the parents to come along as well. So what do you say when you have parents who want to come along? I would say "no." More emphatically I would say "no" if it is a boyfriend or girlfriend who wants to tag along. I once had a case where a female student had her boyfriend (not enrolled in the program) bring her to the airport, and right at the departure gate they got into a huge fight having to do basically with his jealousy about her going. I was stunned to see her decide right there that she would give in to the boyfriend, and she simply turned around and walked out of the airport and out of the program.

So what do you do with this group once it is formed? Prior to the event itself there is the necessity, of course, for some preparation (which, to continue the theater metaphor, can be a bit like rehearsals for the reality of the group experience). It is important to get information to the students, but also important to get them together to begin to interact with each other and with you. I have over the years experimented with a variety of get-acquainted activities or role-playing exercises. They have worked with varying degrees of success, and none to my knowledge has done any harm. These activities can be those done with the orientation for study abroad in general.

My recommendation to others is to find (or invent) something that works well for your particular personality and interests. The important thing is to inculcate some sense of group cohesion and acquaintance before you are off and running. One factor that has emerged in recent years that can alter how you prepare the students is that some, and perhaps many, students will already have traveled and/or studied abroad before they come along on your program. Their experience can be a resource on which to draw in preparing the group. But one also has to watch for such students adopting a blasé or superior attitude toward once again being abroad.

Even on a short program there is time for problems to develop with group dynamics. Coping with these problems can be very time and energy consuming, especially if you are alone and the sole director of the group. Nip these problems in the bud, if you can. Being direct, honest, gentle, and sensitive is important. If it is at all workable, solicit the help of fellow students. If you have been able to establish a sense in the group at the beginning that this is something like a large family that they are participating in, then you have a better chance of calling on them to do what they can to work out their own differences and disagreements. In longer programs it is essential to establish individuals or committees who function as "ombudsmen" or troubleshooters and problem-solvers in group dynamics, and this can be done in short programs as well. There may be students in the group who already have training in facilitating group dynamics or in intervention, and typically they feel honored to be asked to help. Above all, in the predeparture meetings with the students it is important to discuss candidly what kinds of problems might arise and how they, the students, might deal with such problems.

An important part of the group dynamic derives from the faculty director's relationship to the group. This relationship can be eminently positive and rewarding, but it can also be fraught with complexity and even frustration. Like it or not, you will have to wear a number of different hats in relating to the group. You are the teacher and sort of tour director, but sometimes you may have to function as a parent or even as the dean of student life or the college nurse. You are of course a traveling companion, and you will, more or less depending on your age and inclination, socialize with your students. At what point does fraternizing with the troops compromise their respect for you, and their distance from you? How willing are you to let them see you in your less-than-better moments? How does your patience and sense of humor hold up when things are not going right, such as when a bus doesn't show up or an airplane is very, very late?

Prepare yourself for the experience especially by thinking through the kinds of stress points or crises you might encounter and how you would respond. There may be relatively minor incidents such as students acting silly or boisterous at inappropriate times or sleeping in class or being rude or inattentive in front of a guide or a guest lecturer. How do you respond and what do you do if, 10 minutes before departure, a student tells you that he can't find his passport?

More serious can be the case where a student comes in late at night and drunk, or where a student is openly defiant of program rules or policies. There is no one perfect way of responding to these kinds of problems; much depends on the personality and style of the director. But it is important to let the students know before departure that these kinds of problems will provoke a response from you and may require disciplinary action that might even go as far as expulsion from the program. (Does your institution have procedures in place for what you do if you are going to expel a student and send that student home?) The students must understand that your concern—and theirs—has to be the safety of individuals and of the group. They should also understand that the program and the college have a reputation to protect, that misbehavior could end the program and shut out future students from enjoying it.

Even more serious, of course, are the medical emergencies or accidents. With regard to these, it is very important in the predeparture information sessions to find out who in the group is trained in first aid. Be very certain, as well, of the channels of communication to and the kinds of support from your home institution in the case of emergencies. You need to know whom to call and what you can expect to happen if there is illness or injury.

Here is another bit of "don't underestimate..." advice. Even though you simply must think positively about how the program will go and how the group will function, you still should not underestimate the degree to which the students can get themselves into trouble or harm. Many of us are not by nature skeptical or excessively cautious, but we need to be so when out in the field.

And here is a bit of tough advice on how you relate to your group. You may think that the question is "how much the students need you" and that the answer lies in how you supply that need. But there is also the question of "how much you need the students." Be honest with yourself about whether your behavior is motivated by a need to have the students like you, or by an inordinate desire to impress the students with your own knowledge and experience, or by your own loneliness and your need for companionship. Your relationship with the students will be strengthened by their knowledge that you are secure, self-confident, and not dependent on them. They need to see very clearly that you care for them and like them and that you are willing to share your feelings, but the last thing they need to feel is that they somehow have to be indulging you or propping you up or continuously keeping you company.

Balance is what you need to find. You have to be there for the students, but you should not smother them or intrude on them. And you have to protect your own space and time. You are not there to hold their hands or always to keep them company, but you do have to tune in to when they might genuinely need you to be with them. I gradually discovered in the course of directing several programs that the students often could do quite well without me. I don't mean for days and days at a time, but rather for a significant chunk of a day and perhaps for an occasion of 2 or 3 days. One of the constant features of our month-long program in London is a "free weekend" in the middle of the month when the students are on their own. Some might stay in London, but most will travel to other cities. They must make their own housing and travel arrangements for the 3-day period. This has turned out to be a very successful part of the program. I find as well as I look back over the schedules for each of the London programs that I gradually built into the programs more afternoon free time for the students. Mornings were always devoted to class (or occasionally to tours), and evenings were always spent at the theater (we would see on average 22 plays in 26 days).

One key element in discovering this balance goes back to what you can do in the planning for the program. Again, to use the theater metaphor, it helps to think about setting and scene change and about timing and rhythm. The students will sense very quickly (though it may not be an entirely conscious perception) how well-planned the program is. And my experience tells me that there is a strong correlation between that perception and their degree of comfort in being on their own. A well-planned program gives them the security to do more on their own. You supply their need for security not by holding their hands all day long but rather by creating a clear and strong structure within which they can relax and even strike out on their own.

I must also emphasize that a well-planned program does not necessarily mean a program that is heavily scheduled. Don't confuse careful planning with the mere process of filling up the schedule. A heavily scheduled program can be very badly planned. You can build free time into a program—quite a bit of free time, in fact—provided that it has a purpose, that it is part of the plan.

For example, in my London program there are many afternoons that are unscheduled. However, it is very clear to the students that the objectives of the course, besides going to and studying the theater, include getting to know London and especially its major museums, galleries, and historical sites. Halfway through the month and again at the end I collect and read the journals that the students must keep, and in those they are assigned to write, among other things, about what they do and see on these afternoons on their own. I give them specific guidelines and suggestions on what to see. Each morning in class we also have a "show and tell" time in which students take turns relating to the rest of the class interesting places they have discovered and visited. I have always been impressed and even amazed at the energy and inventiveness the students put into these free afternoons of exploration. I am hard-pressed to remember any occasions when I thought that a student was wasting this special time.

Two caveats about scheduling and how you and the students handle it. First, it matters a great deal what the reputation is for the program. This is a difficult matter to shape or change, but if a program has the reputation of being a party program, then you are likely to get students who come with that expectation only, and much of your effort in planning and management of the program will be frustrated. My own advice on this issue is blunt: if a program really is suffering from the reputation of being a party program, it is an incurable malady and the program should be junked. Better to scrap it and start all over, either at a later time or in a different form. If the program has a reputation built on good planning, high expectations from the faculty directors, and responsible student commitment, then you can do the kind of creative planning that includes unscheduled time that will be used constructively.

A second caveat has to do with what I must acknowledge as a subjective factor. The kind of schedule you devise for the students will be shaped in part by your own comfort level with heavily scheduled or lightly scheduled programs. I discovered that, given the way that I plan and then manage a program, I could make unscheduled time work for the students. Both I and the students seemed to benefit from it. The question in part, then, was "could the students handle it." There was also the question of "could I handle it." Not every instructor will be comfortable with or be convinced of the value of unscheduled time. I come back yet again to the theater metaphor. Every stage production will have imposed on it in some way the vision and the personality of the director. I think that a study abroad program is similarly shaped by the vision and personality of the faculty director.

Much of the success of the program abroad (like the theater production) depends on whether the instructor's vision and personality clicks with the way the program is scheduled and planned. And here I refer to more than making use of unscheduled time. How you, the instructor, relate to the tour guides and hosts, how you run the classes, what kind of schedule you devise, and what sort of personality you project to your students—all of these elements of the program derive from your vision and your own unique personal characteristics. You need to discover what works for you, what is best in your own raw material, and work out a plan for the program and for relating to the students that makes the most of that material.

Are the students, then, merely actors being directed by you? No. After all this attention to how you and I as instructors shape, plan, and manage the program, I must emphasize how much a good program is really the students' program. The students must discover (and you can help them do this) that it is their program and that much of the success of the program depends on what they put into it and do with it. To use a common phrase, the students need to find that they have some ownership of the program. There are a variety of ways to achieve this. For example, in my London program I put the burden of leading discussions on the plays that we see on the shoulders of the students. I divide them into pairs (to encourage teamwork and diversity of viewpoints), and each pair is assigned one of the plays for which they lead the discussion. We also do cooperative work on journal writing. You can also assign certain responsibilities to individuals or small committees—responsibilities, for example, for logistical details (such as making sure baggage is collected in a timely and efficient way for transfers between destinations), for social activities within the group, or for other aspects of group dynamics. This attention to finding ways for the students to claim ownership of the program needs to begin well before departure in the earliest meetings of the group.

One last but not least point: it is important that no one lose sight of the fact that the program is finally an academic program. There is, of course, no way for the students to avoid being torn between the academic expectations you impose upon them and the alluring prospects of immersion in the life and activities of the program site. There are some ways to alleviate this problem. To begin with there should be regular and open discussion of this issue with the students. It helps them to know that you know they are struggling with this. On the instructor's part there should be considerable effort put into designing the course so that both subject matter and pedagogy are adapted to the demands and the opportunities of the site. Typically on site there is no access (or very little) to a library. There may be little access as well to a traditional classroom or to the kinds of technology available in most of our classrooms. I found it a stimulating challenge to figure out how to make a class work in a hotel lounge, and I found it very liberating (after some frustration) to be deprived of a blackboard. Students do not like to haul a lot of textbooks along in their luggage, and once on site the opportunities for sitting down and reading traditional kinds of assignments may be hard to come by. As my London course evolved I gradually moved away from using textbooks to using shorter, photocopied essays, which were more manageable both physically and intellectually. Keep in mind that whatever reading the students can manage to do will be accomplished while riding in a bus or airplane, or sitting on a bed in a hotel room, or down in the lounge or hotel coffee shop, or out in the park. But they can do some reading and the instructor should expect it. Several weeks before departure I would hand out a large packet of these readings, some of which they were required to read before we arrived on site. In my course I had the advantage also of primary subject matter consisting of the theater productions we were seeing every night. In any case, you should not lose sight of the fact that your course is being done abroad for particular reasons, and the content and the pedagogy should naturally be at least somewhat or perhaps radically different from what they would be in a comparable course on campus.

Pedagogy seems naturally to focus on discussion, and one can heavily involve the students in taking responsibilities for leading discussions. In my course I have no examinations but rather evaluate the students on the work they do in their journals and in two relatively short, analytical papers. I am quite enthusiastic about the use of journals in study/travel contexts. I spend time before the program begins and during the program discussing how to write good journals. I give the students specific guidelines (and even a few requirements) on what kind of material should be in the journals. I expect daily writing, and I collect the journals at the mid-point of the month and again at the end to read and evaluate them (reading journals is what I do on the flight home). After the mid-point reading I hold individual conferences to discuss the students' writing. It was always a pleasure to hold conferences in this kind of situation where I had no office, for it would force me and the student into some delightful setting like the sidewalk cafe or the nearby park or the local pub.

Contributors

Elise Amel teaches psychology at the University of St. Thomas. She has taught six courses abroad in England and France, and she is currently working on a program focusing on ecopsychology in Hungary. Elise is the cochair of St. Thomas's Academic Review Committee for International Education. She and her husband have an infant daughter, who she hopes will also have the travel bug.

William W. Hoffa holds academic degrees from the University of Michigan, Harvard University, and the University of Wisconsin, and is founder of Academic Consultants International. He is author and editor of numerous professional publications: essays, interviews, book reviews, and reports on education abroad. He has contributed 17 years of active professional involvement within NAFSA: Association of International Educators, including national election to SECUSSA chair, appointments to other key leadership positions, and presentations at regional and national conferences.

Peter Hovde is director of international education and professor of international relations at Concordia College in Moorhead, MN. He led numerous short-term study abroad courses in public policy and international conflict during the 1970s and 1980s, becoming director of Concordia's overseas programs in 1990. Beyond expanding both the number and the kinds of overseas programs for students, he has focused his professional efforts in two areas. His publication and presentation record mainly focuses on program design and impact, and was instrumental in obtaining and directing three large grants aimed at getting faculty overseas to prepare them to lead study abroad programs. In what little remains of his leisure time, he enjoys golf and lake life with his wife Charlie.

Sue Jackson is director of off-campus programs at Whitworth College in Spokane, WA. She holds a master's degree from Indiana University, is on the trainer corps of NAFSA: Association of International Educators, and has led NAFSA Professional Practice Workshops on "Developing and Administering Quality Short-Term Education Abroad Programs," and "Foundations of International Education: Education Abroad Advising." She has also presented on various topics at NAFSA regional conferences.

Allison Keith is the director of U.S. operations for ACCENT International Consortium for Academic Programs Abroad, a program provider specializing in Western Europe, specifically France, Italy, Spain and the United Kingdom. She has worked with ACCENT since the opening of their San Francisco headquarters in 1991. The San Francisco Center of ACCENT currently oversees the developmental, contractual, and predeparture phases of close to 100 programs annually, of which roughly half are short-term programs. Allison has been a panel member for the NAFSA Professional Practice Workshop "Developing and Administering Quality Short-Term Education Abroad Programs" since 1997.

Joe Kinsella is the director of study abroad at DePaul University, a position he has held since 2000. He was assistant director of study abroad from 1988 to 1996. During his 10 years at DePaul, he was instrumental in growing the number of study abroad offerings from 4 to 24 programs, and focused his professional activities on short-term program pedagogies, experiential learning, and assessment. In 1993 and 1994 he was part of the NAFSA Professional Practice Workshop "Developing Quality Short-Term Education Abroad Programs." Joe is currently completing a Ph.D. in anthropology at the University of New Mexico, working with a group of sculptors from Zimbabwe around questions of aesthetics and postcolonial identity.

Mike Klein (B.A. studio arts, theology, M.A. educational leadership) is the coordinator of volunteer services and adjunct instructor in justice and peace studies at the University of St. Thomas, MN. He directs student programs in community service, domestic and international service/immersion experiences, and social action initiatives. Mike's service-learning courses address the civil rights movement, Native-American land issues, the arts and social change, and justice on the farm. When he is not on campus, he spends time as a mural artist and most importantly as a husband and father.

Ron Lee recently retired from the English Department at St. Olaf College, where he taught courses on drama, especially with a focus on drama in performance, as well as a wide range of courses in the humanities and in literature and theology. During his tenure at St. Olaf he was chair of the English department, served as the associate dean for interdisciplinary and general studies, and was a member of and then chair of the Committee on International and Off-Campus Studies. His graduate degrees are from Oxford University (where he studied as a Rhodes Scholar) and Stanford University. Four years altogether of living and studying in England inspired a deep commitment to study abroad. He was a faculty director three times on 5-month-long programs to Southeast Asia and the Middle East and led the "Theater in London" January program eight times, with the satisfactions and pleasures of the program never diminishing. After wandering the world he decided in his retirement to immerse himself in the grandeur nearer home, the Rocky Mountains of Montana, where he now lives with his wife, Sue Clarke, who was formerly the director of international studies at St. Olaf College.

Susan MacNally, assistant director at the University of Kansas Office of Study Abroad, has worked at the KU OSA for 9 years in a variety of positions, including student data development, publications and outreach, and administering and developing short-term programs. She currently oversees the administration of all KU short-term programs and has developed approximately 25 new short-term programs over the past 5 years. Susan has been a panel member of the NAFSA Professional Practice Workshop "Developing Quality Short-Term Education Abroad Programs" since 1997, and has been a member of the NAFSA trainer corps since 1998. She will finish a 2-year term as Region II SECUSSA representative in May 2002.

Pamela Nice teaches "Encountering Egypt Through the Arts," a short-term study abroad course to Egypt. She also has developed and taught the courses "20th Century Arab Writers" and "Documenting Arab Lives" for the University of St. Thomas. She is currently working on a documentary of Egyptians' perceptions of Americans. She recently received a Malone Fellowship to Syria and a Jerome Travel and Study Grant to Egypt to work on a film. Pam has written many articles, interviews, and book and film reviews on Middle Eastern subjects for Al Jadid and Mizna. Her background is in theater and film.

Patrick Quade has served as the director of international and off-campus studies at St. Olaf College since 1997. He currently serves in this position and holds the rank of professor and chair of the department of theater. He is a graduate of St. Olaf College (1965), the University of Wisconsin (M.A. in 1968), and the University of Minnesota (M.F.A. in 1972). He has led many student and adult-learner groups on programs to various parts of the world. In 1993 and again in 1996 he led the St. Olaf College Global Semester Program, a 5-month-long study program with 28 students in Switzerland, Egypt, Israel, India, Nepal, Hong Kong, Japan, and Korea. He is a veteran of 13 "Theater in London" January short-term study programs. In 1976 and in 1980 he served as the resident director of the Associate Colleges of the Midwest Arts of London and Florence Program.

Mickey Slind is currently a field director for the Institute for Study Abroad, Butler University, Indianapolis, IN. She travels for approximately 25 weeks each year on behalf of the institute's programs and visits over 100 institutions annually. Since 1982, she has worked as a study abroad adviser, program administrator, resident director, and program representative. She has served in various international education positions at Hamline University, St. Paul, MN, and the University of Minnesota, Minneapolis, MN; and with the Institute for Study Abroad. From 1993 to 1996, she was a member of NAFSA's Insurance Advisory Committee. In 1993, she organized and chaired the first NAFSA conference workshop on short-term programs, "Designing and Administering the Short-Term Study Abroad Program." In 1995, SECUSSA presented Slind with its Lily von Klemperer Award for service and commitment to the field of study abroad. In the fall of 2000, Slind was elected to SECUSSA leadership and will serve as chair during 2003.

Melissa Smith-Simonet is originally from New York and a graduate of the State University of New York-Albany. She has been living in Paris since 1987 and has worked with ACCENT since 1989, first as administrative assistant, then Paris program and housing coordinator, and since 1998 as ACCENT Paris director. Melissa is the director of an international team of 11 administrative staff and 15 faculty and is responsible for the management and administration of over 40 study abroad programs per year in Paris. She also serves on the NAFSA workshop panel for "SECUSSA Basic Training for Overseas Directors."

Sarah E. Spencer is assistant director of international education at the University of St. Thomas, MN. She has overseen the growth of the institution's short-term programs, which have increased dramatically from 3 to 32 since her arrival in 1993. She holds a B.A. from St. Olaf College and an M.A. in English from St. Thomas. She has studied and worked in England, as well as traveling extensively. Sarah has co-chaired the NAFSA Professional Practice Workshop "Developing and Administrating Quality Short-Term Education Abroad Programs" since 1997, frequently presents at regional conferences, is a member of NAFSA's trainer corps, and also serves as the Region IV SECUSSA representative. She is currently developing a workshop on advanced topics in short-term study abroad.

Julie Taylor is associate director of campus relations for the American InterContinental University. Her previous positions include associate director of study abroad at the University of Illinois at Urbana-Champaign and coordinator of study abroad at Ohio University. She has been active in NAFSA since 1995 and has been a member of the SECUSSA trainer corps since 1998. She has been a frequent presenter at regional and national conferences and has contributed to foundations and professional practice workshops, including "Developing and Administering Quality Short-Term Programs." She holds a B.A. in French and Psychology from Central Washington University and an M.A. in International Affairs from Ohio University. Her overseas experiences include teaching English in Japan and Chad and studying at the Université de Savoie, France, as a participant in the International Student Exchange Program. She currently resides in Washington state.

Kathy Tuma is the assistant director of the International and Off-Campus Studies Office at St. Olaf College, Northfield, MN. She has worked with St. Olaf's short-term programs for all of her 28 years at the college (yes, they had airplanes that could fly across the oceans that long ago). St. Olaf continually ranks as one of the nation's top private, liberal arts institutions in sending students abroad. In 1995, Kathy had the privilege of participating in and learning from the Fulbright Program for Administrators in Germany. She first presented a session on short-term programs at the region IV NAFSA conference in 1995. In 1996, she presented the first short-term study abroad workshop at the national NAFSA conference and has done so every year since. In addition, she is a member of NAFSA's trainer corps. Beyond working to help promote the cause of quality short-term programs, Kathy has presented other professional practice workshops including "Foundations of International Education: Education Abroad Advising and Administration of Education Abroad Programs." She has also participated in a number of other workshops and sessions related to health, safety, and liability issues.

Anders Uhrskov has been associated with DIS, Denmark's International Study Program, which is affiliated with the University of Copenhagen, since 1977. He holds a Cand.mag. degree in political science from the University of Copenhagen (1977), and has held various academic positions, including associate professor at Statens Kursus (1977–1978), and visiting scholar at the University of California-Berkeley (1985). He has also been a member of the NAFSA Board of Directors (1988–1991); the Board, Denmark-America Foundation (since 1992); Academic Selection Committee; and Crown Prince Frederik's Fund (since 1993). He holds an honorary doctoral degree from Whittier College (1999) and has presented with the NAFSA Professional Practice Workshop "Developing and Administering Quality Short-Term Education Abroad Programs" for 3 years.

Dawn White is director of international education services at Portland State University, where she oversees the administration of study abroad programs as well as services to international students and scholars. A regular presenter of sessions and workshops at NAFSA's national conferences and in Region I, Dawn cowrote (with John Pearson and Nancy Stubbs) the "NAFSA/AT&T Travel Tips" booklet published in 1998 and the revised "Basic Facts on Study Abroad," published in 1997 by NAFSA, CIEE, and IIE. She served Region I as chair in 1996-1997 and has held other leadership positions in her region.

Web Resources

[Source: University of Kansas.]

Culturegrams	• Individual country descriptions	http://www.culturegrams.com
U.S. State Department	• How to apply for a U.S. passport • Entry requirements to foreign countries for U.S. citizens (includes visa requirements) • U.S. State Department Travel Warnings • Tips for travelers for different world regions from the U.S. State Department	http://travel.state.gov
Centers for Disease Control	• Health Information by country	http://www.cdc.gov
Embassies	• U.S. embassies and national embassies in the United States	http://www.embassyworld.com
Mobility International	• Information on traveling abroad for people with disabilities	http://www.miusa.org
Lesbigay Links	• Links to sites dealing with issues involving the lesbigay community and international travel	http://www.indiana.edu/~overseas/lesbigay
Insurance	• Offers information on 28 different plans and allows you to compare each plan online. This site does not include information on every travel insurance plan available.	http://www.insuremytrip.com
	• Travel insurance offered by a local travel company specializing in student travel.	http://www.studyabroadinsurance.com
	• Offers trip cancellation insurance	http://www.kitt-travel.com/insurance.htm
	• Offers trip cancellation insurance	http://www.travelguard.com
IAMAT: International Association for Medical Assistance to Travelers	• Nonprofit organization that provides medication information around the world.	http://www.iamat.org
U.S. Postal Service	• International shipping rules, regulations, and rates. Good links, too.	http://www.uspsglobal.com
Currency conversions		http://www.xe.net/ucc/
Global Information Network	• Time zones, telephone codes, and more	http://www.ginfo.net
Map Quest	• Maps of various cities around the world	http://www.mapquest.com/
Tourism	• Tourism offices worldwide • Hostels by country • International Youth Hostels • Travelocity • European and British rail passes	http://mbnet.mb.ca/lucas/travel/tourism-offices.html http://www.hostels.com/hostel.menu.html http://www.iyhf.org/ http://www.travelocity.com http://www.railpass.com/ http://www.raileurope.com
Travel Guides	• Lonely Planet home page • Rough Guides • Let's Go • Fodors	http://www.lonelyplanet.com http://www.roughguides.com http://www.letsgo.com http://www.fodors.com